Montréal
Palais de la Civilisation
30 May-4 October 1987

GOLD
OF THE THRACIAN HORSEMEN

Treasures from Bulgaria

LES ÉDITIONS DE L'HOMME

THE SOCIÉTÉ DU PALAIS DE LA CIVILISATION WOULD LIKE TO THANK ALL THOSE WHO PARTICIPATED IN THE PRODUCTION OF THIS CATALOGUE.

IN PARTICULAR, THE SOCIÉTÉ WOULD LIKE TO ACKNOWLEDGE THOSE MEMBERS OF THE BULGARIAN CULTURE COMMITTEE WHO FURNISHED THE INTRODUCTORY TEXTS AND THE CATALOGUE NOTES, AS WELL AS THE MAJORITY OF THE PHOTOGRAPHS.

THE SOCIÉTÉ WOULD ALSO LIKE TO SHOW ITS APPRECIATION FOR THE WORK DONE BY VÉRONIQUE SCHILTZ WHO, AS THE INVITED SCIENTIFIC ADVISOR, COORDINATED ALL THE WRITING, WROTE THE INTRODUCTION TO THE CHAPTER "THRACE FROM THE NEOLITHIC TO THE EARLY BRONZE AGE" AND WHO PROVIDED VALUABLE CONSULTATION THROUGHOUT THE PRODUCTION OF THE CATALOGUE.

IN ADDITION, APPRECIATION IS SHOWN TO THOSE WHO GAVE THEIR RESPECTIVE TALENTS TO ASSURE THE QUALITY OF THE CATALOGUE:

PAULE NOYART: PRODUCTION DIRECTOR
KATHERINE SAPON: ART DIRECTOR
JEAN BERNIER: EDITING
JILL CORNER: TRANSLATION OF TEXTS
SHEILA FISCHMAN: TRANSLATION OF CATALOGUE NOTES
PATRICIA JUSTE AND PETER O'BRIEN: PROOFREADING
VÉRONIQUE SCHILTZ AND ANNE NERCESSIAN: BIBLIOGRAPHY
LISE GILBERT, ASSISTED BY LAURENT TRUDEL: LAY-OUT
COMPOSITION TECHNOLOGIES: TYPESETTING
MICHEL LAMBERT: LIAISON WITH BULGARIA; COVER PHOTOGRAPH

THIS CATALOGUE HAS BEEN PRODUCED FOR THE SOCIÉTÉ DU PALAIS DE LA CIVILISATION BY LES ÉDITIONS DE L'HOMME, UNDER THE DIRECTION OF BERNARD PRÉVOST.

PUBLISHED IN MONTRÉAL, 19 MAY 1987

Données de catalogage avant publication (Canada)

Main entry under title

Gold of the Thracian Horsemen

2-7619-0681-0

1. Art, Thracian – Exhibitions.   2. Thrace – Antiquities – Exhibitions.
3. Bulgaria – Antiquities – Exhibitions.

N5899.T5O7314 1987   709'.39'8   C87-096178-0

*This exhibition has been mounted under the auspices of
the President of the People's Republic of Bulgaria*

HIS EXCELLENCY TODOR ŽIVKOV

and of the Governor-General of Canada

HER EXCELLENCY THE RIGHT HONORABLE JEANNE SAUVÉ, P.C., C.C.,
C.M.M., C.D.

*The exhibition has been organized by the Société du Palais de la Civilisation,
for the city of Montréal, with the collaboration of the Council for Culture,
Science and Education of the People's Republic of Bulgaria.*

The honorary presidents are

the Prime Minister of Bulgaria

HIS EXCELLENCY GUÉORGUI ATHANASSOV

the Right Honorable Prime Minister of Canada

MR. BRIAN MULRONEY

and the Honorable the Premier of Québec

MR. ROBERT BOURASSA

HONORARY COMMITTEE OF THE PEOPLE'S REPUBLIC OF BULGARIA

HIS EXCELLENCY PETER MLADENOV

Minister for Foreign Affairs

MR. GUÉORGUI YORDANOV

Deputy Prime Minister,
Deputy Chairman of the Council of Ministers,
Chairman of the Council for intellectual development and
Chairman of the Comity for Culture

HIS EXCELLENCY BOÏKO TARABANOV

Ambassador of the People's Republic of Bulgaria to Canada

MR. LJUBOMIR PAVLOV

First Vice-president of the Council for Culture,
Science and Education

MR. MILAN MILANOV

Vice-president of the Council for Culture,
Science and Education

HONORARY COMMITTEE IN CANADA

THE HONORABLE FLORA MACDONALD

Minister of Communications

THE HONORABLE LISE BACON

Minister of Cultural Affairs
Deputy Prime Minister of Québec

MR. JEAN DORÉ

Mayor of Montréal

MRS. KATHLEEN VERDON

Member of the Executive Committee of the City of Montréal
Member responsible for cultural affairs

MR. JEAN-PAUL GOURDEAU

Chairman of the Société du Palais de la Civilisation

SOCIÉTÉ DU PALAIS DE LA CIVILISATION

ORGANIZING COMMITTEE IN THE PEOPLE'S REPUBLIC OF BULGARIA

PROFESSOR ALEXANDRE FOL

*Director, Institute of Thracology in
the Bulgarian Academy of Sciences*

PROFESSOR SVETLIN ROUSSEV

Managing Director of Fine Arts Galleries

MR. ZAHARY ZAHARIEV

Managing Director for International Cultural Activities

MR. RUMEN KATINČAROV

Director for Historical and Cultural Heritage

CREATED IN ANCIENT TIMES, PRECIOUS TO POSTERITY

The imperishable treasures in the exhibition "Gold of the Thracian Horsemen—Treasures from Bulgaria," marvellous works of art created millennia ago, move us to wonder and admiration, as they will move generations to come.

Archaeological research has shown us that the Thracian people, who were, according to Herodotus "the most numerous nation in the world after the Indians," were endowed with such creative genius that we may well describe their land as one of the cradles of civilization.

The cultural heritage of the world is greatly enriched by the extraordinarily beautiful creations of the Thracians. The masterpieces shown here were made over a period stretching from the end of the Chalcolithic era (the fourth millennium B.C.) up to the Roman occupation of the Balkan peninsula. These magnificent works from the dawn of time are, in their universal human qualities, important to us and to posterity. We need their human and spiritual values, for they make us the heirs of a great culture which is still to some extent unknown and insufficiently appreciated.

The Thracian works of art are mute but eloquent witnesses to man's endless quest for beauty and harmony. Each of these objects, made by the skilful hands of Thracian craftsmen, depicts an aspect of the struggle between good and evil, in which both men and animals take part. We see in them ordeals and victories, moments of grief and triumph, living scenes fixed forever in metal. They give us priceless insights into the times of our ancestors, those legendary times when the horseman-god of the Thracians still rode across the land, when the silver-tongued lyre of Orpheus sounded and Boreas, the formidable north wind, blew—the times of the heroes of Homer's Iliad.

The creations of the ancient Thracians are evidence of their rich spiritual life. The act of union with the universe, whose essential principle was represented by the Mother-Goddess, was concluded by a sacrifice. And what sacrifice could be more valuable than a human life? What fight could be worthier than the fight against oneself? Thracian art offers us images of mankind's eternal search for self-fulfilment.

The exhibits you see here, ladies and gentlemen, come from the National Museum of History in Sofia, the museum of the city of Varna and other collections. They represent only a small part of the priceless treasures held in the museums of Bulgaria. We have every reason to believe that the heritage of centuries past, evidence of the astonishing talent of our ancestors, inspires through its spirit and its example the art and culture of our own time, and therein is the guarantee of its survival. We go back to the dawn of human civilization to discover the message of those who went before us, and to pass it on to our posterity. And in this way we discover the fundamental meaning of life, of art, of creation.

Bulgaria has passed through thirteen centuries of history, a long path marked by tragic ordeals and astonishing recoveries. Our people created their own spiritual values, while keeping what earlier generations had bequeathed them. Mr. Todor Jivkov, President of the Privy Council of the People's Republic of Bulgaria, has stated: "Everything that immortalizes the creative genius, the art and the optimism of our ancestors must be preserved as a sacred heritage, which we have the duty to pass on to future generations."

Having emerged from a true social and economic transformation on to the path of progress and growth, our socialist country is seeing today an extraordinary flowering of science, education and the life of the intellect. It is with good reason that this is beginning to be called a new golden age of Bulgarian culture.

The People's Republic of Bulgaria offers to the cultural exchange between peoples and countries the most important achievements of a culture thousands of years old which was born on Bulgarian soil.

We see this as a valuable symbol of knowledge and of mutual trust which helps to bridge the gap between peoples and links us to the future of the world.

For when nations meet each other, and show their wish for mutual understanding, it is easy for them to learn a common language of friendship and peace.

The People's Republic of Bulgaria speaks this language. We feel honoured that this language of mutual comprehension should be the one spoken here, at this exhibition of Thracian masterpieces in the world-famous city of Montréal.

GEORGI YORDANOV
Vice-president of the Council of Ministers
President of the Council for Culture, Science and Education.

The origin of the Thracians — an ancient race of valiant warriors and artists inhabiting what is now present-day Bulgaria — reaches back to the first millennium B.C. The poet Orpheus, sweet singer of mystic songs, tells of their legends and folklore, and it is said that his music had the power to move even inanimate objects.

Through the generosity of the government of the People's Republic of Bulgaria we are privileged to enter the mysterious world of this proud, high-spirited people, who possessed such a remarkable sense of beauty. Many of the works you will see in this exhibit are marvels of the goldsmith's art, and demonstrate why gold remains to this day one of the most fascinating and breathtaking of all mediums. In these artifacts — whether they be for war, symbolic burials, or more daily concerns — we are able to glimpse the secrets that turn precious metal into works of art.

We wish to express Montréal's warmest thanks to the government of Bulgaria and to its representatives in Canada. We are proud to host this exhibit and to discover a fascinating era in the culture of their beautiful country.

JEAN DORÉ
Mayor of Montréal

KATHLEEN VERDON
Member of the Executive Committee

For the third year in a row, Montréal's Palais de la Civilisation is the setting for a remarkable exhibition, giving the public an opportunity to see the archaeological and cultural treasures of a great civilization. The Egypt of the Pharoahs and the China of the mighty emperors gave us unforgettable images of their grand and glorious past: "Gold of the Thracian Horsemen" presents us with a new world to be discovered, a marvellous world of Greek myths and legends.

Thanks to the generous participation of some thirty Bulgarian museums, the Société du Palais de la Civilisation is able, for the first time in North America, to present a collection of varied exhibits which testify to the creative energy and originality of the peoples of ancient Thrace. Our thanks are therefore due to the government of the People's Republic of Bulgaria and to the Council for Culture, Science and Education for having undertaken to prepare and mount especially for Montréal this wonderful exhibition of gold and silver objects from Europe's rich cultural heritage.

An exhibition of this scope requires the expertise and enthusiastic involvement of many people. We wish to offer our special thanks to Mrs. Véronique Schiltz, scientific consultant for the exhibition, for her indispensable help. Her scholarship and feeling for Thracian art have enabled us to offer the public an exhibition worthy of the Thracians and their treasures.

It is our hope that this direct contact with the masterpieces of these people, with their age-old history, will enable us all to understand and truly appreciate the unique role played by the Thracian horsemen in the history of the great peoples of ancient Europe.

JEAN-PAUL GOURDEAU
Chairman of the Société du Palais
de la Civilisation

"It is through art," said Oscar Wilde, "that we can realize our perfection." The National Bank, as a strong supporter of the arts, is proud to be associated once again with Montréal's Palais de la Civilisation as the principal sponsor of the "Gold of the Thracian Horsemen" exhibition.

This exquisite exhibit provides an opportunity to discover archaeological treasures of a civilization that left its mark on the history of art as well as humanity. At the crossroads of Eastern and Western civilizations, the Thracians, described by Homer in the Iliad, still evoke admiration today, thrilling us with the delight of discovery. The treasures of this ancient civilization are proof that even in the space age, art is timeless.

By supporting this exhibition, the National Bank recognizes the importance of artistic expression and its power to transcend the limits of time and space, bearing witness to the universal dimension of man.

We are proud to play a role in making these treasures available to the public and to have a hand in extending Montréal's influence across Canada and around the world.

MICHEL BÉLANGER
Chairman of the Board
and Chief Executive Officer
National Bank of Canada

THRACE IN THE ANCIENT WORLD

SCYTHIA

SEA OF AZOV

THRACE

EUXINE SEA

ILLYRIA

ITALY

COLCHIS

MACEDONIA

PHRYGIA

ASIA MINOR

GREECE

EUBOEA

LYDIA

SICILY

IONIA

LYCIA

SYRIA

CRETE

PHOENICIA

LIBYA

EGYPT

IRON GATES

RUMANIA

POROÏNA

BUCHAREST

AGIGHIOL

VIDIN

PERETU

DANUBE (ISTROS)

SILISTRA

DOBROUDJA

LOM

RUSE

TOLBUHIN

DURANKULAK

ORSOJA

DANUBE

ORJAHOVO

RAZGRAD

KASPIČAN

ROGOZEN

SVEŠTARI

MIHAILOVGRAD

PLEVEN

BOROVO

ŠUMEN

SADOVEC

LETNICA

VARNA

ČERVEN BRJAG

VALČITRAN

TARGOVIŠTE

NESEBAR *MESEMBRIA*

LUKOVIT

ALEXANDROVO

VRACA

LOVEČ

TORNOVO

KARLUKOVO

SEVLIEVO

VARBICA

TRAN

TETEVEN

BULGARIA

SOFIA

SEUTHOPOLIS

KAZANLAK

SLIVEN

BURGAS

BLACK SEA

PANAGJURIŠTE

ROZOVEC

NOVA ZAGORA

PERNIK

STRELČA

KARANOVO

JAMBOL

SOZOPOL *APOLLONIA*

DUVANLI

STARA ZAGORA

KJUSTENDIL

BREZOVO

PAZARDŽIK

TUNDŽA

PHILIPPOPOLIS (PLOVDIV)

MARICA

BLAGOEVGRAD

HASKOVO

STRUMA (STRYMON)

ASENOVGRAD

MEZEK

SVILENGRAD

GOCE DELČEV

KÂRDŽALI

TURKEY

SMOLJAN

MOMCILGRAD

KRUMOVGRAD

MESTA (NESTOS)

BYZANTIUM

GREECE

ABDÈRE

MARONÉE

MACEDONIA

VARDAR (AXIOS)

PHILIPPES

CHERSONÈSE DE THRACE

SEA OF MARMARA

MONT PANGÉE

AÏNOS

CHALCIDICE

OLYNTHUS

THASOS ISLAND

AEGEAN SEA

CYZICUS

BITHYNIA

LAMPSAQUE

PARION

MYSIA

TROY

PHRYGIA OF THE HELLESPONT

YUGOSLAVIA

The underlined names correspond to the ancient names used in the catalogue.

BRIEF COLLECTION OF ANCIENT TEXTS ON ORPHEUS AND THE THRACIANS

(Book IV, 94-96.)

(Book V, 3-8.)

94. As to their claim to be immortal, this is how they show it: they believe that they do not die, but that he who perishes goes to the god Salmoxis, or Gebeleïzis, as some of them call him. Once in every five years they choose by lot one of their people and send him as a messenger to Salmoxis, charged to tell of their needs; and this is their manner of sending: Three lances are held by men thereto appointed; others seize the messenger to Salmoxis by his hands and feet, and swing and hurl him aloft on to the spear-points. If he be killed by the cast, they believe that the god regards them with favour; but if he be not killed, they blame the messenger himself, deeming him a bad man, and send another messenger in place of him whom they blame. It is while the man yet lives that they charge him with the message. Moreover when there is thunder and lightning these same Thracians shoot arrows skyward as a threat to the god, believing in no other god but their own.

95. For myself, I have been told by the Greeks who dwell beside the Hellespont and Pontus that this Salmoxis was a man who was once a slave in Samos, his master being Pythagoras son of Mnesarchus; presently, after being freed and gaining great wealth, he returned to his own country. Now the Thracians were a meanly-living and simple-witted folk, but this Salmoxis knew Ionian usages and a fuller way of life than the Thracian; for he had consorted with Greeks, and moreover with one of the greatest Greek teachers, Pythagoras; wherefore he made himself a hall, where he entertained and feasted the chief among his countrymen, and taught them that neither he nor his guests nor any of their descendants should ever die, but that they should go to a place where they would live forever and have all good things. While he was doing as I have said and teaching this doctrine, he was all the while making him an underground chamber. When this was finished, he vanished from the sight of the Thracians, and descended into the underground chamber, where he lived for three years, the Thracians wishing him back and mourning him for dead; then in the fourth year he appeared to the Thracians, and thus they came to believe what Salmoxis had told them. Such is the Greek story about him.

96. For myself, I neither disbelieve nor fully believe the tale about Salmoxis and his underground chamber; but I think that he lived many years before Pythagoras; and whether there was a man called Salmoxis, or this be a name among the Getae for a god of their country, I have done with him.

3. The Thracians are the biggest nation in the world, next to the Indians; were they under one ruler, or united, they would in my judgment be invincible and the strongest nation on earth; but since there is no way or contrivance to bring this about, they are for this reason weak. They have many names, each tribe according to its region. All these Thracians are alike in all their usages, save the Getae, and the Trausi, and those that dwell above the Crestonaeans.

4. As for the Getae who claim to be immortal, I have already told what they do; the Trausi, who in all else fulfil the customs of other Thracians, do as I will show at the seasons of birth and death. When a child is born, the kinsfolk sit round and lament for all the tale of ills that it must endure from its birth onward, recounting all the sorrows of men; but the dead they bury with jollity

and gladness, for the reason that he is quit of so many ills and is in perfect blessedness.

5. Those who dwell above the Crestonaeans have a custom of their own: each man having many wives at his death there is great rivalry among his wives, and eager contention on their friends' part, to prove which wife was best loved by her husband; and she to whom the honour is adjudged is praised by men and women, and then slain over the tomb by her nearest of kin, and after the slaying she is buried with the husband. The rest of the wives take this sorely to heart, deeming themselves deeply dishonoured.

6. Among the rest of the Thracians, it is the custom to sell their children to be carried out of the country. They take no care of their maidens, allowing them to have intercourse with what men they will: but their wives they strictly guard, and buy them for a great price from the parents. To be tattooed is a sign of noble birth; to bear no such marks is for the baser sort. The idler is most honoured, the tiller of the soil most contemned; he is held in highest honour who lives by war and foray.

7. These are the most notable of their usages. They worship no gods but Ares, Dionysos, and Artemis. But their princes, unlike the rest of their countrymen, worship Hermes above all gods and swear only by him, claiming him for their ancestor.

8. Among those of them that are rich, the funeral rites are these:—They lay out the dead for three days, then after killing all kinds of victims and first making lamentation they feast; after that they make away with the body either by fire or else by burial in the earth, and when they have built a barrow they set on foot all kinds of contests, wherein the greatest prizes are offered for the hardest fashion of single combat. Such are the Thracian funeral rites.

XENOPHON, *ANABASIS*

After sacrificing some of the oxen which they had captured and other animals too, they provided a feast which was quite a good one, though they ate reclining on low couches and drank out of horn cups which they had come across in the country. When they had poured the libations and sung the paean, first of all two Thracians stood up and performed a dance to the flute, wearing full armour. They leapt high into the air with great agility and brandished their swords. In the end one of them, as everybody thought, struck the other one, who fell to the ground, acting all the time. The Paphlagonians cried out at this, and the other man stripped him of his arms and went out, singing the ballad of Sitalces. Then some more Thracians carried the man out, as though he was dead, though actually he had not been hurt in the slightest.

There was a lot of snow here, and it was so cold that the water which they brought in for their dinner, and the wine in the jars, froze, and a number of Greeks lost noses and ears through frostbite. It was then easy to see why the Thracians wear fox skins round their heads and ears, and why they have tunics that cover their legs and not only the upper part of the body, and why, when they are on horseback, they wear long cloaks reaching down to their feet instead of our short coats.

Translation: A. D. Godley
© 1957, Harvard University Press

(Book VI, 1, 4-6.)

(Book VII, 4, 3-4.)

Translated by Rex Warner
© 1949 by Rex Warner
Reproduced with the kind permission of Penguin Books, Ltd.

OVID, *THE METAMORPHOSES*

(Book XI, 1-66.)

The songs that Orpheus sang brought creatures round him,
All beasts, all birds, all stones held in their spell.
But look! There on a hill that overlooked the plain,
A crowd of raging women stood, their naked breasts
Scarce covered by strips of fur. They gazed at Orpheus
Still singing, his frail lyre in one hand.
Her wild hair in the wind, one naked demon cried,
"Look at the pretty boy who will not have us!"
And shouting tossed a spear aimed at his mouth.
The leaf-grown spear scratched his white face,
Nor bruised his lips, nor was the song unbroken.
Her sister threw a stone, which as it sailed
Took on his music's charm, wavered and swayed;
As to beg free of its mistress' frenzy,
Fell at the poet's feet. At this the women
Grew more violent and madness flamed among the crowd:
A cloud of spears were thrown which flew apart
And dropped to earth, steered by the singer's voice.
The screams of women, clapping of hands on breasts and thighs,
The clattering tympanum soon won their way
Above the poet's music; spears found their aim,
And stones turned red, streaked by the singer's blood.
No longer charmed by music now unheard,
The birds, still with the echoes of Orpheus' music
Chiming through their veins, began to fly away—
Then snakes and wild things (once his pride to charm)
Turned toward their homes again and disappeared.
Now, as wild birds of prey swoop down to kill
An owl struck by a blinding light at noon,
Or as when dawn breaks over an open circus
To show a stag bleeding and put to death by dogs,
Such was the scene as Maenads came at Orpheus,
Piercing his flesh with sharpened boughs of laurel,
Tearing his body with blood-streaming hands,
Whipping his sides with branches torn from trees;
He was stoned, beaten, and smeared with hardened clay.
Yet he was still alive; they looked for deadlier weapons,
And in the nearby plains, they saw the sweating peasants
And broad-shouldered oxen at the plough.
As they rushed toward them, peasants ran to shelter,
Their rakes and mattocks tossed aside
As the maddened women stormed the helpless oxen
To rip their sides apart, tear out their horns.
Armed with this gear they charged on Orpheus
Who bared his breast to them to cry for mercy
(A prayer that never went unheard before);
They leaped on him to beat him into earth.

Translation: Horace Gregory
© 1958, Viking Press, Inc.

Then, O by Jupiter, through those same lips,
Lips that enchanted beasts, and dying rocks and trees,
His soul escaped in his last breath
To weave invisibly in waves of air.
　　The saddened birds sobbed loud for Orpheus;
All wept: the multitude of beasts,
Stones, and trees, all those who came to hear
The songs he sang, yes, even the charmed trees
Dropped all their leaves as if they shaved their hair.
Then it was said the rivers swelled with tears,
That dryads, naiads draped their nakedness
In black and shook their hair wild for the world to see.
Scattered in blood, and tossed in bloody grasses,
Dismembered arm from shoulder, knee from thigh,
The poet's body lay, yet by a miracle the River Hebrus
Caught head and lyre as they dropped and carried them
Midcurrent down the stream. The lyre twanged sad strains,
The dead tongue sang; funereally the river banks and reeds
Echoed their music. Drifting they sang their way
To open sea, and from the river's mouth
The head and lyre met salt sea waves that washed them up
On shores of Lesbos, near Methymna: salt spray in hair,
The head faced upward on strange sands, where a wild snake
Came at it to pierce its lips and eyes, to strike:
Phoebus was quicker, for as the snake's tongue flickered
He glazed the creature into polished stone,
And there it stayed, smiling wide-open-jawed.
　　The poet's shade stepped down from earth to Hades;
To stroll again the places that it knew,
It felt its way toward fair Elysium.
There Orpheus took his Eurydice, put arms around her
Folding her to rest. Today they walk together,
Side by side—or if they wish, he follows her, she, him,
But as they move, however they may go,
Orpheus may not turn a backward look at her.
　　Lyaeus could not let the killing of Orpheus
Pass without revenge on his mad murderers.
Angered by loss, he captured Thracian women
Who saw him die, trussed them with roots,
And thrust their feet, toes downward, into earth.
As birds are trapped by clever fowlers in a net,
Then flutter to get free, drawing the net still tighter
Round wings and claws, so each woman fought,
Held by quick roots entangling feet and fingers,
Toenails in earth, she felt bark creeping up her legs,
And when she tried to slap her thighs, her hands struck oak;
Her neck, her shoulders, breasts were oak-wood carving;
You'd think her arms were branches—you're not wrong.

THRACIAN FIGURES IN GREECE: THE PARADOXES OF ORPHEUS

In April 1791, a young officer boarded a ship in the harbour of Saint-Malo, France. The sky, we are told, was overcast, a soft breeze was blowing, and a heavy swell was pounding the rocks a few cable-lengths from the boat. The young man was twenty-three years old, and dreamed of discovering the New World. His name was François René de Chateaubriand. Years later, in his *Mémoires d'outre-tombe*, he would recall that voyage to the "Hyperborean shores," the memory of which, somewhat enhanced by his romanticizing, was to enrich his writings. He describes his emotions on seeing the American coast "faintly outlined by the tops of maple trees above the water," and recounts his adventures, evoking the picturesque figure of Monsieur Violet, "the new Orpheus," who taught French dances to the Iroquois and was paid in beaver pelts and bear hams. He also tells of his encounter, on the shores of the Genesee River not far from Ontario, with a rattlesnake charmer, about whom he writes: "The Greeks would have made my Canadian into Orpheus, changed his flute to a lyre and the snake to Cerberus, or perhaps Eurydice."

Greek Orpheus, Thracian Orpheus, even Canadian Orpheus . . . From Aeschylus to Pindar, Euripides to Plato, Ovid or Virgil to Dante, Milton to Rilke, Supervielle to Cocteau, the image of Orpheus has never ceased to haunt the Western imagination, appearing in the greatest works of literature, as well as in painting, sculpture, music and even film. From the dawn of time he has been legendary: when, in the sixth century B.C., his name appears for the first time, in a mutilated fragment from the Greek poet Ibykos of Rhegion, he is already "Orpheus of the famous name."

A complex, multi-faceted figure in whom each of us finds our own likeness, continually reinvented by Western culture down through the centuries, Orpheus is no longer either Thracian or Greek, but universal. Who better to be our guide than this eternal traveller between the twin shores of life and death? Who better to help us not merely to know but to discern, not just to understand but to feel, and how better to approach this exhibition in which, although nowhere to be found, he is nonetheless omnipresent?

In the pages which follow, my Bulgarian colleagues discuss the importance of the Thracians—their history, culture, religion, and burial rites, together with their art, and the difficulties in interpreting it. This catalogue, which is primarily their work, sets out to present the very latest research and opinions of the most eminent Bulgarian thracologists. All of these scholars show enthusiasm in vindicating and elucidating Thracian culture, particularly those cultural manifestations which are today part of the Bulgarian heritage. The vision they offer us is first and foremost a literally dazzling look at objects and treasures discovered in their own land. In daily contact with these marvels, these scholars have studied them at first hand, and although these scholars are only minimally, if at all, direct descendants of the Thracians—a people who have long since disappeared, overwhelmed and absorbed by the great migrations of the first millennium A.D.—nevertheless Bulgarian thracologists feel an intimate link, almost a sense of complicity, with their all-but-ancestors.

For my part, I would like to take a different but complementary viewpoint, that of the ancient written tradition, in order to look at Thrace more indirectly. I admit my own sense of complicity, which is decidedly with the ancient Greeks, and take from Greek texts images which, though misleading as are all images, nevertheless contain their own truth. Like the story of Orpheus, these images have a power greater, though in a different way, and in the end no less true, than reality.

Let us first take the name of Thrace itself. In its historical sense, it is applied to the Roman "diocese" established in the third century A.D. by Diocletian, when he distributed the imperial power among four jurisdictions, thus setting up the tetrarchy. At that time Thrace consisted of the territory today occupied by Bulgaria, northeastern Greece and the European part of Turkey.

But in the legends of antiquity, Thrake, the heroine from whom Thrace took its name, was the sister of Europa. (A lovely image, which creates this link of sisterly equality between Thrace and the rest of the continent.) Both girls were daughters of Okeanos, the primordial river that bounded with his waters the circle of the earth. Hesiod, in his poem the *Theogony*, tells us that Okeanos was also the father "of the turbulent rivers Nile, Alpheos, Eridanos of the deep eddies, Strymon, Maeander, and Ister of the beautiful flowing waters." The Strymon (Struma) and the Ister (Danube) are thus included among the greatest rivers. In these two images, Thrace is seen as a continent watered by mighty rivers, and indeed this was the case: the land stretched far beyond Bulgaria to the north, into territory that is now Rumanian. The Danube and its tributaries constituted the essential channel of communication for this immense land deep in the heart of Europe. In this sense Thracian civilization, like that of Egypt, was also born of a river, and the Danube (which is today the northern border of Bulgaria) in antiquity ran through the middle of Thrace.

One of the oldest and most famous of Greek legends, that of the journey of the Argonauts, testifies to the importance of the Danube. According to a tradition passed on by Aristotle in the fourth century B.C., Jason and his companions, not content merely to hug the coast of Thrace and cross the Bosphorus on their return journey, followed the course of the Danube far inland. The existence of very early coastal navigation is also proven by archaeological finds off the Bulgarian coast of the Black Sea, where in the waters of more sheltered parts of the coastline a large number of stone anchors have been discovered.

For the Greeks, Thrace was a distant land of inaccessible yet easily-reached borders, a strange and barbarous place which nevertheless held vague memories as the one-time cradle of their race and heritage. Hence their relationship with the Thracians was from the start paradoxical.

The image of Boreas is an appropriate reflection of this ambiguity. Boreas was the icy wind from the north that swept down on the Aegean Sea. The idea of Thrace as a cold land runs throughout ancient literature up to the Roman period, and one does not need to be a great Latinist to grasp the implications of the adjectives most often employed by Roman poets to describe Thrace: *frigida, gelida, glacialis, nivosa*. How the Greeks dreaded that cruel north wind! In the sixth century B.C. Hesiod warned sailors and farmers against "these troublesome frosts which appear on the ground when Boreas blows, when from Thrace, the motherland of horses, it sweeps down upon the vast sea and whips it up, while the earth and the woods moan." But the Thracian Boreas was also the sacred breath of Zeus, and hence a familiar personage in Athenian legend. The ravisher of Oreithyia (daughter of Erectheus, the first king of Athens, who instituted the great festival of the Panathenaea), Boreas had by her two sons, the Boreads, who became companions of Jason and Orpheus on the expedition of the Argonauts. Together with these human offspring, Boreas also sired, with Greek mares, colts so light and swift that they could gallop over wheatfields without bending the ears of grain, and over the sea without leaving the slightest ripple.

Ares the destroyer, the fearsome god of war and carnage, was also a denizen of Thrace. In the *Iliad* he is usually on the side of the Trojans, who were allies of the Thracians, and part of the tradition links Thrace (or at least the Black Sea) with his daughters the warlike Amazons. Yet he was also the son of Zeus, with a sanctuary in Boeotia at Thebes, and in Athens a hill, the Areopagus, bore his name.

Greek though he was, Apollo spent part of the year among the swans and griffins in the distant land of the Hyperboreans, somewhere in the north beyond Thrace and Scythia. And was he not, according to some sources, the father of Orpheus?

The latest addition to the Greek pantheon, apparently from abroad, was Dionysos the unknown, god of delirium and intoxication, which were so foreign to the Hellenistic yearnings for order, reason and lucidity. Dionysos was linked to the Asiatic world of the Phrygians, themselves originally from Thrace. But the way he is depicted, with his suite of satyrs and maenads, and the rites with which he was worshipped, show direct affinities with the Thracian world. He is very close to local divinities, such as Sabazios and most importantly Zalmoxis. He has been the enemy of Lycurgus, king of the Edonians of Thrace, and is thought to have had there one of his principal sanctuaries. Was it not by his order that the maenads, unleashed, tore Orpheus to pieces?

The most popular figure in ancient Greek folklore, Herakles the strong-man, the fairground Herakles, the all-purpose superman who became the metaphor for human destiny fully accomplished after many trials, is also linked with Thrace. In his *Third Olympian*, Pindar writes of "The grey-green olive crown that once the son of Amphitryon (Herakles) brought from the shady source of the Ister (Danube), as a proud emblem of the games of Olympia," and later speaks of the hind with golden horns that the hero was to conquer "in the land of Istria." Reading these verses, we are reminded of the rhyta from Panagjurište shaped like the heads of does, one of which in fact has on its neck a depiction of the fight between Herakles and the Ceryneian Hind. Herakles also mastered the mares of Diomedes which, deadly savage toward strangers, ate human flesh. The hero fed them on their own master, Diomedes, the son of Ares and legendary king of the Bistonians.

During the Trojan War another Diomedes, this time a Greek, was Ulysses' accomplice in stealing some magnificent steeds. Homer tells us how, having surprised the traitor Dolon, the two thieves had him lead them through the enemy lines into the Thracian camp, where they killed Rhesos the Thracian king and seized his horses, which were "like the rays of the sun."

The importance of the horse in Indo-European societies cannot be overemphasized. It is demonstrated not only by these two stories, but also by the quantity and richness of the harness trappings in this exhibition, and the number of representations of mounted men, especially of the Thracian horseman himself. The horse, which was early broken to harness and, by the latter half of the second millennium B.C. was ridden, actually changed the course of history, its mobility and speed helping to accelerate the process of conquest and migration. It was both the weapon and the prerogative of an entire victorious aristocracy, a cavalry which was soon to become chivalry. The image of the wooden figure brought into Troy, thus causing the downfall of the city, is a fine one: who could have refused a splendid horse?

Once the war was over, Ulysses set off to return home to Ithaca. The *Odyssey* shows him landing on the coast of Thrace, in the land of the Ciconians. He and his companions embark on an orgy of looting, and feasting on mutton, beef and delicious wine. But the coastal Thracians call to their aid their neighbours from inland, who flock to their rescue "thicker than leaves and flowers in springtime." They send the Greeks away, who take with them "seven talents of worked gold and twelve amphorae of a very strong wine, a divine nectar," which Ulysses is given by Maron, a priest of the local Apollo, in exchange for saving his life. This is undoubtedly one of the sordid adventures that originally incited the Greeks to set foot on these northern shores, but the nature of the booty taken is revealing.

Aside from these links with epic poetry, Greek tradition is remarkably consistent in associating the lyre and the birth of lyric poetry with the northern lands. Almost all the great antecedents of legend, except perhaps for Amphion, were Thracian, or had something to do with Thrace. As well as the obvious example of Orpheus, we have the case of Philammon, and of Thamyris, whose name appears in the *Iliad*. The latter was a Thracian bard who, because he claimed to be better at singing than the Muses, was deprived both of his sight and of his voice. Musaeus, inventor of dactylic rhythm, and the priest-king Eumolpos, who established the Mysteries of Eleusis and founded the great priestly line of the Eumolpides, were both Thracians. Later, and probably not purely through coincidence, other poets, this time real ones, found themselves drawn to the north. Alcaeus, exiled in Thrace, writes of the river Hebrus in a fragment of a lost poem possibly telling the story of Orpheus:

Hebrus, loveliest of rivers, close to Ainos
You fling yourself into the turbulent sea,
Pouring out a shining bath of Thracian foam,
And the maidens come to you in bevies,
They rub with their delicate hands
The flesh of their magnificent thighs
And your divine water has for them
The power of a beautifying lotion.

Archilochus went to seek his fortune on the island of Thassos, and later Anacreon fled his native city of Teos and the Persian yoke to take refuge in Abdera, where he calls his beloved by the tender name of "my Thracian filly." These three poets are unquestionably real historical figures, whose travels took place at the great period of Greek colonization to the north of the Aegean: there must have been many other such travellers.

What was the historical reality underlying this northern tradition, which by its very existence testifies to the rich vein of poetry attributed to Thrace? It must hark back to the ages before writing, when oral poetry, words inextricably linked with music, became incarnate in the poets, who were both priests and bards. But what significance had they for the Greeks, for whom they were foreigners? It is tempting to see here the dim memory of a distant time, before the Dorian migration from the north in the twelfth century B.C. which the Greeks called the "return of the Heraclidae," or possibly even earlier, of a far-off time when the peoples who were to become Greeks, Thracians and Phrygians were in direct contact with each other, perhaps indeed were one nation, and where no one was considered a barbarian.

Of incomparable beauty, dazzlingly magnificent even in its raw state, impervious to time or decay, easily worked by simple cold-hammering, gold has always fascinated mankind. Splendid, but too soft to be made into weapons or tools, immortal but useless, it is paradoxically the apotheosis of the gratuitous. It is beauty in its pure state, sunlight held in the hand. This entirely symbolic value is what constitutes its pricelessness. Gold cannot become anything but an adornment, jewellery, something to be displayed. But it is also a means of entry, a passport to the world of the gods, and therefore, as the example of Varna makes plain, to the state of royalty. Numerous ancient Greek expressions—golden name, golden age, golden Aphrodite, the *Golden Verses* of Pythagoras—make gold the metaphor for perfection. But being a land poor in gold deposits, Greece was obliged to look elsewhere for the precious metal. An important factor in the process of Greek colonization of the periphery of the Mediterranean and the Black Sea was in fact the quest for Eldorados or promised lands, and this quest, in antiquity as in modern times, has produced brave adventurers who ran great risks.

Thrace figures in many of these golden legends, notably in the oldest and most celebrated of them all, an epic journey known to Homer, mentioned by Pindar, and told in detail in the middle of the third century B.C. in the famous *Argonautica* of Apollonius of Rhodes. Orpheus participated in the expedition led by Jason in the ship Argo to search for the Golden Fleece. He had a decisive role in the success of the undertaking, for this lyre not only heartened the oarsmen, soothing their quarrels with its harmony, but also calmed the raging waves. His singing was even lovelier than that of the Sirens, so that the Argonauts were able to escape their deadly seductions. He also sang to sleep the terrible dragon that guarded the Fleece. It is true that tradition places the Golden Fleece and the kingdom of the murderous Medea in Colchis, at the foot of the Caucasus. Nevertheless, as has already been stated, the Argonauts sailed along the Thracian coast and crossed the Bosphorus on their way to Colchis, and on the return journey took their boat down the Danube.

We cannot omit here, though it comes from the Thraco-Phrygian world, the story of Midas, the legendary king of Asiatic Phrygia, a land peopled in the earliest times by settlers from Thrace. As the result of an incautious wish he had expressed after saving Silenus—a wish which was granted by Dionysos—Midas turned everything that he touched into gold. He would have died of this gift, which turned even his food into gold before it reached his mouth, had he not dived into the Pactolus to rid himself of so burdensome a power.

What can we make of all this? Let us first take the image of the Golden Fleece. Far from being the creation of some poet's wild imagination, it corresponds to an exact reality. For ancient gold cleansers, sheepskins which were hung across gold-bearing rivers to catch grains of gold dust and even nuggets served the same purpose as does the sluice for modern prospectors, and it is fascinating to imagine them heavy with their precious cargo. There is no doubt that this procedure was originally known in Thrace, where the rivers, still virgin and unexploited, ran with gold like so many Pactoles. Soon afterwards, this practice was superseded by mining for reefs of gold. Both ancient sources and modern research agree entirely on this point: the north of the Aegean, the Danube, and the Balkan peninsula were for the ancients among the most important gold-producing lands. In the period with which we are concerned, evidence of mining has been found not only at the famous gold mines on the Greek island of Thasos, but also at the foot of Mount Pangaeus, in the region of the Strymon in southwest Bulgaria, and also in the northeast and the outskirts of Sofia, where studies have been made of a whole network of ancient narrow passages dug in the alluvial deposits of the old river bed. The gold mines of Transylvania, which were renowned in the Roman period, seem to have been exploited relatively later. They formed one of the main reasons for Trajan's conquest of Dacia, a campaign whose major events are depicted in bas-relief on Trajan's column in Rome.

Thucydides describes the links of privilege that were established between those united by a common interest in this sort of enterprise. In the chapter he devotes to the Odrysian kingdom and to the expedition of Sitalkes (429 B.C.), he explains, speaking of himself (he was then a military commander) in the third person: "He possessed the rights to exploiting gold mines in that region of Thrace, and because of this fact had some credit with the principal personages on the continent." But the precious metal could also come from much farther off, arriving in Thrace in the form of ingots or manufactured objects which might be gifts, tribute, or booty from raids far away. Thucydides gives us an idea of what the revenues of the Odrysian king amounted to in the last quarter of the fifth century: "The tribute paid by the whole of the barbarian land and by the Greek subject cities, in the reign of Seuthes (who reigned after Sitalkes and raised the tribute to its highest level), represented, as far as one can estimate, the equivalent of four hundred talents of silver, paid in gold or silver, without counting all the cloth embroidered or plain, or the other gifts in kind, and these were offered not only to the king himself but to all the Odrysians of some degree of authority, and to the nobles." And he concludes: "Of all the European monarchies situated between the Ionian gulf and the Black Sea, this was the wealthiest in its revenues of silver and its prosperity in general."

Collected, demanded, offered, won, stolen . . . who can say from what gold or silver the objects we see today were really made? The important thing is that they have come down to us. For if gold is immortal, things made from it, exposed to the greed of men, melted down and recast a thousand times over, are extremely vulnerable, their survival constantly endangered. Another paradox springs to mind here: it was the barbarians who were best able to protect their gold. It is not in Greece itself, but on the periphery of the Greek world, among the Thracians, Scythians and Etruscans, that we find the gold masterpieces of antiquity. This is partly because the barbarians' taste for gold caused objects to be created which would otherwise not have existed. Another reason is that by burying these creations with their dead (in defiance of the sumptuary laws which Greece had since the sixth century B.C. and which prohibited gold to be placed in tombs), the so-called barbarians saved from the ravages of time not only their own heritage but also part of the Greek patrimony. Where now are the works of Phidias, or the gold from the Zeus of Olympia or the Athena of the Parthenon? But the kantharos and the cup of Duvanli, the treasure of Panagjurište, have survived. And although the forms of the latter cannot truly be understood in the context of Greece only, nevertheless many aspects of the decoration and workmanship are glorious evidence of Greek genius.

Through their profound faith in immortality, the Thracians, these "barbarians," succeeded in making immortal the heritage of their time. And it was another sort of barbarism, a real barbarism, which impelled people terrified by the enemy's approach to bury hastily in the ground their most precious possessions, thus paradoxically saving them for posterity. Such was the case at Rogozen.

What is surprising is the manner in which Greek comedies present the most grossly caricatured image of Thracians. Aristophanes, wishing to put into his *The Birds* (414 B.C.) a particularly barbarous god, calls him Triballus and makes him a complete savage, capable only of abdominal rumblings. The Triballoi, a Thracian tribe from the northwest of present-day Bulgaria, were more prone to be defamed in this way since they lived far inland, south of the Danube, and hence were the least known to the Greeks. Even among the Thracians, the Triballoi had the reputation of being particularly redoubtable warriors. A Greek proverbial saying to censure very bad manners was: "We are not among the Triballoi." And yet it should not be forgotten that it is in their territory that the greatest number of extremely sophisticated treasures, notably that of Rogozen, have been found. Once again, this is the paradox of barbarity. It is true that the Odrysians were scarcely better treated. In *The Acharnians* (425 B.C.) Aristophanes introduces an Athenian ambassador on his way back from the court of king Sitalkes, with whom the Greeks had made an alliance in 432. The Greek recounts how, kept in Thrace by the snow that covered the entire country, and the ice that made the rivers unnavigable, he spent his time drinking with the king and his son. The latter, longing to eat Athenian sausages, urges his father to help the Athenians. Suddenly there erupts on to the stage, in the purest tradition of gross farce, the "Thracian reinforcements": an army of bloodthirsty Odomantes brandishing before them the most manly of "weapons," a phallus. They take advantage of their lightning visit to relieve the main protagonist of his supply of garlic.

Quite different, however, is the picture of Thrace given in the tragedies. Though it is only fleetingly mentioned in the works we have by Aeschylus and Sophocles, it is much in evidence in the work of Euripides, who at the beginning of the last quarter of the fifth century B.C. presents a true portrait of Thrace and the Thracians. The writer sometimes achieves this by thumbnail sketches: "The Hebrus rolling with silver," "the fertile bed of Strymon," near "Mount Pangaeus of the gold nuggets," "snow-covered Thrace, the land where one man shares his bed with many wives each in her turn." But two tragedies, *Hecuba* and *Rhesos*, belonging to the Trojan cycle, are set in Thrace. The latter, written not in the epic but rather the tragic mode, takes up the well-known episode from the *Iliad* which has already been alluded to here. The description of the king in his splendour, echoing the lines of Homer, can be fully grasped by

Catalogue no. 421.
Gold phiale from the Panagjurište Treasure.

anyone who has seen the treasures excavated in Bulgaria: "I see Rhesos, like a god, standing in a harnessed Thracian chariot. A golden yoke supported the necks of his horses, which were more dazzlingly white than snow. From his shoulders hung a buckler glittering with ornamented gold plaques. A bronze Gorgon, like that on the goddess's shield, was placed on the headstall of the horses and inspired terror with its countless bells. As to the strength of his army, one could not estimate it even by counting numbers, for it was a spectacle without end."

Euripides' description, often almost ethnographic in its attention to detail, is reminiscent of the attention paid to Thrace by his great contemporary Herodotus. We will not dwell here on the latter's long account, which is nearer to true history than to literature: it will be allowed to speak for itself elsewhere. It is true that Euripides' decision to introduce Thrace onto the Athenian stage was a reflection of renewed interest in the country at that period. What is perhaps less recognized is the fact that in so doing, he must have set off a considerable reaction. By describing Thrace, he provided all those Greeks from Thrace, or Hellenized Thracians, with a literary image of themselves to which they could not remain indifferent. He made himself not only a mirror, but also a resonator, an amplifier of an image which he sent back magnified, doubled in grandeur. The concrete results of this phenomenon may be measured when one considers how important Euripides was in spreading themes and legends out to the periphery of the Greek world, and how great was his impact on pictorial representation throughout the fourth century.

Finally, let us come back to Orpheus. If, as seems probable, there is a historical basis for believing that he existed, what was he? A poet, undoubtedly, and a religious reformer, perhaps even a king; but beyond these, which are of course only hypotheses, everything is vague. Was he a Thracian magician who succeeded in being understood by the Greeks? A Greek converting barbarian Thrace to his own way of belief? Once again, the reality is less important than the idea, the principle of duality, which is preserved in all versions of the myth. In a land of warrior horsemen, Orpheus goes forth on foot, without thunderbolts, weaponless. In this land of carousing huntsmen, he tames animals with his bare hands and refuses to touch blood or meat. In the midst of barbarism he is above all the civilizer, and the notes of his lyre bring sense and meaning to the mindless din of the world, his cadences and melodies transform into music the savage sounds of brute nature. Called and called again, Eurydice comes back to life, revived by the sound of her name repeated, chanted, sung. Rhythm gives back her bones their firmness, melody clothes them with flesh. Soon she will be brought out of the dark, dank kingdom of Hades. But Orpheus looks back; perhaps he stops singing; and Eurydice, caught from behind, dissolves once again into the mist. "Why did Orpheus turn back before he was safely out of hell? He mustn't have been quite sure of himself after all!" cries the five-year-old Eurydice El Etr in astonishment. Her question, which seems to echo Plato's explanation of why Orpheus lost everything, "because he seems to have had a weak spirit, like a zither player," harks back to the original truth of the myth. There was perhaps a time when Orpheus did not turn back, when he kept on, and Eurydice, renewed, came like Alcestis out of the underworld.

As adolescents in the Florence of Lorenzo the Magnificent, Leonardo da

Vinci and his young companions from Verrocchio's studio, Botticelli, Perugino, Filippino Lippi, walked every day across the square of the cathedral. There, at the foot of Giotto's bell-tower, they could see, carved in stone by the chisel of Luca della Robbia, an Orpheus in ecstasy, playing the lyre among listening swans and lions, while above his head the leaves bend down to hear him. The presence of Orpheus in the heart of the city of the Medici is deeply significant. The figure of Orpheus, with whom according to John Warden (*Orpheus, The Metamorphoses of a Myth*, Toronto, 1982) the neo-Platonist philosopher Marsilio Ficino identified himself, was for the thinkers of the Quattrocento a beacon. Theologian and humanist, lover and creator, Orpheus the civilizer helped them bridge the gap between pagan thought and Christian faith, between the search for the beauty of the senses here below and the call to perfection from above, between the mediaeval world and that of the Renaissance.

But in every version of the myth, Orpheus dies, whether through the vengeance of Dionysos in the person of his maenads, or through the jealousy of the Thracian women, whom he had left inconsolable. Enraged women fling themselves upon him, rend him asunder. Torn to pieces, Orpheus dies. With eyes closed and the singing mouth now mute, his head is carried down the Hebrus to the sea, to be cast up at last on the shores of Lesbos. But his body remains there on the soil of Thrace, the soil of Bulgaria. Reverently the Muses approach, take up his lyre. Carefully the archaeologists search the ground, bend over the scattered remains, take up, gather and rebuild the fragments into a coherent whole. The gold of Thrace shines on the shores of the St. Lawrence, and in the sky there blazes the constellation of the Lyre.

VÉRONIQUE SCHILTZ

I would like to express my deepest gratitude to my Bulgarian colleagues for their collaboration: to Anne Nercessian who provided me with valuable bibliographic information, to Chantal Mercier for her kindness as well as her efficiency in typing the manuscript, and to Pierre Chuvin who so generously put at my disposal his immense erudition.

The excavations at Rogozen.

Painted decoration on the northern lunette of the Sveštari funeral chamber. A goddess gives a gold crown to a horseman.

THE MOST NUMEROUS PEOPLE IN THE WORLD, AFTER THE INDIANS...

The Thracians were the inhabitants of an immense territory stretching between the Carpathian Mountains, the Prut and Dnestr rivers, the Aegean Sea and northwest Asia Minor. Herodotus, the "Father of History," said of them in the fifth century B.C., "They are the most numerous people in the world, after the Indians." "Thracians" is an ethnic term, appearing for the first time in Homer's *Iliad* where it designates, in Hellenized form, the neighbouring peoples to the north of Hellas. We even know the names of the principal tribes of Thrace: the Odrysians, the Triballoi, the Getai, the Bessoi and the Bithynians.

But linguistic research alone is inadequate to solve the problem of the origin of the Thracians. The study of archaeological data is much more productive, and indeed, fascinating. The excavation of a large number of burial mounds, more than five hundred of them in Bulgaria alone, proves that from the end of the fourth millennium B.C., at the beginning of the Bronze Age in southeastern Europe, there is a historical record of continuous habitation in this region. Such a continuity suggests that the Bronze Age people of the area were the direct ancestors of the Iron Age tribes, which is to say, the Thracians, mentioned from 1200 B.C. onwards by neighbouring peoples. The study of some of the burial mounds excavated in Bulgaria seems to prove an even more exciting fact: the existence of a direct link between the Bronze Age and the preceding epoch. This means that the people who left us the famous necropolis of Varna, dating from the end of the Chalcolithic era (3500 to 3000 B.C.). are the same people who initiated ancient Bronze Age culture. Some archaeologists and linguists believe today that the origins of the Thracian people are to be found in the period extending from the Chalcolithic to the end of the Bronze Age. If this hypothesis could be confirmed by new data, it would solve definitively the problem of establishing the origin in time and space, the starting point, of the Indo-European peoples. Such a proof would constitute a considerable advance for scholarship, which has been trying for decades to find the answer to this ethno-genetic puzzle involving Europe and Asia Minor.

Thracian society had no written language. For carving inscriptions and religious texts in stone, metal or slate they used the Greek alphabet. Thus the written evidence we possess is not the work of the Thracians themselves, but of Greek and Roman authors. On the other hand, year after year new excavations are providing a wealth of information. It is necessary, therefore, in studying the Thracians, to use an interdisciplinary methodology which, when employed to decipher the history of societies without a written language, requires meticulous attention to detail. Correct reading of texts by foreign authors, and precise interpretation of the symbolism of objects and monuments, are essential. These are difficult tasks which continually give rise to new problems.

The interdisciplinary method has shed light on the structure of Thracian society, which, during the later Chalcolithic and Bronze ages was based on a clan structure. In the Iron Age, from 1200 B.C., the community restricted to a single clan became enlarged, with several clans or families occupying the same unit of territory. This might well be called a prototype of a class-based society, since it is predicated on the juxtaposition of two groups: those who own or control the means of production, and those who have only precarious access to

Fresco of the frieze, Sveštari funeral chamber.

them. The owners of the means of production were the Thracian royal dynasties and the nobility, whose power was based on armed force. The workers, who operated the means of production, were the masses, those who produced material goods and were subject daily to heavy forced labour in the army, in building, in mining and working metals, in agriculture and animal husbandry. Slaves in the traditional sense were rare in Thrace, prisoners of war being immediately sold off in enormous slave markets, and the houses of the wealthy being staffed by domestic servants. The few exceptions to be found only confirm this general rule.

It was this simple social structure which determined the nature of the Thracian states, the most important of which were established on the territories of the tribes mentioned above: the Odrysians occupied the south and southeast of Thrace, the Triballoi the north and northwest, the Getai the north and northeast, and the Bessoi the region of Rhodope. Most of our written, archaeological and epigraphic information relates to the Odrysian dynasty. This was the best-known Thracian dynasty in southeast Europe: equally famous in northwest Asia Minor were the Bithynians. Thracian kings were independent monarchs, who could also govern their different provinces through intermediaries or representatives. However, they preferred to travel about their domains at the head of their armies, in order to exercise complete military, political and economic control throughout the territory as a whole. As a general rule, the kings had no capital city but maintained numerous fortified residences called royal cities, which of necessity housed a central keep or citadel as well as stores of victuals and arms, shelter for livestock, and workshops for gold- and silversmiths. In these workshops were made the Thracian "treasures," which also include objects deposited in the treasury such as diplomatic gifts, tax payments and the spoils of war. These masterpieces of metalwork were also symbols of royal power, and the rhyta, phialae and cups sometimes bear royal inscriptions with the name of the craftsman, the place where the object was made, and the name of the owner, that is, the king.

The most important buildings in the royal cities of Thrace were connected with religious rites, and seem to have formed an integral part of the palace. Ancient sources give us only a brief description of Thracian holy places, but archaeological explorations have uncovered a number of them. They consist of an altar, sometimes merely a large stone in the middle of a sacred wood. In the mountainous regions, these places of worship are even more rudimentary, always set among rocks and laid out for sacrificial ceremonies involving the ritual killing of animals, with basins and troughs to carry away the blood. The most sacred victim was the horse, for in the Indo-Iranian world to which the Thracians belonged culturally and historically, the horse was the semantic equivalent of man. The bull, symbolizing the male principle, and the ram, representing the king's possessions, were also sacrificed to the Thracian divinities.

The king was the main protagonist in Thracian acts of sacrifice; the priests, who were probably very few in number, only officiated in remote sanctuaries where their role was in general to prophesy. But why was this principal part in the ritual allotted to the king?

The role was assigned to the king as a result of Thracian mythological thinking. Like other ancient peoples, the Thracians had four conceptions or models of the world: the cosmogonic, the mythological, the religious and the social. According to the Thracian cosmogonic model, the universe was created by the great Mother-Goddess, who conceived by herself. The mythological model comes into play after the birth of the Goddess's son, the Sun. This is the point at which the celestial and terrestrial principles of the cosmos are established: the sun begins its course across the sky, and the natural order of things commences. The Thracian religious model or conception was based on a belief in the Sun, child of the Mother-Goddess, as the incarnation of perfection and therefore of immortality. The Thracians believed in immortality, and not only for the soul. To attain this state, it was necessary to perform actions to purify both body and soul. These actions, however, were not possible for everyone, and it was this distinction which formed the basis of the social conception of the world, according to which only the leader of the tribe could attain perfection, while the rest merely aspired to it. This was why only the king (or the leader of the people) could perform sacrifices, those acts of supreme importance as confirming the religious relationship with the great Mother-Goddess.

As has been stated, all ancient peoples created for themselves four models or images of the world. In some cases, these models were maintained even after conceptual, that is, deductive, thinking came into play side by side with mythological thinking. The way in which these models functioned, however, differed from one culture to another. With the Thracians, the functioning of the four concepts or models was subordinate to the acts of the great Goddess's son, who in the heavens was the Sun, and on earth the King. The Thracian king united in his person the three fundamental missions dictated by the mythological view of the universe. These were the mission of the procreator or begetter, that of the maker, or creator of the terrestrial world, and that of the hero who bestows on mankind the gifts of civilization he has stolen from the gods or from nature, such as fire. In carrying out these three missions all in one, the Thracian king was, therefore, not a deified ruler but rather a mediator linking the gods with men.

It was the Thracian social and political structure that determined the nature of their art, the essential theme of which was the basic cosmogonic myth of the great Mother-Goddess and her son. This theme is further developed in the actions of the king and of other protagonists. Unfortunately, many aspects of this art are still a mystery to us. The number of ancient symbols is limited, but their content is extremely varied. For this reason, it is very difficult at the present stage of research to arrive at a correct reading of the form, ornamentation, figures and colours of Thracian metalwork, sculpture and painting. Additional evidence of the true significance of Thracian art came to light with the discovery of the treasure of Rogozen in northwest Bulgaria, which gave new meaning to a certain number of images and conventional iconographic schemas, and demonstrated the ease with which the Thracian craftsmen incorporated borrowed forms into the Thracian cultural context. Skill such as this is the best proof of a culture's vigour and creativity, and is explainable by the historical and geographic circumstances of the land of Thrace.

Thrace was in effect a crossroads between Europe and Asia, not only in the sense of being simply a corridor, but more particularly in being a place where contacts were established, within the country as a whole and via certain of its regions. Contact with the Greeks was particularly intense in the area of the Sea of Marmara (in antiquity the Propontis), along the shore of the Black Sea (the Pontus Euxinus), and along the great rivers that flow into the Aegean: the Marica (Hebros), the Struma (Strymon), and the Mesta (Nestos). It was through these regions that the Thracians established relations not only with the Greeks but also with the major centres of Western Asia and Asia Minor. There was a continual exchange of objects, ideas and skills.

Northeastern Thrace, adjoining territory occupied by the Scythians, was an important area of cultural contact where such borrowings took place constantly. Some scholars even maintain that after 500 A.D. a Thraco-Scythian cultural community was established there. Recent discoveries prove that northwestern Thrace was also a special contact zone, with the Danube (the ancient Istros) and the routes along its banks forming the main channels of communication. It is becoming apparent that communication between the Thracians and the Celts, the most powerful of the peoples of central Europe, was longer established and more productive than had hitherto been thought.

It is hardly surprising, then, that there should exist archaeological evidence of the remarkably expressive art of these peoples. But the idea of culture is infinitely vaster than the idea of art, and this is what we find disconcerting when we discover among the treasures of Thrace objects which are undoubtedly imports. Some scholars maintain that such objects, which are usually of Greek or Persian origin, or from Asia Minor, cannot be called Thracian because they do not belong to Thracian art. While it is perfectly true that they cannot be called Thracian art, nevertheless they form part of Thracian culture.

Culture is defined in numerous ways by different academic disciplines. Specialists in ancient history have the least problem with the term, since for them culture is the behaviour of the peoples they study. Since in antiquity this behaviour was strictly ritualistic, ritual practices made use of any potentially effective object without concern as to its provenance—whether it was purchased, a gift or booty. As soon as a form, an ornamental motif, an image, an attribute or a colour was found to serve the ideological purposes of a society in the ancient world, it became a behavioural tool for the members of that society and consequently a part of its culture.

As has already been stated, the primary characteristic of Thracian culture considered as human behaviour was the belief in immortality. Furthermore, the aspiration to immortality obliged mankind to transcend itself, which meant, according to the Thracian doctrine of immortality known as Thracian Orphism, to perfect oneself in virtue. In our day, we would call this "improving oneself," and it is surely one of the wisest teachings handed down to us moderns from antiquity.

Professor ALEXANDRE FOL

General view of Seuthopolis.

20

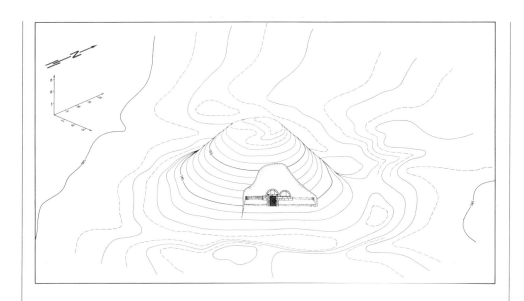

Sveštari burial mound.

THE MOST RECENT ARCHAEOLOGICAL DISCOVERIES IN BULGARIA

Sveštari caryatid head.

Bulgaria is exceptionally rich in historical remains, and represents a real treasure trove for archaeologists. Situated in the heart of the Balkan peninsula, a natural corridor between East and West, it has always been a favourite place for human habitation and settlement, with the result that it possesses numerous traces of the various peoples who have lived there or have merely passed through the country. It was only after Bulgaria was freed from Ottoman domination in 1878 that archaeological research began. The foundations for research were laid during the last two decades of the nineteenth century, but the sites did not begin to be fully excavated until after the Second World War, and it is the diggings undertaken in the past thirty years that are the most significant. Specialists from abroad, as well as Bulgarian archaeologists, have taken an active part in studying the ancient sites: Soviet, German, Polish, British, Japanese, Italian and French experts have worked and are working alongside Bulgarians in mixed teams.

Archaeological research is carried out within one of three great fields—prehistory, antiquity or the Middle Ages, and the periods or regions to be studied are determined by archaeological criteria as the work progresses.

The excavation of tells around Kazanlak, Gradešnica, Pernik, Stara Zagora, etc., has provided valuable information on the chronology and cultural characteristics of the Neolithic period (the sixth and fifth millennia B.C.). Research carried out at Kazanlak has revealed the lay-out and structure of Neolithic dwellings, as well as the biggest collection of Neolithic sickles in Europe (around seventy of them), with stag horn handles and flint blades. In 1985 there began in Sofia the excavation of an important group of Neolithic sites comprising the biggest settlement known in Europe, dating from the sixth millennium B.C. and covering one hundred and seventeen square metres. It consists of two areas, the living quarters and annexes. As well as a great deal of evidence about daily life—pottery, utensils of various sorts, a hearth, a millstone, a loom—the dig has revealed a workshop where flint, horn and bone tools were made, a sacred pit or grave, and a platform. There is a large oven surrounded by fourteen flint store pits capable of holding fourteen tonnes of grain. Two hundred and fifty kilograms of carbonized grain have been found on the site, representing the largest quantity ever discovered.

An extremely well-preserved Neolithic house uncovered at Stara Zagora has been given a special protective treatment and is open to visitors. Thus, for the first time, one can see clearly the lay-out and contents of dwellings of this epoch. Richly decorated terracotta objects of various shapes found in the course of excavations in a Neolithic village near Gradešnica in the district of Varna have greatly added to our knowledge and helped date the earliest evidence of agriculture in the northwest of Bulgaria. It has thus been possible to establish that Neolithic agriculture was of local origin, and did not come from Asia Minor.

While providing valuable information on Balkan Chalcolithic society in the fifth and fourth millennia B.C., the excavation of a fourth-millennium necropolis near Varna has also raised a number of questions. The two hundred and sixty-five graves, real or symbolic, that have been excavated have yielded a great number of copper, stone, bone or horn tools, six and a half kilograms of gold objects, mostly head ornaments, and other objects characteristic of the period.

There are also human masks made of flint and ornamented with gold appliques, stone sceptres with gold handles, and flint vases decorated in gold. These discoveries have substantially changed our view of the Chalcolithic period and the structure of society at the time.

Over the past three years, the study of a group of Chalcolithic sites at the village of Dolnoslav in the Plovdiv region has aroused considerable interest, and for good reason. What has been found there, aside from the dwellings and everyday objects typical of the period, includes an impressive number of flint utensils, and buildings in a special architectural style which archaeologists believe to be places of worship. In the latter have been uncovered over eight hundred idols, whole or in fragments, altars with phallic symbols, sacrificial platforms, and plaster debris with traces of paint. This is undoubtedly the first place of worship dating from the later Chalcolithic period ever discovered in Bulgaria. Although these excavations have only just begun, they have already increased our knowledge about the beliefs of the indigenous population in the fourth millennium B.C., a population composed basically of farmers and herdsmen.

Near Orsoja, in the Mihajlovgrad region, archaeologists have found a large necropolis dating from 1600 to 1400 B.C., the biggest Late Bronze Age one in Bulgaria. Over two hundred and twenty graves for cremation have been studied. The ashes of the dead, and the offerings intended for the dead, were placed inside terracotta receptacles often ornamented with incised designs. The number and variety of the offerings is remarkable: more than a hundred and seventy vessels, flint and bronze knives, bronze and copper pieces of head ornaments, and many other items. The funerary vessels had been buried in irregular rows along a southwest to northwest axis, which implies that the location of the tombs had been apparent at ground level. The pottery from this necropolis has elements in common with that from the mid-Danube region, a point in favour of the argument for an ethno-cultural community in the Late Bronze Age.

In recent years, a huge research programme has facilitated exploration of regions in southeast Bulgaria which had hitherto been little studied, and has enabled a map to be drawn up which describes over seven hundred and fifty Megalithic buildings, mostly dolmens, some of which have been excavated. They mostly consist of one or two chambers with a small entrance passage (a dromos), and were originally covered by a burial mound of earth or stone. The size of these structures is particularly impressive, some of the stone slabs covering them weighing more than ten tonnes, evidence of the remarkable skill of the builders. These findings illustrate the Thracian desire to construct durable edifices, as do numerous rock-hewn tombs discovered in the same region. Most of the latter have dome ceilings, a tradition which continued up to the Hellenistic period. Both dolmens and rock tombs were plundered almost entirely in ancient times. However, some finds have proved them to date from the First Iron Age (1100 to 600 B.C.). The enormous votive-altar stones found recently also belong to Thracian Megalithic civilization. To judge from their orientation, some of these must have been devoted to sun-worship, a finding which completes our knowledge of the rituals and beliefs of the ancient Thracians.

One of the most important ventures of Bulgarian archaeology in recent years has been the excavation of the Thracian city at Kabyle, near Jambol. This city lies in a particularly fertile area where the oldest traces of human habitation go back to the end of the second millennium B.C. The religious and administrative centre of the city was an acropolis on a natural hill, where the remains of a sanctuary sacred to Artemis Phosphoros, the tutelary goddess of the city, have been found, as well as other edifices which probably served administrative purposes. The acropolis was encircled by a strong wall built of thick stone blocks fitted together without mortar. The latest excavations indicate that by the fourth century B.C. the city had become an important political, commercial and economic centre of southern Thrace, and that it maintained close links with a large number of Greek cities. The city was rebuilt at that time, and the agora, the various temples and the lay-out of the city reflect classical traditions. It was the residence of a number of Thracian chieftains who must have minted their own coinage there. A rampart and other monumental constructions from the Roman epoch, notably the largest early Christian basilica in Bulgaria, testify to Kabyle's continuing importance in later times.

There exist in Bulgaria around fifteen thousand burial mounds and tells, most of them dating from 600 to 400 B.C., the most highly developed period of Thracian civilization. Only a small part of this heritage has as yet been subjected to systematic excavations. Researchers are increasingly using modern geophysical and electronic apparatus, and, for digging, mechanical means, which cuts down considerably on the time required for preliminary work. Thus it took only three seasons to study thirteen burial mounds on the outskirts of Strelča, in the Pazardžik region, which contain more than fifty tombs. More than five hundred and fifty objects were unearthed there, notably flint, bronze and silver vessels, weapons, and pieces of gold head ornaments. These finds have led to the formulation of the hypothesis that there existed in this region a precious-metal workshop the products from which were sold in the north of the Balkans.

The largest burial mound, called Žaba Mogila, which stands close by the village of Strelča, has provided valuable indications about Thracian tumular architecture. The large stone tomb found under the mound was clearly the mausoleum of some local Thracian dignitary. Built from perfectly cut stone blocks, some of which are decorated with complex sculptural reliefs, the tomb is one of the most beautiful monuments of Thracian architecture of the fifth and fourth centuries B.C. Unfortunately, it was plundered in antiquity; a chariot found near the entrance, however, is the oldest known Thracian chariot. The same burial mound was found to contain, on the opposite side from the tomb, a place of worship established at the same period as the tomb and altered later.

The theory developed at Strelča was resoundingly confirmed in 1982 by a discovery made with the help of geophysical apparatus, near the village of Sveštari in the district of Razgrad, which brought to light the largest Thracian tomb in the whole of Bulgaria. The excavations took three years. The tomb consists of a passage (dromos), an antechamber and the burial chamber itself, with another room adjoining the latter. It is chiefly remarkable for the richness of ornamentation. The antechamber is decorated with rosettes in relief, the passage adorned with painted capitals. It is, however, the decoration of the main chamber that is the most exceptional. There are two benches carved out of the rock itself, surmounted by a small shrine with three sculpted doors. On the walls of the chamber are ten female figures more than a metre high dressed in lavishly pleated robes. These caryatids are connected to Doric and Corinthian columns with capitals. Capitals ornamented with eagles occupy the four corners. The paintings that formerly adorned the corners are now only partially preserved. In the lunette above the caryatids, a scene from heroic legend painted on the rock itself shows the goddess holding out a golden crown to a kingly horseman in the midst of two files of warriors and servants carrying burial offerings. As the tomb was pillaged in ancient times, our main sources of information are the stylistic details and the few objects brought to light by the excavations. The tomb dates from the third century B.C.

Chance has also lent a helping hand in events. In 1974, an extraordinary treasure was found not far from Borovo in the district of Ruse, when agricultural work turned up a magnificent set of silver drinking vessels consisting of three rhyta of exceptionally fine workmanship, a jug and a cup. The rhyta end in protomes, shaped respectively like a horse, a sphinx and a bull. The jug is decorated in relief with scenes of the cult of Dionysos, one of the divinities most venerated in Thrace. The cup is decorated with a typical Thracian motif: a doe being attacked by a griffin. All these items were made by immensely talented artists, and in both shape and ornamentation are very elegant. Three of them bear a Greek inscription with the name of king Kotys I, who reigned between 383 and 360 B.C. It seems most probable that they came from one of the royal workshops of the first half of the fourth century B.C.

Bulgarian experts on Thrace had another stroke of luck in 1986. The most sensational discovery of recent years, and not just for Bulgaria, was made in January of that year in the village of Rogozen, district of Vraca. It is a truly splendid treasure trove of one hundred and sixty-five objects in silver, some in silver gilt, with a total weight of over twenty kilograms. This treasure was divided into two lots, buried five metres apart. The first lot, composed of sixty-five items, was found by pure chance, and the second, numbering a hundred objects, was brought to light following a systematic archaeological excavation of the surrounding area. In total there are a hundred and eight phialae, fifty-four jugs, and three goblets. The ornamentation, embossed in relief, is different in every case. This incredible variety of motifs and decorative elements makes the Rogozen treasure an invaluable source of information on the toreutics of the fifth and fourth centuries B.C. The Thracian craftsmen who created these masterpieces in silver were astonishingly imaginative. Rarely is a shape repeated. Geometric elements, vertical grooves, beading, egg and dart designs, meanders, are found side by side with plant motifs, lotus leaves and flowers, palmettes, rosettes and acorns. The images of animals, real or imaginary, are no less varied: birds, bulls, griffins, sphinxes, and so on. Various scenes from mythology adorn the jugs and the phialae, with Thracian gods and goddesses alongside Greek divinities depicted in Thracian style. There are hunting scenes, chariots pulled by winged horses, goddesses riding panthers or taming dogs. It is noteworthy that even on pieces the decoration of which is Greek in subject, the inscriptions bear the names of Thracian kings. Study of the Rogozen treasure enriches our knowledge of the spiritual life of the Thracians, of their myths

The Rogozen Treasure.

and culture as a whole, especially since this find has almost tripled the number of Thracian silver objects found. It constitutes a priceless source of information on the history, art and customs of the Thracians. The treasure, which must have been amassed over several decades, clearly formed part of the dynastic inheritance of the Thracian overlord of the territory now known as northwest Bulgaria. Buried in haste at some point during the course of the second half of the fourth century B.C., it has come to light once more to illustrate, if only partially, the splendour and magnificence of that royal court.

Underwater archaeological research along the Thracian shore of the Black Sea has produced very valuable information. The base at Sozopol, specially established for this purpose and equipped with the latest technology, has fully lived up to expectations. Investigations carried out at key points along the coast have enabled us to build up a complete picture on the basis of accidental finds. The discovery of about a hundred stone anchors and lead weights has led us to modify our theories on the Thracian attitude to the sea. It would appear that during the first millennium B.C., and probably well before that, there was considerable traffic of ships on the Black Sea, and not only for trade purposes. Underwater exploration has produced objects dating from the Bronze Age and the beginning of the Iron Age, and has revealed the existence of harbour installations. It has also been proven that the greater part of the ancient Thracian city of Mesembria, present-day Nesebar, which later became a Greek colony, now lies underwater. The oldest walls date from the sixth century B.C. It has thus been possible to calculate the extent of the city: it covered about forty hectares, and was therefore one of the largest Thracian cities on the Black Sea coast. Work is expected to begin soon on exploring a number of submerged prehistoric cities, in particular, those on pile-dwellings of the Chalcolithic and Bronze ages under Lake Varna.

In order to find out more about Thracian religious life during the Roman period, researchers have carefully examined a large number of sanctuaries dating from the second and third centuries A.D. In one of them, on the outskirts of Targovište, there have been found more than two hundred votive reliefs, with inscriptions which show that, despite a long period of subjection to heavy Greek and Roman influence, the Thracians remained faithful to their own religious traditions and concepts, notably to the cult of the "Thracian Horseman." During the early centuries of the Christian era, this figure often merged with a popular divinity from the Graeco-Roman pantheon such as Apollo. Nevertheless, the way he is described links him with the very beginnings of Thracian religion.

The sanctuaries around Pernik, some of which were dedicated to Asklepios, show a similar situation. Besides magnificent reliefs executed by local artists, there has been discovered here a huge architectural complex including a temple with a wide courtyard in the centre of which stands a massive stone altar. The lay-out and building technique link this with the finest traditions of the pre-Roman epoch. This sanctuary is at present open to visitors.

Systematic excavations have been carried out in most of the great Roman cities in Bulgaria—Nicopolis ad Istrum, Oescus, Marcianopolis, Novae, and so on. Studies are being made of the fortification systems as well as of town planning and urban topography. At Oescus, not far from the village of Gigen (dis-

Lamp in the form of a head, painted black (beginning of fifth, end of fourth centuries B.C.).

trict of Pleven), a forum has been uncovered, with a temple to Fortuna built during the second half of the second century A.D. A theatre and stadium of the same period, both remarkably well-preserved, have been discovered at Philippopolis, present-day Plovdiv, where there has also been unearthed an immense forum one hundred and thirteen metres long with a large basilica paved in mosaic, and a considerable part of the road system. The complex dates from the second and third centuries A.D., but continued to be used much later. The ancient theatre at Plovdiv has been restored and during the summer is used for performances of Greek plays as well as modern productions by authors from all over the world.

At Devnja, a large private building covering a surface area of fourteen hundred square metres has been unearthed. It occupied a whole neighbourhood of the ancient city of Marcianopolis. Five rooms still have their beautiful mosaic floors depicting animals and birds, sometimes exotic ones, as well as scenes from mythology including the rape of Ganymede, Zeus, Antiope, Medusa, and an allegory of the seasons. Both mosaics and building date from the third to fourth centuries A.D., and constitute some of the most remarkable in the country. A protective structure has been built over this edifice, so that the historic remains can be viewed *in situ* and compared with other mosaics discovered in the Roman city.

Several thousand objects: bone and bronze pins, sewing and knitting needles, rings, buttons, and flint lamps, have been found in a large workshop of the Roman period near the modern city of Radomir. The presence of coins struck in various cities of the empire and dating from the first to third centuries A.D. shows how wide the market was for the products made here.

The ceramic workshops at Butovo, Hotnica and Pavlikani (district of Veliko Tarnovo) are extremely interesting, both for experts and the general public. They contain several dozen kilns from the fifth to fourth centuries B.C. and the second and third centuries A.D., as well as fragments of ceramic, moulds, tools and other utensils. These finds have made it possible to build up a complete picture of the production process and also to identify the shapes of local pottery, the borrowings and traditions, and to evaluate the influence of Roman ceramics in Thrace. The workshops at Pavlikani may be visited.

In connection with the celebrations for the thirteenth centenary of the founding of the state of Bulgaria in 681, researchers concentrated their efforts on buildings from the mediaeval period, notably at Pliska (seventh to ninth centuries), Preslav (ninth to eleventh centuries) and Turnovo (ninth to fourteenth centuries A.D.).

At Pliska, new parts of the royal palace have been excavated, as well as constructions and fortifications going back to the time the city was founded. At Preslav, monuments of Bulgarian art of the ninth and tenth centuries, and monastery workshops, have been found. Some of the latter produced icons in painted ceramic and in relief, others pottery, others again, glass objects and jewellery. The skill of Bulgarian craftsmen was allied to a great desire for self-expression, which is what gives these images their national character. It is noticeable in the decoration of different vessels, and in the numerous drawings to be found on the defensive walls and on those of houses at Pliska and Preslav. Anonymous artists depicted here the world that surrounded them, and also the world in which they believed. Alongside hunting scenes, battles, horses, there are imaginary animals, images of saints, and also boats and scenes from everyday life.

Near the village of Ravna (district of Varna) a large monastery dating from the ninth to tenth centuries has been studied since 1978. Over a surface area of seventy-five hundred square metres there has been uncovered one of the oldest Bulgarian churches, built in 889, not long after the conversion of the Bulgarians to Christianity. The rows of monks' cells, the abbot's residence, the refectory, the scriptorium where translations were made and manuscripts copied, a bathroom, and storehouses have been revealed. The most interesting discovery, however, has been that of inscriptions and drawings numbering over two thousand which are carved on the walls of the church and of other buildings. The inscriptions are in the Bulgarian tongue written in Cyrillic or Glagolithic characters, or in Greek, or in both languages. This is the first time so large a number of inscriptions from this period have been found in Bulgaria. They are of a religious nature, but some also contain everyday or instructive references. All of this proves that here was one of the great cultural centres of the first Bulgarian kingdom, the inhabitants of which were proud of their learning and spread the alphabet among the ordinary people.

One of the most significant recent excavations is that at Preslav, of a public building where several hundred Bulgarian and Byzantine lead seals have been found. These date from the tenth to eleventh centuries and will enable us to answer important questions about diplomatic relations in the Middle Ages.

In recent years several monuments from the period of the second Bulgarian kingdom (twelfth to fourteenth centuries) have also been studied. The mediaeval city of Šumen has been entirely excavated and preserved. Established as a fortress in the ninth or tenth century, the city became in the centuries following an important administrative, religious and trade centre. The ramparts of the mediaeval capital of Veliko Turnovo have also been uncovered and restored, as have the patriarchal seat, the royal palace, workshops and churches, thus recreating the picture of a flourishing mediaeval city which was the pride of the nation from the twelfth to the fourteenth centuries.

This brief survey of the latest archaeological discoveries in Bulgaria cannot claim to be complete. A large number of monuments from different periods remain to be investigated. However, the results obtained up to now are considerable. Bulgarian archaeologists are delighted to be able to present to the Canadian public at least some of the results of their labours.

ALEXANDRE MINČEV

The entrance to the Sveštari dromos.

29

THE THRACIAN TOMBS

The great expanse of the eastern and central part of the Balkan peninsula was inhabited from the earliest times by the Thracians, one of the numerous branches of the Indo-European family of peoples. The Bosphorus and the Dardanelles, the Aegean Sea and the Sea of Marmara to the south of the coast of Thrace facilitated contacts with the Greek Islands and Asia Minor, while to the east the Black Sea coast opened access to the steppes of Scythia and the Caucasus, and to the north the Danube, that oldest of communication arteries, linked Thrace with central Europe. Thrace was, therefore, not only the cradle of an ancient civilization but also an important crossroads where cultural influences from West and East met and mingled. Information from the writers of ancient times, together with the results of the excavation of sites and necropolises, are eloquent testimony of the high level of Thracian civilization.

This civilization reached its zenith between the fifth and third centuries B.C., a period during which political, social, and economic life flourished in Thrace. On the one hand there was an ongoing process of town planning, which led to the building of well laid out fortified cities: the capitals of Thracian dynasties, such as Seuthopolis, city of Seuthes III, Kabyle, the city of Spartokos, the city of Philippopolis, and others. Then again, this activity led to the building of monumental tombs covered by a burial mound. The lay-out and decoration of these tombs are extremely varied. The more than fifteen thousand burial mounds which have been located up to now in Bulgaria conceal under their earthworks monumental tombs containing rich burial offerings as well as graves with much more modest contents.

Funerary building in Bulgaria goes back to a very ancient tradition. The first burial mounds were raised at the beginning of the Bronze Age (in the fourth millennium B.C.), while the oldest caves, dolmens and rock-cut tombs date from the beginning of the first millennium B.C.

This ancient tradition, based on a firm belief that life goes on beyond the grave, influenced the later development of Thracian funerary architecture and ritual in later times.

Up to the present time approximately forty tombs have been uncovered which were built during the relatively short but brilliant epoch between the fifth and the third centuries B.C. They represent a major source of information on the funeral rites, architecture, art and ideology of the Thracians. In addition, they are evidence of the class structure of the society, and provide new data on the development of a ruling class.

The study of the tombs also presents many problems in regard to dating, classification, origin and development. Almost all the tombs are those of rulers or members of the nobility. They were the setting for ritual ceremonies in honour of the deceased, to whom rich gifts were offered: valuable tableware, weapons, horse trappings if the deceased was a man, jewellery and gold head ornaments in the case of a woman. In a sense, the tombs constituted temples to heroes, to which after the funeral rites people came to pay homage to the deified dead.

Thracian tombs of the fifth to third centuries B.C. show great diversity in lay-out and structure, with some elements in common. Most of them have a dromos or access passage, an antechamber and a main chamber. Burial was

View of the dromos of a Thracian tomb with triangular arch.

by interment, men often being accompanied by their horses. The tombs were made of stone blocks, and occasionally of brick, and are sometimes adorned with a painted decor. They may be classified in two large groups: tombs with a rectangular chamber, and those with a circular one.

Tombs with rectangular chambers seem most numerous. We know of a total of twenty-three, most in southern Bulgaria: on the outskirts of Vetren (district of Pazardžik), Kalojanovo (district of Sliven), Tatarevo (district of Haskovo), Philippovo (district of Plovdiv), Magliž (district of Stara Zagora), etc. In most cases, one or two antechambers and a dromos precede the main chamber. The method of roofing over the burial chambers varies. Sometimes it is by triangular vaulting formed by leaning blocks of stone, or by large oblique slabs joined by a horizontal block. The tomb at Philippovo presents a rather special sort of roofing, with stone blocks laid diagonally from the four corners of the chamber forming a vault called a "galate," typical of the architecture of Asia Minor. The antechambers of the two tombs at Varna display, as at Svestari, a "cradle" vault. But most often it was the triangular or false vault which was chosen because it was easy to build.

From the end of the fourth century B.C. advances in stone-cutting and the appearance of baked bricks, mortar and plaster allowed more sophisticated building. Façades began to be decorated, and the interiors of tombs to be painted.

In the second category of tombs, circular ones with a dome (tholos), the tomb at Mezek is particularly interesting. It is as remarkable for its size (29.95 metres in total length) as for its arrangement, with a long passage (20.65 metres), two rectangular antechambers and a circular main chamber with a beehive-shaped dome. Dating from the end of the fourth or the beginning of the third century B.C., it contained very rich offerings: bronze tableware, candelabras, the statue of a wild boar, gold jewellery, amphorae, etc.

Domed tombs present the same variety of materials and of methods for constructing the vault. Together with carefully cut stone blocks, in the tombs of the Seuthopolis region baked bricks of a special shape designed for circular buildings were used. In some tombs the vaulting begins at the base of the wall, in others it rests on a frame. The vault at Kazanlak is in the shape of a beehive. The tomb at Strelča is the first example of a sophisticated façade. The entrance is framed by stone blocks carved with a row of beading, Ionic and Lesbian string courses and an ivy pattern, evidence of the existence of a local school of stone masons. The sculptural decoration of the tomb at Svestari confirms the existence, at the beginning of the Hellenic period, of sculpture workshops in other regions of Thrace.

The problem of the origin of dome tombs has always aroused debate among researchers. Their resemblance to Mycenaean tombs suggests that the prototype should be sought in the Mycenaean tholos, and their appearance in Thrace could be explained by the persistence of a very ancient form which was revived to fulfil the needs of the Thracian nobility. However, many scholars believe that Thracian dome tombs constitute a separate architectural type, the appearance and development of which were largely the result of local forms of megalithic building, notably the dolmens and rock tombs, unconnected with any influence from abroad. It is undeniably true that the rectangular and dome tombs of the fifth to third centuries B.C. show a development of the main principles of local megalithic funerary building. Both types co-existed in Thrace in the classical and Hellenistic eras and influenced each other both in lay-out and in construction and decoration methods.

The discovery in the tombs of monumental wall painting opens a new chapter in the cultural history of Thrace. Imitation marble veneer is well-known in ancient wall painting from the classic period onwards, being very popular in the Hellenistic era, and Thrace followed the fashion. Traces of it can be found in over ten tombs as well as in the palace at Seuthopolis and the houses of Mesembria.

The oldest tombs have only plain plastering with friezes of simple motifs. A little later, different parts of the walls were highlighted by means of colour, as in the tombs at Kalojanovo and Ruen. This style, known as "architectural," was followed by the extremely elaborate painting of the tomb at Kazanlak.

Numerous articles have been published about the Kazanlak tomb, and the problems of its exact dating, the interpretation of the main scenes, and the artisans, have aroused considerable interest. V. Mikov and Ludmila Živkova have studied in detail the decorative scheme of the paintings, which demonstrate for the first time a total concept of decorating the structure of a wall by plastic and pictorial means. Though he was to a great extent limited by the demands of the Ionic style, the artist often allowed himself a certain licence. Thus most of the decoration is found on the vault itself, which is unusual for the period. Though using this small space to the maximum extent, he was nevertheless obliged to go beyond the architectural framework. Above the ornamental frieze of the dromos he placed another frieze of figures, showing a parade of horsemen and foot soldiers in battle order. On the string course of the dome the principal frieze is composed of rosette and bucrane motifs, while below the cornice is inserted a lower frieze, also of figures. These are all indications of the Thracian origin of the artist. An analysis of the style of the painting as well as parallels with the decoration of the Ptolemaion and with the sanctuary of Arsinoé at Samothrace (286-281 B.C.) enable the Kazanlak tomb to be dated as being from the third quarter of the third century B.C. In the centre of the big frieze, there is a couple holding hands. The whole composition revolves around this central group of the deceased Thracian dignitary and his wife who face the entrance. The man, wearing a crown, is shown almost full-face, seated on a low chair before a table laden with dishes and fruits. In his right hand he holds a metal cup, and in his left hand holds that of his wife, who is seated on a richly ornamented throne. A woman holding a platter of fruit is approaching the man from his right, followed by a servant carrying a jug and a cup. Behind him there appear trumpet players preceding a group of two horses with men holding the reins. On the other side, two maidservants approach the seated woman bringing her a box of toiletries, a jewel casket and a veil. In the background is a chariot, the driver of which has stopped to soothe the horses which are prancing.

This rich picture which fills the large frieze of the domed chamber is most often interpreted as the scene of a funeral banquet. Others see it as a wedding feast. Perhaps it is less a question of considering these two conceptions as opposites than of seeing them as one, the unification of marriage and death, both of which mark the start of a new life. Thracian faith in immortality is here expressed through the image of a deified ruler, become a hero, whose wife accompanies him to his new eternal life.

With its typically Thracian architecture, and the richness and variety of its paintings, the Kazanlak tomb represents one of the masterpieces of Thracian art of the early Hellenistic period. The style of the tomb and the lay-out of the decoration, faithful to the traditions of Hellenistic painting, are evidence of the refined taste of the local nobility, while at the same time, the subject and composition reflect the religious beliefs and ideology of the Thracians.

The decoration in two other tombs found near Kazanlak at Magliž and at Kran show the next stage in the development of wall painting in southern Thrace. The Magliž tomb is remarkable for the complexity of its lay-out and for its size. The rectangular burial chamber is connected to two other rooms built of brick and covered by a false vault. Access is via a long stone dromos. All the walls are covered with plaster, but it is the painting in the main chamber which is the best preserved. Above the blocks of the plinth a wall painted in Pompeian red has a string course in relief with plant motifs and a frieze with a succession of palmettes and amphorae. The three variants on the "architectural style" —the linear, the coloured and the plastic—are thus all represented at Magliž. The walls here are for the first time modelled by means of stucco pilasters. Another detail of the decoration of this tomb is the frieze of amphorae and palmettes. The amphorae are of the agonistic type associated with burial rites. They date from the second half of the third century, while the decorative details date the tomb from the third quarter of the third century.

The tomb at Kran is also later. The painting in the dromos is well preserved, and the partition wall is divided by a plinth and stucco slabs above which the wall is painted in Pompeian red and white.

These three tombs as well as the two with brick domes at Seuthopolis which date from the early third century lead us to assume the existence of an important school of architecture and painting in the region of the modern city of Kazanlak. It must have been active from the end of the fourth century and throughout the third century, and not only the tombs but also all the buildings of Seuthopolis, the city of Seuthes III, are evidence of its brilliance. This group of buildings enables us to follow the development of architectural planning and decoration during this period and the troubled epoch which followed.

In the north of the country, architecture and funerary decor reached their high point with the recently excavated tomb at Sveštari (district of Razgrad). This Thracian royal tomb was one of the most sensational discoveries of recent times (cf. M. Čičikova, "La découverte d'une tombe royale thrace" *Archéologie* no. 190, Dijon, 1984). Its architecture and the richness of its paintings and sculptures make it an outstanding achievement of Thracian art. It is also considered to be among the finest examples of Hellenistic funerary architecture.

This tomb represents a new version of the traditional lay-out, with its three almost square chambers covered by a vault the height of which varies according to the size of the chamber. At the same time, a number of elements are typical of Hellenistic architecture of the period. The Sveštari tomb reveals a marked penchant for the monumental and the decorative, evidenced particularly by the lay-out of the main burial chamber. The "architectural" style

Fresco of the tomb at Kazanlak.

Sveštari caryatids.

here is created with solid architectural elements. The Doric order is represented by columns partially within the wall, an architrave and a frieze with alternating triglyphs and metopes. The sculptural decoration blends harmoniously with the architectural ting. Between the columns, above a plinth and a row of orthostats, there is a series of limestone panels with caryatids in high relief. These ten female figures 1.2 metres high are shown full-face in a pose of solemn gravity with their arms raised as if to support the vault. Although the gesture and the robes are all the same, the faces vary, being very individual and expressive. In the originality of representation and composition and in the specific nature of their dress with its plant motifs, the Sveštari caryatids illustrate both the artistic and religious ideas of the time. These figures depict one of the aspects of the great Mother-Goddess, shown as the divinity of vegetation and fertility, mistress of life here below, and beyond death. Her presence in the tomb symbolizes the continuity of life and the cycle of rebirth.

Figures of caryatids are also found in other tombs, notably in Asia Minor and southern Italy. They belong to the burial ritual, and are designed as deities upholding the celestial canopy over the burial of the deified dead. They may also symbolize the forces of destiny that guide dead heroes into the hereafter.

This theme of the apotheosis is developed in the lunette on the northwest wall. As in the great frieze at Kazanlak, the Sveštari figures appear as though suspended in space, with no surrounding context. The principle of the composition is the same, with the figures divided into two groups. The large female figure in the centre probably represents the Mother-Goddess. She is approaching a horseman to whom she is offering a gold crown. Behind her is a procession of four women carrying various offerings: a box of toiletries, an oenochoe, a half-open jewel casket, a big metallic vessel and a sort of tripod. The horseman, who represents the deceased, is wearing a short garment covered by a chlamys. He holds the reins in his left hand, and his right arm, slightly bent, is stretched out towards the goddess. Two men, apparently shield-bearers, follow him carrying weapons. The religious nature of the scene is unmistakable: this is a dead king in the process of becoming a hero. Such an interpretation is confirmed by the lay-out of the burial chamber in the manner of a religious building (a heroon with a portico), and by the presence of a little shrine (naiskos).

The naiskos consists of two pilasters crowned by capitals, a cornice, and a pediment painted red with a Gorgon's head sculpted on the tympanum, with a triple stone door. This structure of religious implication overhung the great bench which was the funeral bier of the deified ruler.

Parallels to the architecture and decorative motifs of the Sveštari tomb are found in the most famous buildings of the Hellenistic era such as the Didymeion at Milet and the already mentioned monuments of Samothrace, which enables us to date this tomb from the second quarter of the third century B.C.

Designed to house the remains of the king of Thrace, the Sveštari tomb was begun while he was still alive, but his premature death obliged the Thracians to make use of it—even before the decorative details were complete. Thus we are able to follow the progress of the work as it was being carried out, and to learn a great deal about the stages of construction of the figures and motifs.

In the technical mastery of its construction, its rich combination of architecture, sculpture and painting, and by the use made of Hellenistic models, the Sveštari tomb stands witness to the great skill of the Thracian artist and to the talent with which he used all the resources of his time. Even though he had recourse to Hellenistic models, he was able to adapt them to the artistic, aesthetic and religious ideas of the Thracian people.

In conclusion it should be noted once again that the development of architecture and funerary decoration went hand in hand with the political and economic rise of the Thracian state in the fifth and fourth centuries B.C. The entry of Thrace within the sphere of the Hellenistic world gave a new direction to Thracian political and cultural development. Thrace was not content merely to belong to this great cultural community, but took an active part in the process of its formation. Against the background of Hellenistic traditions in architecture and painting, the tombs at Kazanlak, Strelča and Sveštari show the development of specifically Thracian elements, which grew out of local architectural, artistic and religious traditions. These tombs constitute, therefore, remarkable monuments to the brilliance of Thracian Hellenistic art.

MARIA ČIČIKOVA

THE THRACIANS AND THEIR ART

The Thracians, one of the most numerous peoples of antiquity according to Herodotus, step into the pages of history with the Homerian epic: they were Priam's allies in the Trojan War. We possess, however, little detailed information about their customs and way of life up to the fifth and fourth centuries B.C. It was not until the Thracian coast was colonized during the seventh and sixth centuries B.C. by the Greeks, most of whom came from Asia Minor and the islands of the Aegean, that they aroused any interest in the colonizers. It would seem from the sources we have that the everyday life of the Thracians who inhabited the centre and eastern part of the Balkan peninsula was little different from that of the peoples of Asia Minor, the northwest of which was also peopled by Thracians. The Thracians of Thrace also had a family structure based on polygamy, lived in villages, practised agriculture and animal husbandry, and were organized in tribes each led by a king, as in pre-Achaemenian Asia Minor. Several Greek legends mention Thracian kings from before the Trojan War, that is, before 1200 B.C. The picture the Greeks give of Thracian royalty differs in many ways from their own idea of kingship.

The Greek legends emphasize how closely linked the Thracian kings were with the religious life of the people. Instead of recalling their conquests and their exploits in war, they depict them as singers and priests. Such is the case with Thamyris, Mousaios and Eumolpos. The last of these, having left Thrace for Attica, settled in Eleusis where he established the famous Mysteries held in honour of Demeter and Persephone which were so famous in antiquity. Orpheus, the most celebrated of Thracian kings for his singing and religious songs, appears in the Greek historical tradition as the reformer of the Thracian religion. Herodotus too states that in the distant past there existed in Thrace mystic brotherhoods surrounding the king. Thus Zalmoxis, king of the Thracian tribe of the Getai who inhabited the Danube delta, summoned together the leading men of the tribe to banquets to teach them that neither he nor his guests nor their descendants would die, but would reach a land of comfort and happiness after departing this life. Thereafter the Getai made Zalmoxis a god.

This evidence makes it clear that kings in Thrace were not only military leaders but also presided over the religious life of the tribe. Nevertheless the tradition of royal power among the Thracians did not appear to be of very ancient origin until an epoch-marking discovery in 1972 completely altered our approach to the question. This was the excavation of the Chalcolithic necropolis of Varna on the Black Sea coast. To appreciate the importance of this discovery, it is essential to keep in mind the way of life of the population which, before the Thracians, inhabited the east and centre of the Balkan peninsula from the seventh to the third millennia B.C. These people had a highly developed culture, making pottery of elaborate and varied shapes, often painted and even sometimes polychrome. They worshipped images of stone or clay, and used polished stone tools, stag horn picks, and horn sickles reinforced with flint chips. This culture was as advanced in the humble villages as in the fortified settlements, as is shown by the large number of tells with their numerous archaeological levels protected by wicker fencing, which recall somewhat the tells of Asia Minor. The dwellings, all similar, each have two rooms, one of which generally contains an oven and a mortar. The alleyways were paved

Following page: Varna, tomb no. 4.

with wood.

Metal makes its appearance here almost as soon as in Asia Minor, which means that these were the most advanced metalworkers in Europe. This hypothesis has been confirmed by the discovery in Bulgaria of the oldest open-work copper mines in Europe. The graves of the period are relatively modest, containing few grave goods: some terracotta receptacles and stone tools. The skeletons are mostly curled up in the foetal position.

THE FIRST KINGS AND THE OLDEST GOLD

The Chalcolithic necropolis at Varna dates from the years 3600-3200 B.C., a period which, in Bulgaria, corresponds to the last phase of the Chalcolithic era. The excavations are still going on, but up to now around two hundred and fifty tombs have been studied, about fifteen of which contain gold objects. Five of these tombs, each of which contained more than a kilogram of gold, are richer than those in succeeding millennia at a period when the mining and working of gold had become infinitely easier. In addition, there is a significant modification in these tombs: the skeleton lies supine with arms and legs stretched out. In most of the graves an axe-sceptre, apparently unused, lies at the head of the deceased. It is made of stone, and the short wooden handle, which has disappeared, can be reconstructed due to the gold rings which encircled it at regular intervals, while the ends were covered by cylindrical gold ferrules. The evidence indicates that the dead man was buried with his sceptre, the badge of power. There are also dozens of gold appliques, some shaped like horseshoes, or two horseshoes joined; others have the form of circles, discs or balls, while three remarkable examples are the shape of horned animals. Curiously, there are cenotaphs alongside these rich tombs, containing no bones, but masks of dried clay in the shape of a human face, with two gold plaques over the eyes, one over the mouth and underneath a row of small gold fragments to represent teeth. One of these masks was crowned with a diadem. The tombs also contained bracelets made of a simple band of gold, coiled or forming two grooves. Sometimes these objects have a border with a grain motif. We can therefore postulate the existence of a primitive metallurgy in copper and gold which was certainly not limited to burial goods. Some of the terracotta vessels had been decorated with a paste of gold dust applied with a brush in a technique found much later. Thus the community to which this necropolis belonged indicated clearly, by means of gold, the rank of the dead: there is no doubt that these were kings who, in the patriarchal society of the Chalcolithic era, received from their subjects tributes in gold, and who maintained workshops capable of producing their copper axes and gold insignia. The Varna necropolis is of enormous historical importance. The gold in it is older than that found in the tombs at Mycenae, in the pyramids of Egypt or even in the royal Hittite tombs of the twenty-fourth to the nineteenth centuries B.C. in northern Anatolia. The royal necropolis of Varna therefore places not only the discovery of gold but also the origins of the state and of kingly power twelve or thirteen

Excavation site at Karanovo, where artifacts from the Bronze Age were found more than 12 metres underground.

centuries earlier than had been thought.

Gold continued to play a part during the later period running up to the beginning of the third millennium and the Middle Bronze Age, but everything indicates that the kingdom which produced this unique necropolis disappeared.

In fact, we know of no other similar tombs from the later centuries of the Chalcolithic era, and at the beginning of the Bronze Age we see a certain regression in the cultural products of the inhabitants of the central and eastern parts of the Balkans. The native population became mingled with newcomers from the East. Polychrome pottery disappeared, as did the idols, while the forms of ceramic changed: we see the appearance of the askoi, asymmetrical vessels resembling jugs with obliquely cut openings, the kyathoi, cups for serving liquids, and kantharoi with two handles above the rim. An increase in the output of weapons and tools towards the end of the Middle Bronze Age (2000-1600 B.C.) brought about the use of stone moulds. The different cultures of the Aegean basin at that period produced scarcely any notable monuments, except for the most important of them, the Cretan civilization, which stands in a category by itself. On the other hand, in Thrace as throughout the Aegean region, the period between the Middle Bronze Age and the Late Bronze Age (1700-1600 B.C.) saw the unmistakable reappearance of a royal power which is clearly marked by a whole series of archaeological finds.

The most striking Thracian discovery of this period is the Razgrad find, consisting of several dozen moulds almost all of which show signs of prolonged use. We will mention three of them. The two first were used to cast the form known as axe-sceptre: the long, ribbed blade curved in a spiral being of no practical use. This spiral was one of the insignia of royal power which decorated the end of a sceptre similar to those of the kings of the earlier period. Another mould, of which three components survive, was for a sort of sword for which there is no evidence in Thrace, but the ornamentation of which is of particular interest. The decorative motif, similar to that on the axe-sceptre, consists of parallel grooves which narrow to a single groove at the tip of the sword, while they divide and widen out towards the hilt. It is these three moulds which lead us to posit the existence of a royal workshop from which they must have come. A very similar decoration is found on the gold sword from the Persinari treasure in Rumania, which dates from the second half of the seventeenth or first third of the sixteenth century B.C. This parallel groove design is found, though in a simplified form, on a large number of more recent swords and axe-sceptres. It is, however, a motif characteristic of forged objects rather than of cast ones, and it appears for the first time on certain of the gold bracelets from Varna.

THE VALČITRAN TREASURE

The Valčitran treasure is undoubtedly the most remarkable Bronze Age collection from Thrace, and even from the whole area of the lower Danube and the northwest coast of the Black Sea. It appears to be a royal treasury which must originally have contained many more items. Its last owner perhaps only possessed a part of it, probably those objects which were easiest to transport and relatively light in weight (a total of 12.5 kilograms), which he was obliged to bury when threatened by some great danger.

That is how these treasures were preserved for posterity: the four cups, the enormous solid gold kantharos, the triple receptacle (without the lid it must once have had) and the lids of seven other large receptacles. These items are evidence of great skill in the shapes and decoration of the metal. Both receptacles and lids are quite heavy and solid, of perfect shape with a carefully polished surface. All are decorated in the same way, not unlike the design found at Varna: parallel grooves and point motifs are found mainly on the handles and the lids. On the handles the parallel grooves fan out towards the ends. The peduncle which attaches the spherical button to the lids is also grooved, and grooves at the centre of the lids form concentric circles. This way of alternating smooth and grooved surfaces is also characteristic of Mycenaean toreutics, as well as of the older toreutics of Anatolia. However, in the two latter cases the grooves are never in this sort of narrow elongated sheaf, often taking the shape of an S. The cupules of the Valčitran triple receptacle are decorated with horizontally laid Ss, and the hollow handles have ring-shaped grooves. The receptacle was emptied through a single orifice in the middle handle. It must have had a lid, which has disappeared, so that the whole ensemble was designed to resemble a group of three water birds. The artists who made the Valčitran treasure used the same S motif in meander for two large lids. The grooves are combined here with a silver niello design inlaid on the gold background. The shapes of the receptacles of Valčitran are well-known not only in Thrace but throughout the Aegean, and must have been quite common in the region where the discovery was made. As for the decoration, it seems to be the work of a local artist. The perfection of his work shows that he had fully mastered the techniques of the craftsmen of Mycenae and of the Anatolian plateau, but he developed them in his own way. This form of vessel, and this type of decoration on bronze objects, are found throughout the region that stretches from the northwest coast of the Black Sea and the Dnieper to the Balkan and the river Iskar.

The epoch following the appearance of the Valčitran treasure gives us a number of other examples of the insignia of kingly power, such as the bronze swords, some of which have a rapier shape designed for piercing and not for cutting, while others are designed as cutting weapons. The only evidence we possess of gold work at the time is a few pairs of earrings. The Valčitran treasure remains the only Bronze Age find that proves the existence of advanced toreutics. In addition, these receptacles are the only evidence we have of the splendour of Thracian royal banquets. It was indeed at these banquets that dignitaries paid homage to the Thracian king, that they worshipped their divinities through mysteries, performed sacrifices and poured libations, and carried out all sorts of other rites.

The existence of a treasure in gold of such importance, at a time when, with the exception of Mycenae, most treasures consist only of masses of bronze objects and of essential tools, is very significant. It shows that the

Thracian lands belonged to a civilization of which the autonomous development kept pace with that of the civilizations of Mycenae and Anatolia. The axe-sceptre appeared there in the remote past as a sign of kingly power, as it did elsewhere throughout the Aegean basin and in Anatolia. Only northwestern Thrace, west of the river Vit, was the exception: the Late Bronze Age civilization developed there closely linked with that of the tribes inhabiting the regions of the mid-Danube. An illustration of this may be seen in the Orsoja necropolis in the region of Lom. Cremation was practised here, and the ashes placed in urns. There were specific forms of vessels: the askos was replaced here by a small receptacle in the form of a bird which apparently was used for religious purposes. This type of receptacle resembles a crude imitation of the Valčitran triple receptacle. Pottery was generally decorated with white stripes and quite simple geometric motifs. Rather stylized terracotta images reappeared, resembling somewhat the Mycenaean idols and their ornamentation, though no direct contact between the two cultures has yet been established.

BIRTH OF THE NEW THRACIAN ART

In Thrace, as throughout the Balkan peninsula, the period between the twelfth and ninth centuries B.C. belonged to what is called the "Dark Ages." There was a certain regression in material culture. The appearance of iron work, no longer cast like bronze but hammered, marks the end of the ancient metallurgic traditions. From this point on, weapons were made of iron, and bronze was only used for animal figurines, fibulae, amulets, bracelets and other similar objects, often with quite complex decoration: the number of them increased sharply from the beginning of the ninth century B.C. Very rare in southeast and eastern Thrace, they appear in the rock-cut tombs and in the dolmens. They are most often found in the western part of Thrace, along the valley of the Vardar, which is to say, in modern Macedonia, as well as in northwestern Bulgaria.

The geometric style which is their principal decoration is typical of the regions on the periphery of the Aegean, Greek art being the most striking manifestation of it. It should, however, be noted that toreutics, of only mediocre quality between the eleventh and sixth centuries B.C., is represented by some interesting examples which allow us to judge the extent to which it declined. So in comparison with older objects, the gold cup of Sofia, found at the same time as a cauldron from Urartu which enables it to be dated from the eighth or seventh century B.C., shows clearly that the artist was not sufficiently in control of the metal to give it a beautiful shape or an elegant design of grooves. This is the same case with the gold scabbard from Belogradec in the Provadja region of northeastern Bulgaria: obviously the artist intended to reproduce a groove motif barred with transversal striae, but the result has faults of workmanship which make it infinitely less polished than the objects from Valčitran. We can only marvel at how far the art had declined. And yet the cross-shaped ornamentation which appears on the back is very similar to the crosses on the underside of the Valčitran lids, and have pieces of amber in the centre.

Another sort of find from the Early Iron Age shows a continuation of the traditions of the Bronze Age. These are the iron sceptres which have at the upper end a bronze axe. The cutting edge of this type of axe was not really usable, and at the heel the hammer was replaced by heads or whole representations of horned animals—bulls, rams, goats, stags—and less often griffins or horses. It is important to emphasize that in their shape these axes perpetuate the ancient tradition of axe-sceptres for religious purposes of the Razgrad treasure, just like the axe-sceptres of Asia Minor, where the axe kept its typical shape throughout the second and into the first millennium B.C., while the hammer became an animal design or some other decorative element.

In the Vardar valley these axes became amulets with a much smaller blade and a heel in the shape of a figure, with two symmetrical protomae of birds, for in that region, modern Macedonia, water birds were a favourite subject for artists.

In the eighth and seventh centuries B.C. there appeared new kinds of ornaments which would continue to be used up to the end of the fourth century B.C. The most important of these were the gold breast-plates. In the Vardar region they were most often lozenge-shaped and decorated with a rosette flanked by palmettes. To the east of Thrace the shapes are much more varied, being hexagonal, ellipsoidal or semi-circular, all typical shapes in Asia Minor. The finest example of a breast-plate is the one from Mušovica mogila, one of the burial mounds situated near the village of Duvanli in the Plovdiv region. It was found in a woman's grave. Breast-plates from eastern Thrace are also decorated with plant motifs but may have in addition animalist motifs, and even human images which are completely absent in the west.

In short, in attempting to define the breadth of techniques used in Thracian art at this period, we are talking about a genuine renaissance. A notable characteristic is the introduction of animalist elements into the geometric patterns. Many scholars believe that the animalist decoration typical of later Thracian art was borrowed from the Scythians. But the animalist motifs decorating the axes are found within a geometric context and predate the first Scythian animalist art objects, which date from the beginning of the sixth century B.C. and show the influence of oriental art. In addition, we can see the appearance of this geometricized zoomorphic style in another and very important category of characteristically Thracian objects from the fifth and fourth centuries B.C.: horse trappings.

THE DEVELOPMENT OF THRACIAN HORSE TRAPPINGS

From the ninth century B.C. there appear among the rich grave goods in tombs pieces of bronze harness or trappings. Always in pairs, they were placed symmetrically on either side of the headstall adorning the horse's head. In southern Thrace they take the form of a pierced cross or of a triscele, while to the north they are circles or pierced rosettes. One unique example came to light

Catalogue no. 379
Ornamented applique of zoomorphic motifs. Loukovit
Treasure (end of sixth century B.C.)

in the find made near the village of Sofroniĕvo, in the district of Vraca. Among bronze rosettes dateable from the sixth century B.C. was an ellipse decorated with scroll work on the lower part, two wings and a bird's tail on the upper, and in the middle, rising out of a simply engraved pattern, a button and the head of a horned animal in relief, of the same type found on the heel of the bronze axes. All these elements originated in the geometric art of the preceding epoch. The symbol of wings was well-known in Asia Minor, notably in Persian art where it accompanies the image of the king or of a god. It was also widespread in pre-Achaemenian art and appears in the ornamentation of the bronze cauldrons of Urartu (eighth to seventh centuries B.C.), on the appliques of the handles, where a bull's head or a human bust is surrounded by stylized wings. The appearance of this headstall reflects the introduction, in the sixth century B.C., of an animalist decoration based on an ancient local tradition. We can only surmise as to how a typically Anatolian motif got to northwest Thrace, the region farthest away from Asia Minor. Asia Minor harnesses did not, as a general rule, include this type of applique. Their appliques mostly took the form of an animal or of a group of animals. This is probably a local adaptation which, in several variants, became very popular in this northwestern region of what is now Bulgaria.

The fifth century B.C. saw a profound change in the manufacture of harness trappings: bronze was no longer cast, but from then on techniques better suited to silver work were used. Ornamentation also changed in the fifth and fourth centuries. Thus, on the Sveštari headstall, dating from the first half of the fourth century B.C., we see two heads, one of a man and the other of a lion. The Vraca headstall (Mogilanska mogila, 385-359 B.C.) only has one head, that of a lion, while the contemporary headstall from Letnica is decorated with a protoma of a lion attacking a bull. The examples from the Lukovit treasure provide even more elaborate shapes. In the same period, cross or triscele-shaped appliques have, at the ends of the arms, griffins' heads that give them the appearance of swastikas. So a zoomorphic ornamentation, no longer geometric, replaced the older geometric patterns. In southern Thrace the headstall, which came from the northwest, appeared simply in the form of one or two animal heads, without the frame of the ellipsoidal plaque. The most typical design in this category, illustrated by a find from Brezovo (first half of the fourth century B.C.), is that of the headstall in the shape of two lions' heads.

It was also at this period that new designs began to appear on silver appliques. The most informative examples are from northwest Bulgaria. Two symmetrical appliques from the Mogilanska mogila tumulus near Vraca show lions attacking bulls; on the Letnica ornament, a lion fights a griffin while a serpent attacks two beasts. From the Lukovit treasure one ornament depicts a lion killing a stag, the other a horseman stabbing a lioness with his spear. All these appliques demonstrate the existence of close relations between northwestern Thrace and eastern Anatolia, where this sort of object displays very similar designs. The animalist repertoire was further enriched by griffins' heads (Brezovo, Bukjovci, Bednjakovo), or again by two lion paws emerging from a shoulder. Many scholars maintain that this type of harness applique appeared in Thrace as a result of Scythian influence, or even that they were the work of Scythian invaders. Certainly their resemblance to equivalent Scythian finds is undeniable, but a more careful and thorough study of the style leads us to suggest another explanation to account for this relationship.

THE STYLE OF THRACIAN ART IN THE FIFTH AND FOURTH CENTURIES B.C.

As an example, let us analyze the Brezovo headstall. It is made up of two lions' heads. The lower one has two protrusions on its forehead, a wide rose, and deep folds, typical of Achaemenian art, on the cheeks. The mane, composed of small semi-circles striated by parallel lines and arranged in three rows of locks, is also characteristic of the Persian style. It is easy to recognize, in this work of Thracian toreutics, an Achaemenian pattern of decoration. The depictions of lions on other objects show only one or two of these characteristics, often crudely done without any real understanding of the meaning. The Thracian artist imitated the style of Persian art, and moved from very cursory geometric style to a much more elaborate one with oriental traits.

Another significant example is provided by a comparison between the small bronze statuette of a stag from Sevlievo and the Garčinovo matrix. The former shows a body, neck and withers of prismatic form, with lines emphasizing the masses and asymmetrical antlers ending in hooks resembling birds' heads. The matrix shows the stag attacked by a lion, twisting in violent movement, but the same elements are there: the ribbing lines on the prismatic body can be seen on the neck, withers and haunches, and the antlers end in lions' and birds' heads. This latter example displays another trait of the Thracian style: the transformation of the tips of antlers into animal heads.

Trying to create a picture of an imaginary being, a winged stag, the Thracian artist adopted this procedure rather than adding wings to the animal's body, and the stylized figure 8 by which, in Achaemenian art, the withers and ribs of animals became a bird's head with a hooked beak. Rather than use an incomprehensible oriental motif, the Thracian artist preferred to use a much more common animalist trait.

Thracian goldsmiths' work provides many other examples of motifs shared with Persian art. This is the case with the scenes of a lion overpowering a victim (Mogilanska mogila, Lukovit), in which the unrealistic position of the animal which turns one paw forwards and the other backwards is frequently found in Achaemenian art.

All of this shows how difficult it is, in stylistic terms, to establish a dividing line between Thracian and Anatolian art. There is scarcely any difference except in the shape and function of the supports of this zoomorphic decoration. The animalist style covered a wide area, including Thrace, Asia Minor and southern Russia. Its origins were, however, purely oriental, and it was the Orient which served as a source of inspiration for both Thracian and Scythian artists. The oriental style came into Thrace against the background of the already existing geometric style. The change from geometric design to animalist design brought in new forms, such as the harness appliques in animal shapes, which were invented by Thracian artists on the basis of an idea from Anatolia.

It is clear, then, that until the sixth century B.C. Thracian art was geometric, but that from the beginning of the fifth century and up until the conquest of Thrace by Alexander of Macedon there developed through the territory between Persia and the middle Danube an art that was oriental in style. Asia Minor then became, for its neighbours to the north and northwest, a model in matters of style, which gave rise in Thrace to a very special art form that could be defined as "baroque animalist." This style, however, is characteristic of only one part of ancient Thrace, towards the lower Danube region and the Marica valley: it scarcely exists in the southwest of Thrace and the Vardar valley, or in the territories close to the Propontis.

THE GOLD AND SILVER VESSELS OF THE THRACIAN KINGS

The history of Thracian art is, in essence, the history of toreutics. The Valčitran treasure is the proof of this: from the Bronze Age onwards, the Thracian rulers possessed rich collections of gold and silver vessels. Looking globally at the series of finds progressively through time, we see gold gradually giving way to silver as the most valued material for luxury objects. This proves that the Thracians relied mostly on the precious metal which could be mined on their own territory: Thrace was famous for its silver mines.

In the numerous finds and treasures brought to light up to the present day, various kinds of receptacles can be identified. The most common are the phiale, the jug, and, found less frequently and mostly in the eastern part of Thrace, the rhyton. The shapes and decoration of the silver phialai and jugs are very similar to what is found in Asia Minor. The ornamentation consists of grooves radiating out from the boss on phialai and from the flat bottom for jugs; rosettes, the leaves of which may be replaced by buds; lotus flowers, almonds, palmettes, animal and even human heads, all typical motifs of Anatolian toreutics for centuries.

All the phialai found up to now date from after the sixth century B.C. As for the jugs, they appear even later, towards the second half of the fifth century B.C. These two types of receptacle, together with the relatively rare rhyta, were for a long time attributed to the Greek workshops in the colonial coastal cities or in Asia Minor. Some spectacular discoveries have provided pieces bearing very significant inscriptions. These are the Rogozen treasure, consisting of one hundred and sixty-five receptacles dating from the end of the fifth century B.C. up to the mid-fourth century B.C.; the Borovo treasure (385-359 B.C.); and the grave goods of Vraca, of Alexandrovo, and from Agighiol in modern Rumania. In the inscriptions there appear, in the possessive form, the names of three Thracian rulers: the famous king Kotys (385-359 B.C.) and his two successors, his son, Kersobleptes, and Amatokos, who reigned simultaneously over his immense kingdom. Furthermore, we can read the names of the towns where the workshops stood that produced these objects: they are the cities of Apros,

Catalogue no. 423
Rhyton in the form of a stag's head. Panagjurište Treasure (end of fourth, beginning of third centuries B.C.)

Catalogue no. 337
Gold protoma of Pegasus. Alexandrovo Treasure
(beginning of fourth century B.C.)

Argiske, Geistoi, Sauthaba and Beos, the last being the most often cited. Only the first two towns, situated to the south of the Ergene river in the European part of modern-day Turkey, have been identified. The three others were unknown to the Greeks, probably because their more southerly situation made them escape their notice. The large number of pieces bearing inscriptions shows that these were products of the royal workshops of Thrace. Those of the vessels which were intended for other princes or Thracian rulers bore inscriptions, or else were sent as gifts to allies. The three most beautiful ones, showing the highest level of artistry, came from the workshop at Beos at the behest of Kotys. They are two rhyta and a small jug. The latter, part of the Borovo treasure, is decorated with designs in relief arranged in two friezes, one above the other, showing a rather mysterious religious scene: Dionysos and his thiasos between two unknown gods. The gods, served by two Amours, are feasting, while a Silenus plays music. The Borovo treasure is additional proof of the skill of the artists who worked in the royal workshops. It is obvious that we can legitimately attribute to them a large number of the Thracian masterpieces which had been thought to be of Greek provenance. And we can now see more clearly the artistic movements of ancient Thrace: the northwest, which created the repertoire of forms and the ornamental horse trappings; and the southeast, the powerful kingdom of the Odrysians where numerous workshops were established.

This Odrysian kingdom reunited the greater part of Thrace after the Median wars and played an important role in the history of southeast Europe between 475 and 410 B.C. under its kings Teres, Sparatokos, who was the first to strike coinage, Sitalkes, and Seuthes I. In the last decade of the fifth century B.C. the kingdom went through a period of crisis which ended only with the accession of Kotys. His reign coincided with the zenith of Odrysian power, a power which, however, proved to be ephemeral, since in the undistinguished reign of his son Kersobleptes the kingdom fell under the domination of Philip II of Macedon. Its territory, relatively fixed, included the land on either side of the Marica and Tundza valleys, corresponding to southeastern Thrace as far as the Propontis and the Aegean Sea.

The almost total lack of treasures in this part of Thrace, as in the southwest (present-day Macedonia) merits attention. The only treasures that have been discovered on the ancient territory of the Odrysians are basically monetary, consisting of coins struck in Chersonnese in Thrace, at Parion in the Dardanelles, and at Apollonia of Pontis, before the end of the fourth century B.C. The gold and silver vessels found there have come exclusively from grave goods.

As we have stated, the phialai and the grooved jugs were typical works of Thracian toreutics which developed in an original way a tradition borrowed from Anatolian art. Such is also the case with the rhyta. Alongside of this tradition, which rejected the depiction of the human figure and mythological stories, the workshops of the Greek colonies developed a style which made great use of both, and in which mythological scenes with human figures occupied an important place.

THE PANAGJURIŠTE TREASURE

The most brilliant example of this style is the Panagjurište treasure, which came from a workshop at Lampsaque and dates from about 330 B.C. Two of the receptacles, the phiale and the amphora-rhyton, are marked with their weight according to two systems, in stateres for Lampsaque, and in Attic drachmas. Both are extremely fine. The Greek artist, who knew the taste of his rich clients, the Thracian kings, depicted on these pieces various subjects taken from mythology. On the amphora-rhyton there is a scene from the "Seven Against Thebes." One of the rhyta shows Aphrodite, Athena and Hera before the judgement of Paris. Another shows Herakles fighting the Ceryneian Hind, and Theseus in combat with the bull of Marathon. A third rhyton bears a very rare picture, Dionysos with the nymph Eriope and not with Ariadne. The names of the gods are sometimes inscribed beside their image. Thus, the eight Panagjurište rhyta bear Greek ornamentation. On the other hand, their shapes are unknown in Greek art. One of them ends in a goat protoma, another in the horned head of a ram: two others end in stags' or does' heads. All these animal representations are quite stylized, and have little in common with the plasticity of Greek art.

We know of a comparable treasure, which has not been written about and which comes from the region of Sinope, on the southeast coast of the Black Sea. It dates from the end of the fifth or the beginning of the fourth century B.C., and contains objects quite like ours, which are evidence of the existence of graeco-barbarian or mixhellene workshops in northern Asia Minor as well as in southeastern Thrace. These workshops acted as intermediaries for the introduction into Thracian toreutics of mythological scenes and images of gods. These new subjects and motifs were imported into Thrace in the fourth century B.C. While the images on the pieces from the Borovo treasure are not very different, artistically speaking, from those on purely Greek objects, the items in the Rogozen treasure from northwest Bulgaria, the work of an artist unaffected by Anatolian influence, are in a much more barbaric style. Moreover, the human figure only appears very rarely in Thracian toreutics.

The introduction of mythological scenes and images in the decoration of horse trappings took place during the second quarter of the fourth century B.C. At that time there appeared mythological scenes and a whole series of rather strange images, sometimes even completely enigmatic, which nevertheless move us by their primitive vigour.

The beginning of the third century B.C. was the end of the most brilliant era of the indigenous kings and of the flowering of Thracian art. From then on, goldsmiths' work became rarer and less widespread, particularly north of the Hemus in northern Thrace. It lost its oriental character, and there are few creations comparable to the goddess on the phalerai of the Galice treasure in the Orjahovo region.

The Odrysian kingdom had one final burst of splendour towards the end of the first century B.C., when the western regions of Thrace, the valleys of the Vardar and the Struma, were already since 164 B.C. under Roman domination. These regions gradually became the Masia, while the southeast of Thrace became a Roman protectorate under the control of the Odrysian kings. The complications of internal relations resulting from the Roman presence in Thrace paved the way for a gradual transformation, and almost imperceptibly the Odrysian kingdom dwindled into a new province, called Thrace.

From then on, after the first century A.D., the fate of the Thracian people was sealed. The Roman empire established in its provinces a whole network of cities with their own magistrates and priests. Craftsmanship developed, as did a class of wealthy landowners. Where a certain sort of urban life had existed previously, there grew up great urban centres ruled by the Roman authorities.

IVAN VENEDIKOV

"INTERPRETATIO THRACICA" OR THE DECIPHERING OF THRACIAN ART

The Thracians share the fate of all ancient peoples who had no alphabet of their own—their customs, myths and ritual practices are known to us only through Greek, Roman and Byzantine writers. Thus it would be natural to expect all sorts of distortions of information, transmitted through a foreign written tradition and perhaps due as much to the sources themselves as to the translation. So Herodotus describes the Thracian pantheon using the names of Greek gods, but that means merely that only an analysis of their complex nature could have revealed the particular characteristics which allowed the "Father of History" to identify the local divinities with the gods of Hellas. In the same way, Thracian art absorbed the representation of certain heroes and of whole scenes from Greek mythology, which in order to function must have corresponded in some way with Thracian mythic and ritual tradition. Two variants of one of these processes allow us to build up a picture of Thracian mythology and royal ideology—the "interpretatio thracica" of Greek sources (literature and fine arts). The other procedure is based on the etymology of local toponyms and theonyms, a system the possibilities of which are well known to thracologists since Tomašek. Reconstructed fragments of Thracian mythological texts have enabled us to discover the structure of the myths, which opens up possibilities of comparison with other Indo-European mythological systems. The comparative method is already beginning to produce results, and is gradually restoring to Thracian mythology its place in the Indo-European cultural context. Finally, thanks to ethnic and historical continuity, thracology has the advantage of basing these reconstructions on Bulgarian and Rumanian folklore which has preserved, in addition to the realias, the complete mytho-ritual structures of the Thracian heritage.

Nevertheless, the reconstruction of the mythology and royal ideology of ancient Thrace can only be carried out by starting with the images on works of toreutics created by local craftsmen in honour of their rulers. These representations are invaluable, in that they constitute the only "texts" in which Thracian mythology is handed down to us directly. The deciphering of the images and scenes in these masterpieces of zoomorphic and anthropomorphic style should contribute immensely towards bringing us closer to specific Thracian mythological conceptions. Such is the importance of Thracian art as a source of information about "the most numerous people in the world, after the Indians."

The flowering of Thracian art began in the fifth century B.C. and coincided with the beginning of the period of rich burials (the earliest are those in the necropolis of Duvanli). It was then that craftsmen abandoned the bronze of the previous epoch, which had been characterized by a geometric style, and began to make objects in gold and silver. The increasing use of precious metals corresponded to the growing social importance of the nobility and to the power of the king—objects made of gold and silver were considered as signs of social status. Naturally it is the graves and treasures left by the rulers themselves which are the richest—the graves under the burial mound of Mogilanskata mogila or the recently discovered treasure of Rogozen confirm ancient reports of the wealth of the Thracian kings. It is clear that the arts flourished because of the formation of strong Thracian states in the course of the fifth century B.C. This was the period when the most remarkable state organization was established—the kingdom of the Odrysians, occupying the southeastern terri-

Detail of a greave found in a Thracian tomb at Vraca (first century B.C.)

tory of Thrace.

Magnificence and luxury in archaic cultures have more of an ideological than an economic significance. Wealth is the yardstick of the sovereign's power, a measure of the help he receives from the gods and of his ability to ensure the prosperity of his subjects. For this reason ingots, collected as taxes, were often transmuted into valuable cups or head ornaments—for merely the price of the gold used for the vessels in the treasure of Panagjurište, their owner could have maintained an army of five hundred mercenaries for a whole year. For the same reasons, veritable treasures were interred in the burial mounds of the Thracian kings.

The material of which objects are made, as well as their form and function, are evidence of social prestige. But Thracian kings often had recourse also to the figures depicted on these objects to create ideological reasons for their power. Thus the figurative language of Thracian mythology had new motives for evolving and improving. This achievement, which, in the course of a century developed a fairly coherent iconography, proves the role of figurative language in moulding the mythological consciousness of the Thracians. Despite being conservative, iconography accepts the existence of variations on a given theme, which demonstrates its existence as an autonomous active system, and not just as a means of illustrating oral narrative. In this sense, figurative language becomes the equivalent of, and parallels, verbal and ritual language. It is unreasonable to seek exact correspondence between the fragmentary data of written sources (which record the Thracian oral tradition) and the still incomplete data provided by the arts: expressed in each of these languages, the myth may exist in different forms, and even, when simply translated, it will be modified somewhat as a result of the laws of translation. An example of this is found in the representation of a sphinx in the Rogozen treasure. It would seem that the artist, not having a model to copy, created a fantastic creature based on an oral description together with images he had seen. The description combines elements of the sphinx and the griffin: the sphinx resembles the griffin, but has a woman's head and a serpent's tail. The result is a new, strange hybrid image, a "griffin-sphinx."

Like any language, that of images can model reality according to different codes. Its special characteristics allow it to use five codes: spatial, material, zoomorphic, vegetal and anthropomorphic. Sometimes only one code is used, but in most cases they are combined, or complement or repeat each other, eventually creating a coherent mythological picture of the world. Ancient Thrace had no difficulty in deciphering this system of signs and reconstructing the myth, even when the latter was not recounted in detail, as it would have been by oral narration. For us, these pictures are often mute, and we can restore only their structure, never the entire text. So we will probably never know the name of the hero of the appliques of Letnica, nor the articulation of his exploits, but we can be certain that they show him fighting the dragon, crushing the three-headed monster, liberating the waters and marrying the maiden thus saved.

It goes without saying that the Thracian artist does not depict men and animals according to the canons of Greek art. He is not reproducing objective connections, but connections between signs; he does not create in the image of nature, but in the image of the mythological universe; and so it is the laws of mythological thinking, not of nature, which are his model. That is why our reading of these texts in pictures must be based on the rules of their own syntax. Otherwise, one runs the risk of over-modernizing archaic messages.

The iconographic unity of Thracian art is founded on the repetition of the basic signs. This often leads to a mistaken belief that their content does not vary, and hence to the conclusion that the iconography is equivalent to the semantic. It is true that the iconographic repertory is not very large, but there is no need for a large number of realias and images, since the combinations of the latter are innumerable. When added to the transformations resulting from the different codings, the possible number of combinations becomes even greater. Thus, any concrete result will have a concrete semantic, that is to say, the content of the sign will depend on the concrete context in which it is introduced. Hence the phiale in the hands of a hero has the value of an insignia, while in the goddess's hands it can be interpreted as a sign of fertility. At the same time, when situated in a similar context, different signs can have the same meaning. On the Loveč belt, among the horsemen pursuing a wild boar, we can see the tree of life, represented by three lotus flowers, while on a jug from Rogozen, there is the figure of a goddess among the huntsmen (cf. the identification of the goddess with the tree of life in different mythologies). The transformation of the code has only affected one element of the myth, but the result is a new text.

The spatial code of Thracian art is relatively easy to follow. Many scenes follow a symmetrical composition, which makes it possible to mark the left and right and thus to bring in a complementary semantic precision. The frescoes on the friezes of the Kazanlak and Sveštari tombs show a wedding ceremony in which the procession of men is on the opposite side from that of the women. This spatial opposition is repeated by another—the hero and his followers occupy the right-hand side, while the woman and her maidservants are on the left. This leads us to think that the metal worker who made the appliques of the Letnica treasure took into consideration the different meanings of the left hand and the right hand in the mytho-poetic consciousness, for in some cases the horsemen hold their spears in the left hand. In this way it was possible to code a particular ritual situation. Skaïoi, the name of a Thracian tribe, has the etymological meaning of "left-handed ones," which brings us to the Indo-European image of the "one-armed man" reconstructed by Georges Dumézil. The tripartite vertical structure of the universe is often represented by the old phytomorphic symbol called "the tree of life." Several pectorals from Thrace carry this universal tree stylized in different ways and to different degrees. The plant code is often repeated by the zoomorphic code. Thus, on the round appliques of Panagjurište, we see the tree of life stylized as a palmette, flanked by a wild boar on the left, a lion on the right, and surmounted by a bird at the top. In this manner the different spatial zones are coded in a zoomorphic fashion. As we have already seen, the tree itself may be replaced by the figure of the goddess or by one of her ritual hypostases (see the caryatids of the Sveštari tomb.)

The structuring of the universe had an immense importance for all archaic cultures. At different levels and expressed in diverse ways, it brought an element of security into the life of the tribal community and the forces of "culture" over those of "nature." On the gold helmet of Cotofenesti (Rumania), the tripar-

Catalogue no. 204
Amphora (detail). Treasure from the Kukova Mogila, district of Plovdiv (beginning of fifth century B.C.)

tite structure of the universe is clearly expressed in three codes: spatial (superimposition of zones), zoomorphic (the upper zone bears winged demons, the lower fierce griffins, and the middle zone a ram), and narrative (the griffins are devouring the herbivorous animals and the ram is sacrificed.) This complex composition is intended to show how order is reestablished in the world by means of the sacrifice performed in the middle zone, thus separating the lower from the upper zone.

Material coding is the transformation of certain objects into attributes signifying either a particular status or the roles of gods and heroes. The importance of this code in figurative language is comparable to the role it plays in the oral language of mythological consciousness. The creations of Thracian toreutics often display a consistent, if restricted, repertoire of cultural signs, that is, of products of human activity: all sorts of vessels (most often rhyta and phialae, the commonest receptacles in Thracian finds), weapons (spears and bows, but not a single sword!), armour (helmets, knee-pieces, shields, coats of mail, belts), ornaments (earrings, crowns, bracelets, tattooing), chariots, chitons, chlamydes, mirrors, throne chairs. Often, the craftsmen tried to reproduce these objects in a realistic manner. This attempt, however, shows no tendency towards naturalism. Rather, it is a way of actualizing the myth which is proper to mythological thinking and which most frequently appears at the level of "concrete" attributes.

Almost all the cultural symbols cited may be considered as insignia of the royal power. Thus, the spear and the bow are the weapons of the king, and the linking of them as attributes of him, which is absurd in terms of mythological consciousness, indicates the status of the sovereign, who is the only impermanent being requiring constant renewal (the bow is the weapon of the ephebe, the spear of the hoplite). The spear and the bow symbolize the king's military function, while the cup he receives on being invested with his powers indicates his primary function, that of priest. The third function, the economic, is only hinted at in Thracian art, by the yoke of oxen Hermes drives for the king, depicted on the coins of the Oresques. Male personages are usually shown dressed as warriors, though the pointed hat (pilos) is another indisputable sign that the wearer belonged to the aristocracy; nobles were called "pilophoroï." Tattooing was another indicator of social standing (cf. the knee-piece of Vraca).

The plant code uses well-known ornamentation from the decorative repertoire of the ancient world, and reinterprets it at the semantic level. Rosettes, lotus flowers, and palmettes become signs of the tree of life, or simply symbols of fertility. Even when these motifs appear in purely ornamental compositions they have these meanings. Yet we often see alternating palmettes, lotus flowers and female heads (on the breast-plates of Mezek and Varbica, the phialae of Lukovit and Rogozen, scyphos of Strelča) which probably contain the code of the link between the goddess and fertility. The branch, which has a profound mytho-ritual meaning, often appears in works of toreutics. Sometimes it is in the goddess's hand as a sign that she protects fertility (the Rogozen cup): elsewhere (an applique at Letnica) she strikes the young bride and groom with the branch to give them the power of fertility, according to an archaic rite found throughout the ancient world. The crown of ivy on the goddess's head in the Vraca knee-piece or those decorating various receptacles (Borovo, Varbica,

Rogozen) is perhaps a symbol of Dionysos, while the gold crowns, of very fine workmanship, discovered in the tombs (burial mounds of Mezek, Rosovec) and the crowns on the helmets are probably royal insignia. In fact, in the Sveštari tomb the goddess crowns the ruler who approaches her on horseback, while the central scene of the Kazanlak frescoes probably represents the next episode of the royal investiture ceremony: the king, already wearing his crown, gives his arm to the woman he is marrying. The different objects carried by the bride's maidservants could be wedding gifts. Clearly, the crown indicates a state of transition, and a change in social status. For this reason the participants in the kabiric mysteries on the frieze of the Borovo jug wear crowns: after the initiation they acquire new knowledge, a new position in society.

The zoomorphic code is very old, its tradition going back to the Paleolithic age. The scientific term "animalist style," although imprecise, is already sanctified by usage as referring to the art of those peoples who inhabited the steppes of Eurasia during the first millennium B.C. Several hypotheses have been formulated to explain this phenomenon: totemic animals, zoomorphic phase in the evolution of mythological thinking, economic role of the animals depicted. Probably all of these hypotheses have some basis in reality, to the extent that different reasons may have induced ancient man to choose a certain animal as a classifier. We have already mentioned the convenience of zoomorphic classifiers in describing the spatial structure: the bird indicates the upper zone, the ungulate the middle, and the serpent the lower zone. On coins struck by Thracian kings we find an ancient motif: an eagle seizing a serpent or a fish. Here we have a "condensation" of space—the tension between the upper and lower points of the vertically structured universe is resolved by the struggle between the respective zoomorphic classifiers. The other antitheses used by the myth may be defined in the same way—carnivore-herbivore, aerial-aquatic, wild-domestic, together with their corresponding mediators, of which the ram is the most popular in Thracian folklore. The zoomorphic code continued to operate in the epic genre, though at the level of metaphor: heroes are often compared with animals whose qualities they possess (brave as a lion, ferocious as a wild boar).

These associations with species of animals may also be due to other reasons. Among the Indo-Europeans, the wolf is the ancient archetype of the outlaw as well as of the young warrior undergoing his military initiation. In Thrace, this identification is preserved in the myth of Harpalycos and his daughter Harpalyke, while the art often shows this carnivore attacking other animals. As for the bear, it is a very useful classifier for rites of passage, since it sleeps in winter ("dies"), and in any initiation the passing into another social level is effected by the symbolic death of the neophyte. In oral narrative, the latter animal is linked with Polyphonte, a girl who, for having broken the sexual taboo, was punished by loving a bear. Perhaps the mythological genesis of Zalmoksis, the god of the Getai, comes from the same animal; at birth, the god was covered by a bear skin. This act was probably repeated in the course of the mysteries of this divinity, in which neophytes were considered as new born, promised to eternal life. Since myth and ritual are linked to critical moments in the social life of the archaic community, one might expect the bear to be a popular zoomorphic personage in Thracian art, and indeed it does figure as a

Gold jug (Vraca, fourth century B.C.)

protagonist in various scenes of the iconography in the animalist style. The fact that on the Mezek head-piece the bear is associated with the she-goat indicates the establishing of an analogy based on functional resemblance.

There are also many imaginary creatures in Thracian iconography: griffins, horned eagles, dragons, sphinxes. Depictions of them combine the characteristics of various animals that mark different social and cosmological positions. In other words, they unite opposites which are normally differentiated in the ordered universe, and it is this joining of opposite elements which transforms them into forces of chaos. For this reason, their position is generally that of the antagonist, the adversary of order and culture, of life and fertility. Probably as a result of such a confusion of characteristics, the wild boar in Thrace is shown among these creatures: herbivore and carnivore, placid and ferocious, producer and destroyer at the same time. In scenes showing battles between animals, he is always the antagonist, pertaining to the forces of evil and of death, the representative of chaos that burrows into the earth, into the roots of the tree of life. The absence of a clear differentiation of the characteristics of an animal (real or imaginary) transforms it at once into either a mediator or an antagonist. This alternative is scarcely surprising, since, in a concrete context, myth can interpret a trait or characteristic in different ways.

It is natural that the binaries of mythological thinking should be expressed artistically by the combat of animals—one of the main themes of the animalist style. It is one of the ways of resolving the contradictions created by the oppositions between groups of zoomorphic classifiers. Of course, this explanation is too general, and applies only at the structural level. We always have difficulty with the concrete interpretation of these scenes—they may symbolize motifs from the astronomical calendar as well as purely ideological motifs. How, for example, does one interpret the emblematic scene of the horned eagle holding a rabbit in its talons and a bird in its beak (Rogozen, Agighilo, Peretu, Metropolitan Museum, Detroit)? It probably has a multiple meaning: hierarchization of the structure of the elements and of the spatial structure of the world; translation of a political formula of the achemenid type where the victor addresses the vanquished: "Bring me earth and water"; and a zoomorphic coding of the investiture—the horned eagle (the horns are a sign of supreme power) bestows the insignia of power on an eaglet before him. The polyvalence of a sign is a characteristic of mythological thinking, and the solution to the problem of the content of each particular case depends on the whole context in which the sign is introduced.

Zoomorphic coding is useful for representing a broader range of images, but is less helpful for specific mythological narratives. When royal ideology required a more solid and convincing motivation for its ideas, art had recourse to another code, the anthropomorphic, for this purpose. Only in recent years has the traditional opinion which insisted on the absolute domination of the "animalist style" in barbarian art been abandoned. It has been established that scenes in which men appear are in fact numerous: they show the attempts of the Thracians to narrate their myths. Naturally, we cannot expect narrative resembling that of Greek mythological representations of the same period, with their dramatization and psychological analysis, the transformation of structure into event and the rationalization of the myth and the ritual. Any

Catalogue no. 240
Helmet (beginning of fifth, end of fourth centuries B.C.)

attempt to explain in this way the images or the relationships between protagonists in Thracian art leads to a modernizing of its functions and content. The Thracian artist is concerned with meaning, not narration, with representing clearly the relationships underlying the subject of the myth, not elaborating the plot. This is why protagonists are almost always shown full-face, making unequivocal gestures which appear very ceremonious. The story is reconstructed mentally by the spectator, who knows how to decipher the code of images thus created. The text is free of all "interference" that would have resulted from a concern with psychology, idealization, individualization and so on, which would have hindered communication. The information perceived corresponds to the information presented. In other words, "what you see is what you get."

Thracian art is homogeneous from the iconographic and stylistic points of view. This uniformity was the result of the close relations, if not among workshops, at least among Thracian kings. It is probable that they exchanged works of art as gifts, which ensured a rapid interchange of ideas and of iconographic and stylistic concepts. There is no doubt that the workshops of Vraca and Letnica, of Sveštari, of northern Dobroudja and the southern Ukraine communicated with each other. Thus, over a wide territory, a homogeneous culture was formed which appears in a common form for objects, a restricted iconographic repertoire, and similar traits of style. If, for example, we compare the faces of the goddesses on the Strelča scyphos, on a Rogozen jug and on the Poroïna rhyton, we find a resemblance as if they were all stamped from the same matrix. And yet these objects were found in places hundreds of kilometres apart, that is, they belonged to the chiefs of different tribes. An exchange of matrices between workshops is not impossible, as we can see from the discovery of two almost identical specimens showing a winged demi-centaur carrying on his back a strangled wolf: would the same craftsman need two identical matrices?

To correctly decipher the images of Thracian art, we should compare them with the data we have from written sources. Herodotus wrote that the Thracians worshipped Dionysos, Ares and Artemis. We may presume that these Greek names were used for local gods who were the functional equivalents of the Hellenic divinities. We may never know what they were called in the Thracian tongue. It is much more important to know whether the structure of the Thracian pantheon as described by Herodotus is based on an underlying principle. If we apply Dumézil's theory of the tripartite ideology of the Indo-Europeans, we get a very clear functional picture. Ares embodies the second function, the military one, Dionysos possesses in Thrace the functional characteristics of the first type, the sacral, while Artemis, in her capacity as great goddess, may correspond not only to the third function (fertility, riches) but also be a transfunctional divinity. At the level of the epic, these three functions may be glimpsed in the myth of Rhesos, Brangas and Olinthus, sons of the god of the river Strymon. After the death of Rhesos (the typical figure of the warrior) before the walls of Troy, Olinthus dies during the hunt and is mourned by his brother, who builds on the battle site "a great and rich city" and gives it his brother's name. Obviously, Olinthus is a figure belonging to the first function, since he becomes the eponym of a city, while Brangas is a typical personage of the third function, for the city he founds prospers. Finally, in Thrace, the sover-

Catalogue no. 378
Silver applique: lion attacking a stag. Lukovit
Treasure (end of fourth century B.C.)

eign himself appears as a synthesis of the three socio-ideological functions. At the level of the epic our information about Rhesos is the most eloquent, though it is limited; he was the legendary king of the Edonians, "bore arms, went hunting, and possessed many herds of horses." At the ritual level, we can analyze from the same point of view the dowry which Kotys I, king of the Odrysians (first half of the fourth century B.C.) gave his daughter: it consisted of cups (first function), a gold shield (second function), a herd of white horses and a herd of goats, and a jar of millet and store of onions (third function). The description Diodorus gives of Sytalkes, powerful king of the Odrysians reveals the same synthesis of functions: "Through his own courage and his own spirit, he reinforced considerably his power, because he ruled his subjects justly, fought as a valiant and experienced leader in war, and furthermore was careful to increase his revenues." The king had to fulfil all his various functions perfectly.

Nevertheless, Herodotus himself deliberately emphasizes that "unlike ordinary people, the Thracian kings worship Hermes, swear only by his name, and claim their origin from him." In his role as mediator, this Greek god corresponded to the primary function of the king—to serve as a link between the world of men and that of the gods, that is, to be man-god, anthropodemon, hero. Thanks to this position, he can ensure his people the protection and goodwill of the gods, maintain order in the social and natural world, and become himself a sign of stability for his society and the world. It is Hermes who is depicted on the coins of the Deronians—he rides in a chariot pulled by bulls, between a palmette and a rosette, that is, in the middle zone of the universe, or else he drives for the king a yoke of bulls, a sign of the monarch's economic power. It is probable that the hero-king sacrifices a ram—was it not the golden ram, known as a royal insignia since the time of the Atrides, whose fleece attracted the Argonauts to Colchis in order that Jason, having won it, might become the legitimate king? Besides, we know that it was Hermes who sent into the flock the marked animal which according to some sources was born of the Thracian princess Bisaltis. In its role as mediator, the ram corresponds completely with the functions of Hermes, and for that reason is associated with him in numerous myths.

It should be noted that in Greek sources the kings of Thracian myth appear either as belonging clearly to the second function, or entirely to the first. An example of a military hero is Lycurgos, who had experienced "all the sins of warriors" and whose name alone, coming as it does from "wolf," makes possible his identification, typical among the Indo-Europeans, with the members of the male military societies (werewolves) and outlaws. Mythical personages such as Orpheus and Zalmoksis were entirely characterized by the sacral or priestly function. They were the religious teachers of the nobility, prototypes of the mystagogue, who in mysterious societies revealed to the "chosen" the secret of immortality and initiated them into the traditions of the ideological doctrine of "Thracian Orphism." It is understandable that the third function remained marginal for mythological consciousness and that only a faint trace of it can be found in the myths.

The anthropomorphic code appears in Thracian art following the development of claims to a royal ideology which required of art a more concrete repre-

Bronze coin bearing the effigy of Seuthes III (Seuthopolis).

sentation of the principal epic themes. The iconography presents us with two general images: the great goddess and the hero, who are often combined in the same subject. The principal theme of royal ideology—the means of achieving power—provides us with different subjects (mythological variants). Archaic thinking submits the man who claims power to various tests: he must find a sacred object, an insignia, overcoming on the way all sorts of obstacles; he must resolve a series of complicated problems, triumph over monsters and animals. Through accomplishing these tasks, he proves he is worthy of the throne.

In Thracian art the test is most often coded in hunting scenes. The horseman fights an animal which embodies the forces of chaos: the bear (Letnica), the wild boar (the Loveč belt and the Rogozen jug), the lion (Lukovit). Often the hunt is the semantic equivalent of the scene of the "battle of animals," that is, the same mythological structure is depicted by two different codes. Unlike hunting themes in Greek art, the huntsman in Thrace is always dressed and armed like a Thracian nobleman, which is one more way of emphasizing that the theme belongs to the royal ideology. The animals, as we have seen, are the classifiers of the "antagonist," the extreme form of which is the dragon: he is three-headed, ophidian, sometimes in the shape of a fish with the head of a wild boar (Stancesti, Rumania). It appears that a series of appliques from Letnica have preserved the myth of the "vanquisher of the dragon"; each of the appliques presents an episode from the syntagmatic of the myth. The first shows a young girl with a mirror in her hand facing a serpent with three wolf heads. She is probably the princess who, whether as victim or bride, is sacrificed each year to the monster so he will free the waters the people need. Unfortunately, the phalera depicting the fight between the hero and the dragon has not survived, but we can reconstruct the scene from the applique showing a battle between a horseman and a bear—one merely replaces the bear by a dragon. The nereid riding a seahorse is perhaps a symbol of the waters liberated by the hero's victory. There follows a scene of a wedding consecrated under the protection of the goddess—as always, the day after the victory, the hero marries the rescued princess, thus ensuring his power over her father's kingdom. Probably also part of this mythological cycle is the plaque with a horseman holding out a phiale—the feast (or sacrifice) always means the celebration of victory. Finally, the horseman also receives the insignia of royal power—the bow, shown at his back. The particular way he wears his hair, evoking "the Abantes with hair gathered at the top of the head," shows that this is a hero who has made a sacred marriage. In a more limited form the same myth appears on the gold helmets of Baceni: the hero is seated on a throne; the phiale and rhyton show that he is taking part in a feast to celebrate his victory; the bow at his back is a royal insignia marking the second ideological function; and the serpent under the throne symbolizes the vanquished enemy. However, it seems that here it is the herds which served as the pretext for combat: on the other cheek-piece we see a bull's head flanked by two dragons.

Thracian art thus gives us a relatively complete picture of the "fundamental myth" of the Indo-Europeans, in its principal variants. Written sources also testify to its popularity in Thrace. Crossing the country with Geryon's cattle

Herakles grew angry with the river Strymon and barred its course with rocks, after which the river ceased to be navigable. The aquatic nature of the dragon is symbolized by the god of the river; the adversaries use rocks in the fight; the motive for the fight is the coveting of the adversary's herds. The motif of the "fight with the dragon" at the level of the gods is confirmed by the Hellenic insistence on setting the scene of giant-killing in Thrace, in the Flagrian fields of the peninsula of Pallène and Lycophron, and even on stating that all Thracians were called "giants." All the evidence indicates that this idea was conveyed in the zoomorphic code. The town of Argilos in the same region got its name from the mouse that appeared at the time it was founded. Being "gegeneis" (born of the earth), giants were identified with mice in mythological thinking (cf. "the war of the toads and the mice," which in ancient tradition parallels giant-killing).

The other main theme of the royal ideology was of course the investiture, the ceremony in which the god gave the king the insignia of power. In this case the idea of power as a gift of the gods is developed through the material code, made concrete through the introduction of anthropomorphic personages. On several rings (Rosovec, Brezovo), the goddess gives the horseman a rhyton or a cup, categorical attributes of royal power. They are signs of spiritual power, since they are used for the sacrifice, that is, they make the link between the world of men and that of the gods. It is for this reason that valuable cups are the receptacles most often found among the Thracian discoveries: phialae (there are one thousand and eighty-one of these in the Rogozen treasure alone), rhyta and jugs (fifty-four jugs in the same treasure!). These vessels were part of the obligatory inventory for any mystery. On the Borovo jug, the guests at Kabyre's wedding feast hold rhyta and phialae, while the cup-bearers (Amours) use jugs to pour the wine. The Rogozen treasure provides a very interesting example of one of these services. One of the jugs bears the inscription: "ΚΟΤΥΣ ΑΠΟΛΛΩΝΟΖ ΠΑΙΣ" (Kotys the son/servant of Apollo). This is Kotys, king of the Odrysians, depicted as a priest of the Orphic cult of Apollo. Together with this jug there are four phialae, on the omphalos of which in repoussé is the image of Apollo. One of the phialae bears the inscription: "ΚΟΤΥΣ ΕΓ ΑΡΓΙΣΚΗΣ'" (to Kotys from the city of Erghiske). It would seem from the evidence that these receptacles were used during the ceremonies of initiation into the mysteries of Orpheus-Apollo, and Kotys, as the mystagogue, made a gift of them to his guest the king of the Triballoi whom he initiated into the secrets of the Orphic doctrine.

Thus we come to the royal banquet and the gifts exchanged between the ruler and his guests during the feast. Happily, we possess a precise ethnographic description, left us by Xenophon, of a feast at the court of Seuthes. It shows the ritual nature of the king's table: the guests sit around it, the king serves the food, toasts are made, gifts are presented to the king who promises in exchange a richer recompense. Clowns and musicians perform, and the king in person performs an armed ritual dance. It is clear that all kinds of problems were solved during the banquet, which only "brothers" and "guests" were entitled to attend (these institutions are well-known in the practices of kings of other Indo-European peoples). According to written sources, such banquets were held when the king and his retinue visited the fortified residences. It is likely that upon the king's entry into any fortified place he was offered a cup of wine, as was also the custom of the kings of Macedonia. These cups probably bore the names of the kings of the Odrysians—Satok, Kotys and Kerseblept (in the possessive genitive)—as well as the name of the city where the receptacle was proffered (Beos, Erghiske, Gheistai, etc.). This indicates that the Thracian king was always on the march making the sacral rounds of his kingdom, to demonstrate his supreme authority and continually renew his power over his territory. The myth of Orpheus gives us a mythological precedent, for "he took with him on his journeys" the men of Thrace. In Thracian art these tours may be depicted on the coins of the Deronians, where Hermes, the royal divinity (the god of the king himself) travels in a chariot between heaven and earth. Sometimes another name is inscribed on the phiale—"ΚΟΤΥΟΣ ΕΓ ΒΕΟ ΔΙΣΛΟΙΑΣ ΕΠΟΙΗΣΕ." Disloias is probably not the name of the craftsman, since such an artist's vanity was scarcely possible in the royal workshop, and since the quality of the receptacle gives no grounds for such pride. It was perhaps the name of a city governor who was privileged to offer hospitality to the king (see Herodotus' description of a similar institution among the Persians). Thus, valuable gifts mark the route of the royal tour, that is, they coincide, in practice, with the political map of the Odrysian kingdom. As a result, it was quite natural for these inscribed receptacles to become the gifts that the kings Kotys and Kerseblept offered their guests, the rulers of the Getai, the Mysians and the Triballoi. They used them to display their power.

Sacrifice performed by the king was another important part of the royal ideology. Ancient writers put into the mouth of the king the following words: "for kings and the common people should not use the same victims." The words are those of Diegylis, noted for his cruelty, upon sacrificing two Greeks at his wedding ceremony. Kotys I did the same when celebrating his symbolic marriage to the goddess Athena. The severed heads behind the horsemen on the appliques of the Letnica treasure are also evidence of the custom of human sacrifice. Behind two other figures on horseback from the same treasure there are two severed horses' heads, a very significant fact which induces us to think that among the Thracians, as among other Indo-European peoples, there existed royal customs similar to those practised in India—Asvamedha (sacrifice of the horse) and Purusamedha (sacrifice of man). Permitting an alternative, these sacrifices were performed by the victorious king and meant that the neighbouring territories recognized his power. Before their battle against the Roman Crassus, the Thracians killed a horse in front of the lines of warriors and swore to sacrifice captured Roman leaders and to eat their entrails. What was at stake in this battle was "domination over the whole world." In this way, written sources confirm the data provided by works of art, and enable us to place the Thracian mytho-ritual system within the wider Indo-European context. The king performed the principal sacrifices, and other rites for the renewal of power. We have already mentioned the sacrifice of a lamb on the Cotofenesti helmet. The man kneeling on the animal is dressed in a coat of mail and a chlamys and wears a pilos, that is, he has the characteristics of a king. From the structural point of view, the sacrifice is identical to the hunt, in that it corresponds to the possibilities of the first ideological function. This parallel is underlined by the myth of Rhesos—after his death the animals come of their own volition to submit to the knife upon his altar, because when he was alive, the hero was a mighty hunter.

The tension between opposites in a myth may also be resolved by marriage. It is not merely by chance that the marriage rites always include a "war" between the bridegroom and a representative of the bride's clan: the ritual must bring into play all means of cancelling the antithesis "a man of our own people" and "a stranger." For this reason Kotys I and Diegylis, two centuries later, kill (or sacrifice) "strangers"—servants from the social standpoint, and strangers or foreigners from the ethnic point of view. The victims in the Letnica appliques are probably marked as "strangers" by the particular style of their hair. The wedding celebrations depicted in the frescoes of the two great tombs at Kazanlak and Sveštari show the two processions visibly in opposition to each other, the men on the right and the women on the left. A "sexual" code defines the oppositions, which are resolved in the centre of the composition. In the first, the king takes his wife's hand: in the second, the bride-to-be places a crown on the head of the horseman-king. It is not accidental that these gestures "of alliance" are placed exactly in the central focal point of the frescoes—they represent the principal semantic moment of the scene. The scene on a jug from the Rogozen treasure is similar in its content and in the artistic solution it presents: Herakles, recognizable by his club and lion skin, is pursued by an Amazon who is about to stab him with her spear. It is unlikely that this is a Greek myth. We are inclined to think that the Thracian artist used the two Greek personages as signs of the "masculine" and the "feminine," who are locked in perpetual strife. At the ritual level, this battle may be interpreted as a conjugal contest (see Atalanta and her suitors). From the mythological viewpoint, it corresponds to the continual battles between heroes and Amazons, representing groups of young people in the process of initiation. These warrior-women are the code alternative of girls who do not marry; they are thrust into the opposite pole, that of war. In Bulgarian folklore, the valiant girl, the warrior maiden, builds a city with the skulls and bones of brave men she has killed, that is, of her rivals who do not succeed in conquering her in the competition for her hand and "die" as suitors. Could this be a memory handed down over the centuries of the Thracian Amazon who triumphed over Herakles himself?

We come here to a question which is important for all barbarian art from classical antiquity: to what extent were local craftsmen influenced by Greek models? How far did the borrowing go? It is true that there are numerous works by Greek artists among the Thracian discoveries: the gold treasure of Panagjurište, the phiale from Rogozen depicting a scene with Herakles and Augeias, Herakles fighting the lion on the two phalerae of Panagjurište. Yet does this mean that the Thracian clients who had ordered or bought these rare objects were unconcerned about exchanges between the two cultures? In the fourth century B.C., even in Hellas, precious objects were used mainly in temples. The Greek craftsmen intended these treasures for the barbarian market, for the Scythians, Lycians, Thracians, Persians. They were only of use in the conditions of the barbarian culture where they acquired value as signs of prestige, as ritual attributes, and received magic power. For this reason we can consider them as an integral part of the cultural heritage of the barbarians, despite the fact that they were made by Greek craftsmen. Furthermore, in Thrace it was

Greek subjects and Greek mythological personages, of whom Herakles was the most popular, that were the most often depicted. This is easy to explain—the Greek hero became a convenient sign to designate the local hero whose epic life included the same exploits: fight with a bull (Buzes), with a wild boar (Rhesos), with a lion (Lysimachos). In Scythia and later throughout the Hellenistic world, Herakles reflected all the local heroic legends. In Thrace only Dionysos rivalled him in popularity, but this is quite understandable—the whole ancient world regarded him as a Thraco-Phrygian divinity, while Herodotus, as we have seen, placed him in the Thracian pantheon. However, unlike his Greek prototype, in Thrace this god clearly had dynastic traits—pouring wine on his altar in the famous sanctuary at Rhodope, the priests made dynastic prophecies while noting the size of the flame. Artemis too was one of the gods represented in Thrace, although she underwent profound modifications there. On a jug from Rogozen she is shown winged, in the traditional iconography of *Potnia thèron*, but unexpectedly flanked by two pairs of winged centaurs. This iconography may reflect the attributes of the goddess as protectress of initiatic societies, attributes she had had in ancient Greece.

The depiction of Greek subjects was also well-known in Thrace, the frieze of the Panagjurište amphora-rhyton being an example. This probably tells the myth of the "Seven Against Thebes." It should be noted that more than half a century before it appeared on this amphora, the myth was known at the Thracian court: Greek musicians had sung it at the wedding of the daughter of Kotys, famous in antiquity for its splendour. The appearance of this mythological subject on the sides of the vessel of Panagjurište may be explained by the purpose it was destined for. It was used for rites of fraternization between rulers in the course of a feast (note that the participants at a banquet were called "brothers"). It is obvious that in this case a story about a fratricidal war unleashed by the breaking of a peace treaty would have a certain moralizing value—the mythological precedent would serve as a lesson to the fraternizers. Even these isolated examples suffice to convince us that the Thracian clients of the Greek workshops situated on the coast of the Propontis took an active part in the exchanges.

A second group of objects of Thracian toreutics was made by local artisans using Greek iconographic models. Thus on a Rogozen jug we find for the first time in Thrace the myth of the battle of Bellerophon and the Chimera. It is possible that the mythological images concerning Bellerophon originated in Thrace, where many place names still keep the same root. Indeed, writers of antiquity were convinced that the name of the monster "Belleros," from which after the victory Hypnoi took the name of Bellerophon (killer of Belleros), was of Pelasgian origin. As for Pegasus, the winged horse who helped the hero vanquish the Chimera, he too was a popular figure, and appears in the Thracian discoveries. So the different elements of the myth are at home in the locality. But this is not essential. Even if he had taken all the iconography from Greek models (though verbal ones), the craftsman would have adapted it to express an idea which is a common type—the combat of the hero and the antagonist.

We have already mentioned the depiction of the Nereid in the Letnica treasure. As a water demon, in Greek mythology she is always allied with the forces of chaos. The Thracian craftsman put her too into the myth of the combat with the dragon, but as a symbol of water.

We need not add more examples to show that Greek personages and subjects were borrowed only as signs, without the meaning they had in Greek art. The Thracians reinterpreted the Greek iconographic models, less by modifying the style than by giving new meanings to well-known signs. For this reason, we would be wrong in applying to Thracian art the criteria applicable to Greek art: we could easily be as mistaken about concrete content as about the supposed hellenization of the Thracian aristocracy. An analysis of the process shows that the "influence" was a way of adapting a system entirely composed of signs to express a new content. It could be compared to the use of the Greek alphabet by the Thracian kings (first level of borrowing) and of the Greek language for inscriptions on Thracian receptacles (second level of borrowing). In both cases the local rulers used ready-made signs to resolve their own ritual situations. It was not perhaps just a happy accident that the Thracians turned to the Greek language and alphabet on the one hand, and to Greek iconography on the other, at almost the same period in history. The language of the Hellenes, both written and figurative, was the dominant one in the ancient world at the time, and its heritage of signs was naturally used by many barbarian peoples. It is precisely this Thracian interpretation (interpretatio thracica) which modern thracology is attempting to reconstruct. It will enable us to enter into the world of the Thracians, to come closer to the concrete subjects of their myths and to understand the meaning of their ritual acts. Only then will we be able to appreciate at its true value this magnificent exhibition—the spiritual testament of a people who have disappeared from the ethnographic maps of the world, but whose legacy enriched the folklore of the Balkan nations and thus has survived up to the present day.

IVAN MARAZOV

Fresco of the frieze of Kazanlak tomb.

THRACE FROM THE NEOLITHIC TO THE EARLY BRONZE AGE (7ᵗʰ-3ʳᵈ MILLENNIA B.C.)

The flowering of civilization on Thracian soil began remarkably early. What is traditionally called the "neolithic revolution" began there at the end of the seventh millennium B.C. This can be stated not only because of the introduction of a new technology which replaced cut stone by polished stone (no. 9), but also because of the appearance of stock-rearing and agriculture (see sickle, no. 4) in the wide fertile plains of the Balkans, as well as the acquisition of new skills. These skills include the use of fire, and in particular the making of terracotta, illustrated here by a large number of vessels and figurines.

These innovations were accompanied by profound changes both in economic and social life, religious concepts, artistic creativity, and the way of thinking of the populace. This was truly the birth of a real civilization and of the art which reflected it.

Modern methods for the dating of objects — carbon 14 testing, thermo-luminescence — permit us to state categorically that as well as being in contact with Anatolia and the Aegean world, the region of the Balkans and the Danube plain developed very early an autonomous and original culture, which served as a beacon for the rest of Europe.

Tells and necropolises constitute our principal source of information. The most spectacular example is undoubtedly that of the Karanovo tell, an artificial hill more than twelve metres high formed by the accumulation of layers of mud dwellings rebuilt in the same place over centuries. A stratigraphic excavation down through this accumulation reveals several millennia of successive habitations, from the Neolithic period to the Bronze Age. The Chalcolithic or Eneolithic Age (fifth and fourth millennia B.C.), which followed the Neolithic era, is characterized by copper and gold work unusually early in these metal-rich regions.

The excavations at Varna, and the more recent ones of the Durankulak necropolis, which will be studied in detail later in these pages, have completely changed our view of these epochs. Everywhere, the presence of female idols with exaggerated sexual characteristics testifies to the cult of a Mother-Goddess, the great divinity of fertility and fecundity. The appearance of seals or of inscribed objects (nos. 46 to 49) remains mysterious: were they religious symbols? ideograms? or the beginnings of what would eventually become writing? It is hard to be sure, just as it is hard to interpret the precise meaning of "models" such as the ritual scene of Ovčarovo (no. 52) or of the models of houses or steles (nos. 58 to 60).

Around 3200 B.C. radical changes occurred, creating a total break with the preceding period. These changes were linked less to hypothetical climatic changes than to the population movements which at this period affected the whole of Europe, but most especially Thrace, which constituted a sort of corridor. The similarity of certain ceramic shapes (nos. 108 and 109) attests to the existence of contacts with Troy and Anatolia, and with the Aegean world. Finally, the discovery of the remarkable properties of an alloy of copper and tin in the manufacture of weapons, tools and jewellery was to usher in a new era: that of Bronze Age metallurgy, which would reach its full flowering during the Late Bronze Age.

THRACE FROM THE NEOLITHIC TO THE EARLY BRONZE AGE (SEVENTH TO THIRD MILLENNIA B.C.)

1

FEMALE IDOL

Terracotta; ht. 11.5 cm.
Karanovo, near Nova Zagora.
Early Neolithic, 6200-6000 B.C.
Archaeological Museum, Sofia, inv.
no. 4033.
Surface brown, undecorated.
Bibl.: G. Georgiev, "Kulturgruppen
der Jungstein-und der Kupferzeit in
der Ebene von Thrazien
(Südbulgarien)," in *L'Europe à la fin
de l'âge de la Pierre*, Praha, 1961,
p. 64, fig. 1; V. Mikov, "The
Prehistoric Mound of Karanovo," in
Archaeology, 12, 1959, pp. 88-97.

2

TULIP-SHAPED VESSEL

Terracotta; ht. 22.5 cm.
Karanovo, near Nova Zagora.
Early Neolithic, 6200-6000 B.C.
Archaeological Museum, Sofia, inv.
no. 3793.
Surface red, with white geometrical
ornament.
Bibl.: H. Todorova, M. Avramova,
Praistoričesko izkustvo v Balgarija,
Sofia, 1982, p. 6, fig. 1.

3

DRINKING VESSEL

Terracotta; ht. 10 cm.
Karanovo, near Nova Zagora.
Early Neolithic, 6200-6000 B.C.
Archaeological Museum, Sofia, inv.
no. 3722.
Surface red, with white
chequerboard ornament.
Bibl.: H. Todorova, M. Avramova,
op. cit., p. 6, fig. 1.

4

SICKLE

Deer antler handle, flint cutting
surfaces; ht. 21 cm.
Karanovo, near Nova Zagora.
Early Neolithic, 6200-6000 B.C.
Archaeological Museum, Sofia, inv.
no. 3143.
Undocumented.

5

ANTHROPOMORPHIC VESSEL

Terracotta; ht. 25.5 cm.
Gradešnica, near Vraca.
Early Neolithic, 6000-5800 B.C.
District Museum of History, Vraca,
inv. no. A-2022.
High-necked vessel with summary
depiction of a human face. The body
of the vessel is covered with beige
slip with geometrical ornaments
painted in black.
Bibl.: B. Nikolov, *Gradešnica*, Sofia,
1974.

6

7

CUP

Terracotta; ht. 16 cm; diam. 26.5 cm.
Neolithic village in the "Lenin"
section of Pernik.
Early Neolithic, 6000-5800 B.C.
District Museum of History, Pernik,
inv. no. I-176.
Beige slipped surface with brown
geometrical ornament.
Bibl.: M. Čohadžiev, "Die
Ausgrabungen der neolithischen
Siedlung in Pernik," in *NNU,* 52,
1983, pp. 23-29.

THREE NECKLACES AND DISTRIBUTOR

Galabnik, near Pernik.
Early Neolithic, 6000-5800 B.C.
District Museum of History, Pernik,
inv. nos. I-300/3, I-300/4.
a) *Necklace of one hundred and*
   forty-three beads
   Limestone, marble; diam. 6 mm.
b) *Necklace of one thousand four*
   hundred and forty beads
   Marble; diam. 5 mm.

c) *Necklace of three thousand and*
   eleven beads
   Marble; diam. 5 mm.
d) *Distributor*
   Nephrite; length 2.2 cm.
   Three cylinders glued together,
   with holes.
Undocumented.

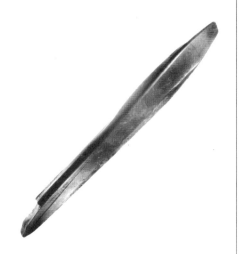

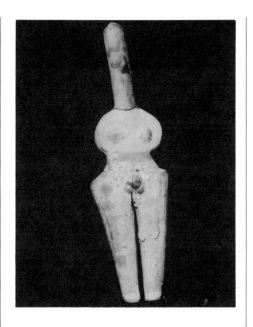

8

9

10

SCEPTRE

*Nephrite; length 36 cm; width
4.8 cm.
Galabnik, Pernik district.
Early Neolithic, 6000-5800 B.C.
District Museum of History, Pernik,
inv. no. I-310.
Dark green ground, polished surface,
front part sharpened.*
Undocumented.

OBJECT OF UNKNOWN USE
(COMPONENT OF SWORD?)

*Marble; diam. 8 cm; thickness
3.4 cm.
Galabnik, Pernik district.
Early Neolithic, 6000-5800 B.C.
District Museum of History, Pernik,
inv. no. I-311.
White, polished surface, biconical
shape, hole down the centre.*
Undocumented.

FEMALE IDOL

*Terracotta; ht. 13.5 cm.
Karanovo, near Nova Zagora.
Late Neolithic.
Archaeological Museum, Sofia, inv.
no. 4035.
Surface light brown, dark brown
trim, elongated head.
Bibl.: G. Georgiev, op. cit., pl. XXXII,
fig. 1.*

11

12

13

FEMALE IDOL

*Marble; ht. 7 cm; width 5 cm.
Karanovo, near Nova Zagora.
Late Neolithic, 5200-5000 B.C.
Historical Museum of Nova Zagora,
inv. no. 3395.
Figure of a woman of which only the
bust has been preserved. Head
trapezoidal; sculptural depiction of
nose, ears, breasts; arms crossed
over belly.
Bibl.: M. Kančev, Praistoričeski i
antični materiali ot mouzeia v grad
Nova Zagora, Nova Zagora, 1973,
no. 15-A-B.*

VESSEL

*Terracotta; ht. 18.5 cm.
Karanovo, near Nova Zagora.
Late Neolithic, 5200-5000 B.C.
Archaeological Museum, Sofia, inv.
no. 3406.
Surface brown, conical
protuberances, handle and four
cylindrical feet.
Bibl.: G. Georgiev, op. cit., pl. XXXI,
fig. 4.*

HEAD OF IDOL, MALE

*Terracotta; ht. 5.5 cm.
Haskovo.
Late Neolithic, 5200-5000 B.C.
District Museum of History,
Haskovo, inv. no. A610.
Surface polished black, bearded
male face in relief.
Bibl.: D. Aladžov, "Arheologičeski
vesti," in Vesti na narodnia mouzej v
Haskovo, I, 1965, p. 244, 3.*

14

RECEPTACLE

Terracotta; ht. 46 cm; diam. 44 cm.
Nova Zagora.
Late Neolithic, 5200-5000 B.C.
Historical Museum of Nova Zagora,
inv. no. KVP 4561.
Surface matte grey, decorated with
white paste inlay of spiral and
meanders.
Undocumented.

THE EXCAVATIONS NEAR THE VILLAGE OF DURANKULAK

The archaeological site of the village of Durankulak (district of Tolbuhin), on the edge of a pool on the Black Sea coast, has been in process of excavation since 1974 by a team under the direction of Dr. H. Todorova. On a large island, levels have been studied dating from the High Middle Ages (ninth and tenth centuries A.D.), the Late Bronze Age (thirteenth and twelfth centuries B.C.), the Early Bronze Age (end of the fourth to the third millennium B.C.), and from the late Chalcolithic era (fifth millennium B.C.). The Neolithic (sixth millennium B.C.) dwellings, where stone was used for the first time in continental Europe, are of particular interest. In the nearby burial ground eight hundred and twenty-six graves, dating from the Neolithic and Chalcolithic eras, have already been excavated. The graves belong to one of three groups, depending on whether the skeleton is stretched out, curled up, or not there (cenotaphs). Clear differences of sex, age and possessions can be noted. Several graves contained rich grave goods: ornaments of gold, copper, chalcedony, malachite, bone, and stone, numerous beautiful receptacles, tools and weapons of copper, flint, stone and horn. The necropolis belonged to the people of the Varna culture, who were in contact with the Cucuteni-Tripolie in Moldavia and the southern Ukraine. The presence of shells of Mediterranean molluscs, spondylus and dentalium, as well as necklaces of Nordic stag's-teeth beads are evidence of intensive trading from the fifth millennium B.C. by means of coastal shipping. The site on the large island near Durankulak was an important staging post on the network of exchanges in prehistoric times.

Bibl.: H. Todorova, "The Eneolithic Period in Bulgaria," in BAR, 49, London, 1978.

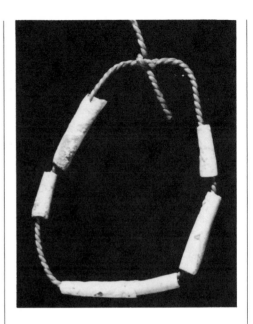

Tomb no. 621, female burial. Necropolis near village of Durankulak, near Tolbuhin. Late Neolithic, 5500-5000 B.C.

15

FEMALE IDOL

Terracotta; ht. 9.5 cm.
Durankulak, near Tolbuhin.
Late Neolithic, 5200-5000 B.C.
National Historical Museum, inv.
no. K-1220.
Surface dark brown, polished.
Female figure, cylindrical head, arms
crossed on belly.
Undocumented.

16

SEVEN SMALL GLASS BEADS

Dentalium, malachite; diam. 1.2 to
2 mm.
National Historical Museum, inv.
nos. K-1296, 1297.
Undocumented.

17

FEMALE IDOL

Spondylus; ht. 2.9 cm.
National Historical Museum, inv.
no. K-1298.
Undocumented.

Tomb no. 643, male
burial.
Necropolis near the
village of
Durankulak, near
Tolbuhin.
Late Neolithic,
5500-5000 B.C.

18

NINETY-ONE SMALL GLASS BEADS

Malachite, spondylus; diam. 5 to
6 mm.
National Historical Museum, inv.
no. K-1357.
Undocumented.

19

ADZE

Stone; ht. 8 cm.
National Historical Museum, inv.
no. K-1356.
Surface dark green, polished.
Undocumented.

20

TWO BRACELETS

Marble; diam. 11.5 cm and 12 cm.
National Historical Museum, inv.
no. K-1360.
Undocumented.

Tomb no. 648, male
burial.
Necropolis near
village of
Durankulak, near
Tolbuhin.
Early Chalcolithic,
5000-4500 B.C.

21

TWENTY-TWO SMALL GLASS BEADS

Malachite; diam. 2 mm.
National Historical Museum, inv.
no. K-1367.
Undocumented.

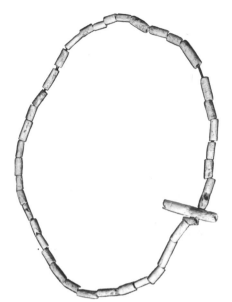

22

FORTY SMALL BEADS

Spondylus; length 1.2 to 1.5 cm;
diam. 5 mm.
National Historical Museum, inv.
no. K-1375.
Cylindrical form.
Undocumented.

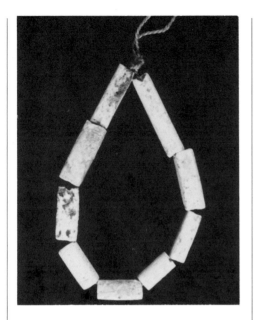

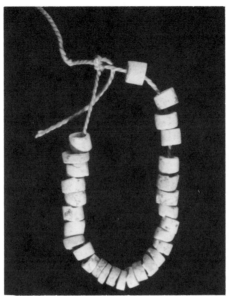

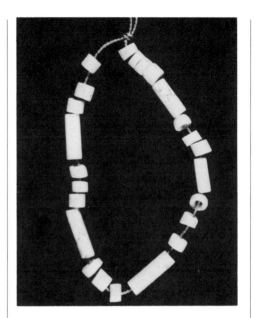

23

NINE SMALL BEADS

Spondylus; length 1.1 to 1.5 cm.
National Historical Museum, inv.
no. K-1377.
Square cross-section.
Undocumented.

24

TWENTY-NINE SMALL BEADS

Stone; diam. 4 mm.
National Historical Museum, inv.
no. K-1378.
Undocumented.

25

TWENTY-THREE SMALL BEADS

Marble; diam. 6 mm.
National Historical Museum, inv.
no. K-1379.
Undocumented.

26

BRACELET

Spondylus; diam. 11.5 cm.
National Historical Museum, inv.
no. K-1372.
Undocumented.

27

TWO NECKLACES OF DEER'S TOOTH BEADS

Ht. 1.1 to 1.7 cm.
National Historical Museum, inv.
nos. K-1370, K-1371.
Undocumented.

28

KNIFE

Flint; ht. 7.2 cm.
National Historical Museum, inv.
no. K-1369.

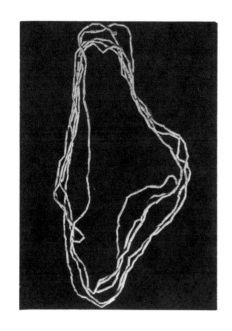

29

NECKLACE COMPOSED OF SMALL BEADS

Dentalium; ht. 1.1 to 2 cm.
National Historical Museum, inv.
no. K-1368.
Undocumented.

Tomb no. 364,
female burial.
Necropolis of village
of Durankulak, near
Tolbuhin.
Late Chalcolithic,
4500-4000 B.C.

30

NECKLACE OF TWENTY-SIX SMALL BEADS

12 gold beads, 3 of chalcedony, 1 of
spondylus, 10 of stone; diam. 2 to
4 mm.
National Historical Museum, inv.
no. 0580.
Undocumented.

Tomb no. 527,

female burial.

Necropolis of village

of Durankulak, near

Tolbuhin.

Late Chalcolithic,

4500-4000 B.C.

Bibl.: M. Avramova, "Nakiti ot praistoričeskija nekropol pri s. Durankulak, Tolbuhinski okrag," in Dobrudža, 3, 1986.

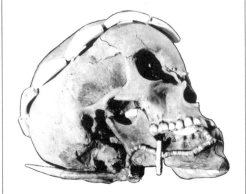

31

SKULL WITH PIN, NECKLACE AND DIADEM

Bone, spondylus, stone; length 11.2 cm; diam. 4 to 5 mm. National Historical Museum, inv. no. 1021.
Undocumented.

32

TWELVE RHOMBOIDAL BEADS FROM BRACELET

Spondylus; length 1.5 to 2 cm. National Historical Museum, inv. nos. K-1012, K-1013.
Undocumented.

33

STRING OF THIRTY-SIX SMALL BEADS

Stone; diam. 4 mm.
National Historical Museum, inv.
no. K-1018.
Undocumented.

34

STRING OF EIGHTEEN SMALL BEADS

Spondylus; diam. 5 to 6 mm.
National Historical Museum, inv.
no. K-1010.
Undocumented.

35

RING

Copper; diam. 2 cm.
National Historical Museum, inv.
no. K-1008.
Undocumented.

36

CUP AND VASE-SHAPED RECEPTACLE

Terracotta; ht. 8.2 cm; diam. 4.5 cm.
National Historical Museum, inv.
no. 1004.
Surface dark brown, polished.
Undocumented.

37

STAND

Terracotta; ht. 19.7 cm.
Necropolis of village of Durankulak,
near Tolbuhin.
Middle Chalcolithic, 4600-4400 B.C.
Archaeological Museum, Sofia, inv.
no. K-0541.
Surface dark brown, polished, with
engraved, inlaid red-and-white
painted geometrical ornament.
Undocumented.

38

VASE-SHAPED RECEPTACLE WITH COVER

Terracotta; ht. 9 cm; diam. 5 cm.
Necropolis of village of Durankulak,
near Tolbuhin.
Middle Chalcolithic, 4600-4400 B.C.
National Historical Museum, inv.
no. K-0540.
Surface grey-brown, with engraved
decoration.
Undocumented.

39

ZOOMORPHIC ALTAR

Terracotta; ht. 8.9 cm.
Jasatepe, near Plovdiv.
Early Chalcolithic, 5000-4500 B.C.
Archaeological Museum, Plovdiv,
inv. no. 2629.
Surface grey, triangular shape with
three feet and animal head,
engraved ornament.
Bibl.: H. Todorova, "The Eneolithic
Period in Bulgaria," in *BAR*, 49, 1978,
pl. I:1.

40

CUP

Terracotta; ht. 16 cm.
Karanovo, near Nova Zagora.
Early Chalcolithic, 5000-4500 B.C.
Archaeological Museum, Sofia, inv.
no. 4032.
Black-painted decoration, with
incisions and inlay in white on red
background.
Undocumented.

41

CUP

Terracotta; ht. 11 cm; diam. 21 cm.
Karanovo, near Nova Zagora.
Early Chalcolithic, 5000-4500 B.C.
Archaeological Museum, Sofia, inv.
no. 3550.
On the outside, decoration painted
in black (graphite) on brown
background.
Undocumented.

42

43

44

TABOR

Terracotta; ht. 52 cm.
Burial mound at Azmak, near Stara Zagora.
Early Chalcolithic, 5000-4500 B.C.
District Museum of History, Stara Zagora, inv. no. 7416.
Surface polished grey-black, with geometrical decoration painted in graphite.
Bibl.: H. Todorova, M. Avramova, *Praistoričesko izkustvo v Balgarija*, Sofia, 1982, p. 32, 17; G. Georgiev, "The Azmak Mound in Southern Bulgaria," in *Antiquity*, 34, 1965.

RECEPTACLE

Terracotta; ht. 16.6 cm.
Fortress of Pernik, Pernik.
Middle Chalcolithic, 4600-4400 B.C.
District Museum of History, Pernik, inv. no. 7813.
Surface grey-black polished, with geometrical ornament painted in graphite.
Bibl.: Y. Čangova, A. Radunčeva *et al.*, *Pernik*, I, Sofia, 1981, p. 20, 6.

STELE FOR WORSHIP

Terracotta; ht. 33 cm.
Burial mound at Poljanica, near Targovište.
Middle Chalcolithic, 4600-4400 B.C.
Departmental Historical Museum at Targovište, inv. no. 2912.
Surface matte grey, two-sided roof, decorated in four zones in "kerbschnitt" technique.
Bibl.: H. Todorova, M. Avramova, *op. cit.*, pp. 32, 49.

45

46

47

HEAD OF AN IDOL

Terracotta; ht. 7.2 cm.
Karanovo, near Nova Zagora.
Late Chalcolithic, 4500-4000 B.C.
Archaeological Museum, Sofia, inv.
no. 4034.
Surface light brown, green eyes with
lines, lips and forehead red.
Bibl.: V. Mikov, "Idolnata plastika
prez novokamennata epoha," in
BIAB, 8, 1934, p. 198, fig. 132.

PLAQUE WITH PICTOGRAMS

Terracotta; diam. 12 cm.
Gradešnica, near Vraca.
Early Chalcolithic, 5000-4500 B.C.
District Museum of History, Vraca,
inv. no. AI2829.
Surface black, pictograms engraved
on both sides.
Bibl.: B. Nikolov, Gradešnica, Sofia,
1974, pp. 68-69.

TWO BASES OF RECEPTACLES WITH PICTOGRAMS

Terracotta; diam. 5.5 cm, 9.5 cm.
Gradešnica, near Vraca.
Early Chalcolithic, 5000-4500 B.C.
District Museum of History, Vraca,
inv. nos. A12831 and A12832.
Bibl.: B. Nikolov, "Signes sur des
ouvrages en argile de l'époque
préhistorique en Bulgarie
occidentale," in Studia Praehistorica,
1986, 8, pp. 181-182, fig. 13, no. 104,
and fig. 14, no. 111.

48

SEAL

Terracotta; diam. 6 cm.
Karanovo, near Nova Zagora.
Early Chalcolithic, 5000-4500 B.C.
Archaeological Museum, Sofia, inv.
no. 4031.
The seal is round. Symbols inscribed
on upper surface in the arm of a
cross.
Bibl.: V. Mikov, G. Georgiev,
"Nadpisat varhu kraglija pečat ot
Karanovo," in *Arheologija*, 11, 1969,
1, pp. 6-13.

49

SEAL

Terracotta; diam. 6 cm.
Ruse burial mound.
Late Chalcolithic, 4500-4000 B.C.
District Museum of History, Ruse,
inv. no. 354.
Round with engraved solar symbol.
Undocumented.

50

HEAD OF IDOL

Terracotta; ht. 4.8 cm.
Vodica, near Targovište.
Late Chalcolithic, 4500-4000 B.C.
Historical Museum of Popovo, inv.
no. 157.
Surface dark brown, mouth open,
eyes and hair marked with engraved
lines.
Undocumented.

51

52

FEMALE IDOL

Terracota; ht. 14 cm.
Burial mound at Poljanica, near
Targovište.
Late Chalcolithic, 4500-4000 B.C.
District Museum of History,
Targovište, inv. no. 1600.
Light kaolin surface. Face painted in
ochre and red as well as the
garment.
Bibl.: H. Todorova, *Eneolit Balgarii*,
Sofia, 1979, p. 76.

RITUAL SCENE

Ovčarovo, near Targovište.
Late Chalcolithic, late 5th-early 4th
millennia B.C.
District Museum of History,
Targovište, inv. no. 1459, A-X, 1-3.
a) *Model of an open-air sanctuary;*
   figures of priestesses, altars,
   tables, chairs and ritual
   receptacles. All figures are
   painted red. Decorated with
   spirals, meanders, triangles and
   other geometric ornaments.
Bibl.: H. Todorova, "Eneolitna
kultova scena," in *Mouzei i
pametnici na kulturata*, 12, 1974,
4, pp. 5-8.

b) *Model of house*
   Terracotta; ht. 6.5 cm.
   Inv. no. 146 d.
   Surface light kaolin, decorated
   with ornament painted red.
Bibl.: H. Todorova, *Ovčarovo*, Sofia,
1976; H. Todorova, "Kultszene und
Hausmodell aus Ovčarovo," in
Thracia, 3, 1974, pp. 39-46; H.
Todorova, V. Vasilev, Z. Janucevicz,
Ovčarovo, Sofia, 1983.

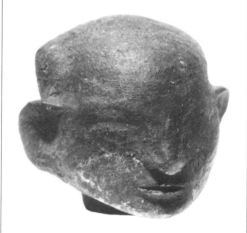

53

54

55

DOUBLE-FACED FEMALE IDOL

Terracotta; ht. 41 cm; width 25 cm.
Starozagorski mineralni bani, near
Stara Zagora.
Late Chalcolithic, 4500-4000 B.C.
District Museum of History, Stara
Zagora, provisional inv.
no. CT.3.b-665.
Hollow figurine of woman, arms
crossed on belly.
Appearance virtually identical on
both sides: eyes and mouth marked
by incisions, ears and nose in relief.
Opening at top of head. Restored.
Undocumented.

MALE IDOL

Terracotta; ht. 15 cm.
Gabarevo, near Stara Zagora.
Late Chalcolithic, 4500-4000 B.C.
Archaeological Museum, Sofia, inv.
no. 2957.
Male figure, surface dark brown and
polished.
Bibl.: V. Mikov, *op. cit.*, p. 198.

HEAD OF IDOL

Terracotta; ht. 7 cm.
Gabarevo, near Stara Zagora.
Late Chalcolithic, 4500-4000 B.C.
Archaeological Museum, Sofia, inv.
no. 2958.
Surface black, previously with red
decoration, now vanished.
Bibl.: V. Mikov, *op. cit.*, p. 198,
fig. 132.

56

FEMALE IDOL

Marble; ht. 33 cm.
Blagoevo, near Razgrad.
Late Chalcolithic, 4500-4000 B.C.
District Museum of History, Razgrad,
inv. no. 770.
Bibl.: G. Georgiev, "Mramorna
čoveska figura ot Blagoevo," in
BIAB, 29, 1955, pp. 1-13.

57

FLAT IDOL

Bone; ht. 15 cm; width 5.1 cm.
Loveč, near Stara Zagora.
Late Chalcolithic, 4500-4000 B.C.
District Museum of History, Stara
Zagora, inv. no. 1-C3-135.
Schematic female figure, with parts
of body indicated by holes and
incised lines; copper greaves.
Bibl.: M. Dimitrov, "Kostena čoveška
figurka ot selo Loveč," in
Arheologija, 4, 1962, 1, pp. 65-67.

58

MODEL OF SANCTUARY

Terracotta; ht. 13.5 cm; width
14.5 cm.
Starozagorski mineralni bani, near
Stara Zagora.
Late Chalcolithic, 4500-4000 B.C.
District Museum of History, Stara
Zagora, provisional inv.
no. CT.3.b-1258.
Double-slit roof with "chimneys"
widening toward the top.
Undocumented.

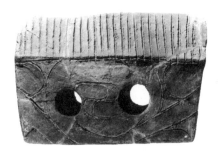

59

60

61

MODEL OF HOUSE

Terracotta; ht. 20 cm.
Kodža-Dermen near Šumen.
Late Chalcolithic, 4500-4000 B.C.
Archaeological Museum, Sofia, inv.
no. 1367.
Surface light brown, incised
decoration.

MODEL OF HOUSE

Terracotta; ht. 6.5 cm.
Vinica, near Šumen.
Late Chalcolithic, 4500-4000 B.C.
Archaeological Museum, Sofia, inv.
no. 4037.
Decorated with incised lines.
Bibl.: A. Radunčeva, "Selištna
mogila pri s. Vinica," in *RP, 6*, 1976,
p. 14, 7/9; L. Perničeva, "Les
modèles de maisons du
Chalcolithique en Bulgarie," in
Arheologija, 20-2, 1978, pp. 1-12.

ZOOMORPHIC RECEPTACLE IN SHAPE OF HEDGEHOG

Terracotta; ht. 10 cm.
Burial mound at Gjundievo, near
Nova Zagora.
Late Chalcolithic, 4500-4000 B.C.
Historical Museum of Nova Zagora,
inv. no. 342.
Surface matte black.
Bibl.: M. Kančev, *Praistoričeski i*
antični materiali ot mouzeia v grad
Nova Zagora, Nova Zagora, 1973,
p. 29.

62

63

ZOOMORPHIC FIGURINE: DOG

Terracotta; length 19.2 cm.
Burial mound at Goljamo Delčevo,
near Varna.
Late Chalcolithic, 4500-4000 B.C.
Archaeological Museum, Varna, inv.
no. 3060.

Surface polished grey-black,
moulded head as lid.
Bibl.: H. Todorova, *Eneolit Balgarii*,
Sofia, 1979, p. 78.

ZOOMORPHIC RECEPTACLE

Terracotta; ht. 11.5 cm.
Karanovo, near Nova Zagora.
Late Chalcolithic, 4500-4000 B.C.
Archaeological Museum, Sofia, inv.
no. 3426.
Surface polished red, moulded head
as lid, linear incised decoration.
Bibl.: H. Todorova, M. Avramova,
Praistoričesko izkustvo v Balgarija,
Sofia, 1982, pp. 26, 43.

64

ANTHROPO-ZOOMORPHIC RECEPTACLE

Terracotta; ht. 15.3 cm.
Goljam Izvor, near Razgrad.
Late Chalcolithic, 4500-4000 B.C.
District Museum of History, Razgrad,
inv. no. 223.
Surface matte red, with painted
linear decoration.
Bibl.: J. H. Gaul, "The Neolithic
Period in Bulgaria," in *ASPR*, 16,
1948, pl. LXII: 6.

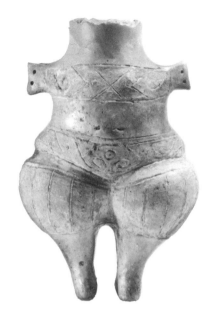

65

FEMALE IDOL

Terracotta; ht. 17 cm.
Radingrad, near Razgrad.
Late Chalcolithic, 4500-4000 B.C.
District Museum of History, Razgrad,
inv. no. 3716.
Surface brown-yellow, massive
body with pronounced steatopygia,
inlaid white engraved decoration.
Bibl.: T. Ivanov, "Mnogoslojnoe
poselenie u s. Radingrad,
Razgradskogo rajona," in *Studia
Praehistorica*, 7, 1984, p. 95, fig. 13.

THE CHALCOLITHIC NECROPOLIS OF VARNA

Excavation of the Chalcolithic
necropolis at Varna has been
going on since 1972. Up to the
present, seven thousand five hundred square metres of the surface have
been studied, and two hundred and sixty–
five graves have been revealed. They have
been classified in groups according to the
usual divisions, depending on the presence
and arrangement of the skeletons in the
graves and the number of objects. The
groups are as follows:
1. Cenotaphs (symbolic graves containing
no body), three of which are remarkable for
their rich contents. Three others contained
terracotta masks with human faces, on
which there are gold appliques.
2. Graves containing skeletons laid supine.
These are mostly male skeletons. Tomb 43
is notable for the richness of its contents.
Clearly the man buried here was a dignitary,
a military or religious leader.
3. Graves containing curled-up skeletons,
which are for the most part female. The
objects accompanying them are different
from those in the preceding group.
More than three thousand gold objects have
been found in the necropolis, with a total
weight of over 6.5 kilograms and assayed at
14 carats. There are also one hundred and
sixty copper tools, ornaments, tools of flint,
stone and horn, ornaments and images of
bone, flint, metal, spondylus and dentalium
shells (kinds of shell-fish), as well as numerous clay receptacles.
This necropolis has provided very valuable
information on the highly organized society
that inhabited the Balkan peninsula at the
end of the Chalcolithic era.
The excavations are still going on.

Bibl.: I. Ivanov, Sakrovištata na
Varnenskija nekropol, *Sofia 1978; I.
Ivanov, "Novye dannye o pogrebal'nom
rituale Varnenskogo eneolitičeskogo
nekropolja," in* Th. Pr., Pulpudeva, *3,
1982, pp. 81-85; I. Ivanov, "Les fouilles
archéologiques de la nécropole*

chalcolithique de Varna (1972-1975)," (Varnenski nekropol i problemy Halkolita), in Studia Praehistorica, *1-2, Sofia; I. Ivanov, "Le Chalcolithique en Bulgarie et dans la nécropole de Varna," in* Ancient Bulgaria, *1983, pp. 154-163; C. Renfrew, "Varna and the Social Context of Early Metallurgy," in* Antiquity, *52, 1978, pp. 199-203; J. G. P. Best, "The Varna Necropolis: Its Historic Significance," in* DITK, *1, 1984, pp. 150-153.*

Tomb no. 1

(cenotaph)

66

BRACELET

Gold; diam. 9.6 cm; width 4 cm; wt. 268 g.
Archaeological Museum, Varna, inv. no. I-1512.

67

BRACELET

Gold; diam. 9.6 cm; width 5 cm; wt. 194.32 g.
Archaeological Museum, Varna, inv. no. I-1513.

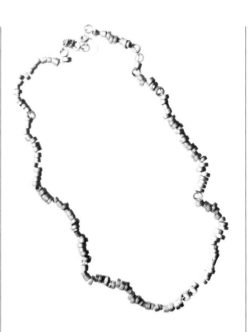

68

BRACELET

Gold; diam. 7.8 cm; width 0.7 cm; wt. 139 g.
Archaeological Museum, Varna, inv. no. I-1515.

69

GOLD BEAD

Gold; diam. 0.9 cm; wt. 0.54 g.
Archaeological Museum, Varna, inv. no. I-1554.

70

ONE HUNDRED AND SIXTY-ONE BEADS FROM A NECKLACE

Gold; diam. 0.3 to 0.5 cm; wt. 30.96 g.
Archaeological Museum, Varna, inv. no. I-1555.
All beads are cylindrical in form.

71

COMPONENTS OF NECKLACE

Shell (dentalium).
Archaeological Museum, Varna, inv.
no. I-1558.

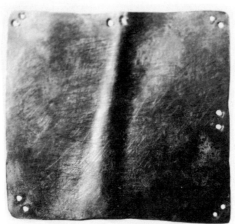

72

PECTORAL

Gold; length 10.3 cm; width
11.3 cm; wt. 189 g.
Archaeological Museum, Varna, inv.
no. I-1514.
Quadrangular with rounded corners.
Attachment holes at each end.

73

SCEPTRE

Varna Museum of Art and History,
inv. nos. I-1516, I-1423, I-1525, I-1517,
I-1540.
a) Ferrules and cylinders for sceptre
*   handle.*
*   Gold; length 7.2 cm; 1.5 to 3 cm;*
*   7.4 cm; total wt. 145.59 g.*
b) Axe.
*   Copper; length 19.2 cm.*

74

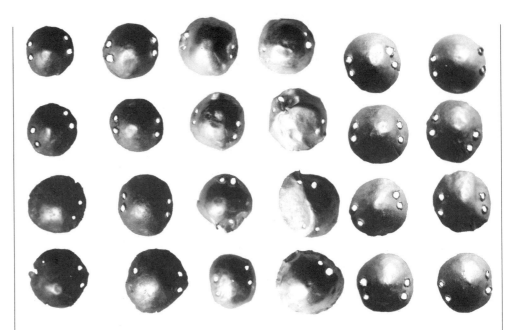

75

SIX RINGS

*Gold; diam. 1.7 to 3.7 cm; wt.
52.12 g.
Archaeological Museum, Varna, inv.
nos. I-1520 to I-1522, I-1553.*

TWENTY-SEVEN APPLIQUES

*Gold; diam. 1.3 to 2.2 cm; wt.
31.36 g.
Archaeological Museum, Varna, inv.
nos. I-1513 to I-1538, I-1559 to I-1562,
I-1566 to I-1573, I-1576, I-1577, I-1582,
I-1585, I-1757 to I-1759.*

*Round, convex; on one ornament,
five attachment holes; on the other
twenty-six, four attachment holes.*

76

SIX APPLIQUES

*Gold; ht. 1.2 to 1.5 cm; wt. 4.88 g.
Archaeological Museum, Varna, inv.
nos. I-1529, I-1530, I-1578 to I-1581.
Trapezoidal, with one or two
attachment holes.*

77

FOUR APPLIQUES

*Gold; width 3.5 to 3.7 cm; wt.
10.36 g.
Archaeological Museum, Varna, inv.
nos. I-1527, I-1528, I-1551, I-1552.
Crescent-shaped; attachment hole at
either end.*

78

SPHERICAL OBJECT

*Gold; diam. 2 cm; wt. 25.09 g.
Archaeological Museum, Varna, inv.
no. I-1518.
The object has a round opening. Its
function has not been established.*

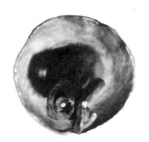

79

NAIL

Gold; ht. 1.7 cm; wt. 8.16 g.
Archaeological Museum, Sofia, inv.
no. I-1519.

80

SPIRAL-SHAPED OBJECT

Gold; ht. 8.1 cm; width 1.2 cm; wt.
3.2 g.
Archaeological Museum, Varna, inv.
no. I-1550.
Function not determined.

81

OBJECT, PURPOSE UNKNOWN

Copper; length 14.9 cm; width
0.8 cm.
Archaeological Museum, Varna, inv.
no. I-1544.
Enlarged in middle; one end pointed
and bent.

82

AXE

*Copper; ht. 14.1 cm; width 3.2 cm.
Archaeological Museum, Varna, inv.
no. I-1541.*

83

WEDGE

*Copper; ht. 14.6 cm; width 2.9 cm.
Archaeological Museum, Varna, inv.
no. I-1542.*

84

CHISEL

*Copper; ht. 14.6 cm; width 1.1 cm.
Archaeological Museum, Varna, inv.
no. I-1543.*

85

TWO AWLS

Copper; ht. 7 and 8.2 cm.
Archaeological Museum, Varna, inv.
nos. I-1545, I-1574.

86

KNIFE

Flint; length 44 cm.
Archaeological Museum, Varna, inv.
no. I-1583.
Trapezoidal.

87

IDOL

Bone; length 18.6 cm.
Archaeological Museum, Varna, inv.
no. I-1549.

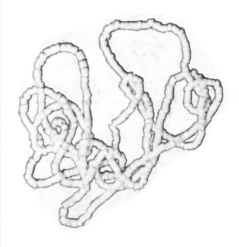

88

FIVE HUNDRED AND SIXTEEN BEADS

Kaolin; diam. 4 to 6 cm.
Archaeological Museum, Varna, inv.
no. I-1557.
Cylindrical form.

89

SCEPTRE

Gold; tot. length 22.5 cm; max.
width 5.3 cm; wt. 85.47 g.
Archaeological Museum, Varna, inv.
nos. VEN 620-627, 667.
The sceptre is composed of several
parts: one cylindrical extremity, one
transverse part with a complex two-
part profile, cylinders intended to
surround a wooden stem and a ring.

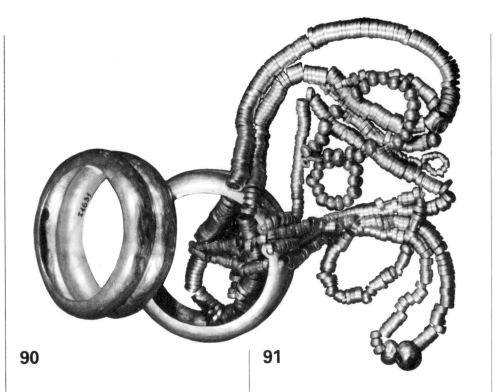

90

TWO BRACELETS

Gold; diam. 6.7 cm; width 2.6 cm; wt. 47.3 g; diam. 6.9 cm; width 2.7 cm; wt. 55.21 g.
Archaeological Museum, Varna, inv. nos. VEN 665 and 666.
Double profile; undecorated.

91

EIGHT NECKLACES COMPOSED OF SEVEN HUNDRED AND FIFTY-TWO BEADS

Gold; diam. 0.3 to 1 cm; tot. wt. 312.5 g.
Archaeological Museum, Varna, inv. nos. VEN 555, 628, 640, 646, 654, 659, 663, 668.

92

DIADEM

Gold; ht. 3.4 cm; wt. 11.72 g.
Archaeological Museum, Varna, inv. no. VEN 652.
Bent rectangular plaque; raised triangular part in the middle; three attachment holes at the ends.

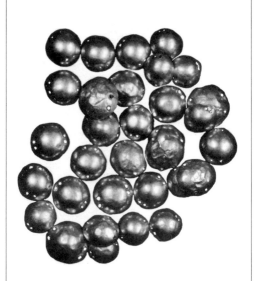

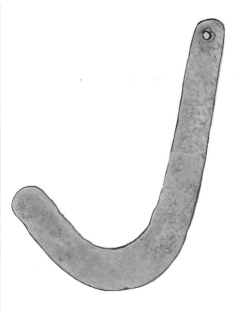

93

94

95

THIRTY-THREE APPLIQUES

*Gold; diam. 1.8 to 2.6 cm; width
0.6 cm; tot. wt. 99.18 g.
Archaeological Museum, Varna, inv.
nos. VEN 547-553, 556, 567, 581-598,
661, 662, 664, 671, 675, 677.
Round, convex; undecorated; four
attachment holes.*

TWO HALF-SPHERES

*Gold; diam. 3.2 cm; wt. 22.28 g.
Archaeological Museum, Varna, inv.
nos. VEN 660, 676.*

UNIDENTIFIED OBJECT

*Gold; length 8.8 cm; width 5.6 cm;
wt. 17.05 g.
Archaeological Museum, Varna, inv.
no. VEN 635.*

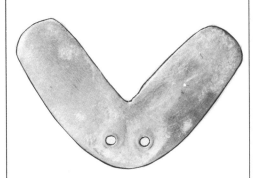

96

MINIATURE "BOOMERANG"

Gold; length 4.1 cm; width 1.2 cm; wt. 5.47 g.
Archaeological Museum, Varna, inv. no. VEN 641.

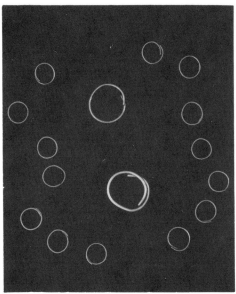

97

SIXTEEN RINGS

Gold wire; diam. 1.6 to 3.6 cm; tot. wt. 27.71 g.
Archaeological Museum, Varna, inv. nos. VEN 568-571, 573-580, 653, 670, 672, 674.

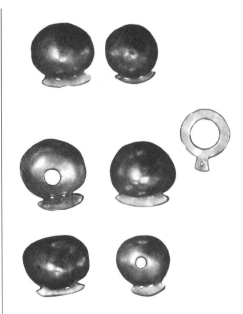

98

SEVEN ANTHROPOMORPHIC APPLIQUES

Gold; diam. 1.5 to 2 cm; width 1.8 to 2.1 cm; tot. wt. 13.94 g.
Archaeological Museum, Varna, inv. nos. VEN 559-604, 657.
Four appliques are convex and have a protrusion with two attachment holes; two are convex with an opening in the middle and have a protrusion which has two attachment holes; the seventh is flat with an opening in the middle and has a protrusion with one attachment hole.

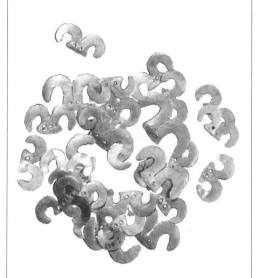

99

THIRTY PLAQUES

*Gold; length 2.8 to 4 cm; width 1.2
to 2.1 cm; tot. wt. 50.37 g.
Archaeological Museum, Varna, inv.
nos. VEN 572, 605-619, 629-633,
636-638, 643-645.
Schematic depiction of a horned
animal head; two attachment holes
in the lower part.*

100

ANIMAL FIGURINE

*Gold; length 6.5 cm; ht. 5.8 cm; wt.
11.7 g.
Archaeological Museum, Varna, inv.
no. VEN 634.
Flat figurine of horned animal
depicted in profile.
Edges decorated with knobs in
relief; two attachment holes in upper
part.*

101

ANIMAL FIGURINE

*Gold; length 3.9 cm; ht. 3.7 cm; wt.
6.74 g.
Archaeological Museum, Varna, inv.
no. VEN 639.
Similar to previous item but smaller.*

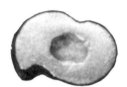

102

ASTRAGAL

Gold; length 1.9 cm; width 1.2 cm;
wt. 33.17 g.
Archaeological Museum, Varna, inv.
no. VEN 642.

103

SMALL CUP

Marble; diam. 11.9 cm; ht. 4.5 cm.
Archaeological Museum, Varna, inv.
no. VEN 649.
In form of truncated cone; rounded
lip.

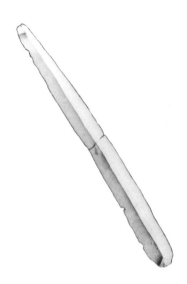

104

KNIFE

Flint; length 29.5 cm; width 2.1 cm.
Archaeological Museum, Varna, inv.
no. VEN 678.
The knife is curved and trapezoidal
in cross-section.

105

ENTHRONED FEMALE IDOL

Terracotta; ht. 12 cm.
Teliš, near Pleven.
Late Chalcolithic, 4000-3900 B.C.
District Museum of History, Pleven,
inv. no. 2538.
Surface matte beige. The idol sits
upon a seat with back.
Undocumented.

106

ENTHRONED FEMALE IDOL

Terracotta; ht. 7.5 cm.
Teliš, near Pleven.
Late Chalcolithic, 4000-3900 B.C.
District Museum of History, Pleven,
inv. no. 1985.
Surface matte beige. The idol sits
upon a seat with back.
Undocumented.

107

108

109

TWO ANTHROPOMORPHIC AMULETS

Bone; ht. 12 cm.
Ezero, Sliven district.
Early Bronze, 3200-2000 B.C.
Archaeological Museum, Sofia, inv.
nos. 1322 and 1323.
Bibl.: R. Katinčarov, "Antropomorfni figurki ot selištnata mogila do s. Ezerovo, Slivensko," in *BIAB*, 33, 1972, p. 71.

TWO-HANDLED VESSEL

Terracotta; ht. 20 cm.
Mihalič, Kardžali district.
Early Bronze, 3200-2000 B.C.
Archaeological Museum, Sofia, inv.
no. 3190.
Surface grey, polished.
Bibl.: V. Mikov, "Predistoričesko selište do s. Mihalič, Svilengradsko," in *RP*, I, 1948, pp. 57-65.

TWO-HANDLED VESSEL

Terracotta; ht. 15.5 cm.
Simeonovgrad.
Early Bronze, 3200-2000 B.C.
District Museum of History, Haskovo, inv. no. 2223.
Surface black, polished, analogous to no. 108.
Bibl.: G. Georgiev, "Konstancia i Troja po danni ot poslednite nahodki," in *BMNH*, 3, p. 334, pl. IV/1.

110

ASKOS

Terracotta; ht. 20.6 cm.
Necropolis at Bereket burial mound,
Stara Zagora district.
Early Bronze, 3200-2000 B.C.
District Museum of History, Stara
Zagora, inv. no. B-77.

Surface black, polished, incised
decoration, white inlay.
Bibl.: *Istoria na Balgarija*, 1, Sofia,
1979, p. 101, fig. 9.

111

ASKOS

Terracotta; ht. 10 cm.
Junacite, Pazardžik district.
Early Bronze, 3200-2000 B.C.
Archaeological Museum, Plovdiv,
inv. no. 2023.
Surface red and brown, incised
decoration.
Bibl.: V. Mikov, "Selištna mogila pri
Junacite, Pazardžisko," in *BIAB*,
1937-39, p. 58.

112

ASKOS

Terracotta; ht. 10 cm.
Junacite, Pazardžik district.
Early Bronze, 3200-2000 B.C.
Archaeological Museum, Plovdiv,
inv. no. 2024.
Similar to previous object.
Bibl.: V. Mikov, *op. cit.*, p. 59.

113

RECEPTACLE

Terracotta, ht. 22 cm.
Necropolis near Tarnava, Vraca
district.
Early Bronze, 3200-2000 B.C.
District Museum of History, Vraca,
inv. no. A1-2708.
Background dark matte brown,
engraved decoration, red and white
inlay.
Bibl.: *Istoria na Balgarija*, 1, Sofia,
1979, p. 100, fig. 1.

114

RECEPTACLE

Terracotta; ht. 11 cm.
Ezero, Sliven district.
Early Bronze, 3200-2000 B.C.
Archaeological Museum, Sofia, inv.
no. 1640.
Background black, decorated with
vertical grooves; cover in the form of
a human head.
Bibl.: *Istoria na Balgarija*, 1, Sofia,
1979, p. 100, fig. 5.

THRACIAN ART IN THE LATE BRONZE AGE (1600-1100 B.C.)

Greek legend links the history of the Achaean kings of Mycenae with that of the Thracian kings. Thus a large number of archaeologists, in studying ancient history in general and the history of the shores of the Aegean in particular starting with the Iliad and the Odyssey, have attempted to explain Thrace and its culture from the Homeric epic onwards.

The epoch of Orpheus, of Maron, of Diomedes whose horses devoured strangers, was the period when Troy dominated the Hellespont. To the east there lay the Hittite state; but the Scythians had not yet settled north of the Black Sea nor the Peonians in Macedonia. During this period, which is still relatively unknown, the life of the Thracian tribes was no different from that of the other peoples north of the Balkan peninsula.

The most widespread art was that of pottery, in which the remote influence of Mycenae can be seen; however, Thracian pottery is different in both shape and ornamentation. The vessels, of rather heavy proportions, are incised and encrusted with white decoration (nos. 131 to 133), as are the bird-shaped receptacles and the female images in long tunics like those of Mycenae (no. 126). This sort of ceramic is found on both sides of the western Balkans and the Carpathians, and also in some parts of the middle and lower Danube. In southern and eastern Thrace the pottery had similar characteristics, but was rougher, as was the culture of those regions. This difference perhaps resulted from the way of life, which was more peaceful in the northwest than in the south and the east.

The bronze weapons of the Thracians at this period were those found throughout the valley of the Danube, notably the tapered sword with two cutting edges and the rapier with a cruciform hilt-guard for thrusts. The rapiers found in Thrace are of the same quality as those found in Greece. For a long time they were thought to have been imported from Mycenae. But compared to the objects common to the Thracians and the Greeks of the Homeric period, Thracian art often had a local character: near the city of Razgrad, at Pobit Kamak, moulds for casting bronze weapons have been discovered (nos. 134 and 135). The elegant decoration shows that these weapons were made for Thracian chiefs, and is evidence of the technical expertise of the bronzesmiths. It would appear that these moulds were buried on purpose when Thrace was invaded by a people who did not possess such sophisticated things. Some objects cast in similar moulds have parallels in Rumania. Another treasure, that of Valčitran, shows even more clearly the high level of skill attained by the craftsmen, not only in casting metal but also in toreutics.

115

116

117

DRINKING VESSEL

*Terracotta; ht. 9.5 cm; diam. of
opening 3 cm.
Ezero, near Sliven.
Middle Bronze, 2000-1600 B.C.
Historical Museum of Nova Zagora,
inv. no. 2247.
Belly spherical, bottom flat, neck
cylindrical, opening raised. Handle
extends beyond the body of the
vessel and terminates in a button.*
Bibl.: M. Kančev, *Praistoričeski i
antični materiali ot mouzeia v gr.
Nova Zagora*, Nova Zagora, 1973,
no. 57-b.

DRINKING VESSEL

*Terracotta; ht. 10 cm.
Junacite, Pazardžik district.
Middle Bronze, 2000-1600 B.C.
Archaeological Museum, Plovdiv,
inv. no. 2033.
Background brown-black, polished,
ends in a point, two handles and
engraved fillet decoration.*
Bibl.: V. Mikov, "Selištna mogila pri
Junacite, Pažardzisko," in *BIAB*,
1937-1939, p. 58.

DRINKING VESSEL

*Terracotta, ht. 7 cm.
Junacite, Pazardžik district.
Middle Bronze, 2000-1600 B.C.
District Museum of History,
Pazardžik, inv. no. A 3241.
Form similar to previous vessel but
with only one handle.*
Bibl.: V. Mikov, *op. cit.*, p. 75.

118

DRINKING VESSEL

Terracotta; ht. 9.6 cm.
Ezero, Sliven district.
Middle Bronze, 2000-1600 B.C.
Historical Museum of Nova Zagora,
inv. no. 1913.
Analogous to no. 115, but smaller.
Bibl.: G. Georgiev, N. Y. Merpert, R.
Katinčarov, D. Dimitrov, *Ezero.*
Rannobronzovo selište, Sofia, 1979,
tabl. 12.

119

JUG

Terracotta; ht. 14.5 cm.
Nova Zagora, Sliven district.
Late Bronze, 1600-1100 B.C.
Historical Museum of Nova Zagora,
inv. no. 5265.
Background brown-black, polished,
decorated with "false-corded" white
inlay.
Undocumented.

120

DRINKING VESSEL

Terracotta; ht. 9.5 cm.
Razkopanica burial mound, village of
Manole, Plovdiv district.
Late Bronze, 1600-1100 B.C.
Archaeological Museum, Plovdiv,
inv. no. I-135.
Similar to no. 115.
Bibl.: P. Detev, "Selišnata mogila
Razkopanica," in *BIAB*, 17, 1950,
p. 182.

121

KANTHAROS

*Terracotta; ht. 17 cm; diam. 18.5 cm.
Razkopanica burial mound, village of
Manole, Plovdiv district.
Late Bronze, 1600-1100 B.C.
Archaeological Museum, Plovdiv,
inv. no. 2945.
Background dark brown, polished,
decorated with vertical grooves.*
Bibl.: P. Detev, *op. cit.*, p. 182,
fig. 123.

122

DRINKING VESSEL

*Terracotta; ht. 8.5 cm.
Izvor, Plovdiv district.
Late Bronze, 1600-1100 B.C.
Archaeological Museum, Plovdiv,
inv. no. 1277.
Surface dark brown, polished,
biconical body, flat lip, high handle,
incised ornaments and white inlay
work.*
Bibl.: P. Detev, "Praistoričeski selišta
i nahodki v Južna Balgarija," in *GPM*,
3, 1960, p. 350, fig. 6.

123

JUG

*Terracotta; ht. 16.5 cm.
Kutela, Smoljan district.
Late Bronze, 1600-1100 B.C.
Archaeological Museum, Plovdiv,
inv. no. I-64.
Surface dark grey, polished,
spherical body, vertical handle,
mouth strongly slanted, inlaid
decoration of circles and tangents
with an engraved band of chevrons.*
Bibl.: D. Končev, "Trakijski mogilni
pogrebenija v Rodopite ot
staroželjaznata epoha," in
Arheologija, 3, 1960, p. 53, fig. 2.

Orsoja ceramic.

Near Mihajlovgrad.

Late Bronze,

1600-1100 B.C.

Bibl.: T. Filipov, Nekropol ot kasnata bronzova epoha pri selo Orsoja, Lomsko, Sofia, 1976; T. Filipov, "Idolna plastika ot kasnobronzovija nekropol pri s. Orsoja," in MPK, 1978, 2, pp. 9-17.

124

THRONE

*Terracotta; ht. 8.5 cm.
Historical Museum of Lom, inv. no. 541.
Base square, forefeet anthropomorphic, incised ornaments with white inlay.*

125

MODEL OF BOAT

*Terracotta; length 9.5 cm.
Historical Museum of Lom, inv. no. KVP 7301/3.
Background beige, incised ornaments with white inlay.*

126

FEMALE IDOL

Terracotta; ht. 9.5 cm.
Historical Museum of Lom, inv.
no. 518.
Background matte red, incised
ornaments with white inlay outlining
the costume.

127

MODEL OF TABLE

Terracotta; ht. 6 cm; width 13 cm.
Historical Museum of Lom, inv.
no. 491.
Background dark matte brown, form
oval, incised ornaments with white
inlay.

128

ZOOMORPHIC VESSEL WITH LID

Terracotta; ht. 7.5 cm.
Historical Museum of Lom, inv.
no. 494.
Bird-shaped, background matte red,
incised ornaments with white inlay.

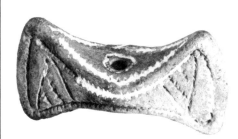

129

MODEL OF AXE

Terracotta; length 6.5 cm.
Historical Museum of Lom, inv.
no. 499.

130

DOUBLE VESSEL

Terracotta; width 14.2 cm.
Historical Museum of Lom, inv.
no. 20179.

Undecorated; a handle joins the two
bodies of the vessel.

131

JUG

Terracotta; ht. 8 cm.
Historical Museum of Lom, inv.
no. 67.
Background matte beige, mouth
with protruding lip, tall handle with
protuberance, four bosses on the
most swollen part of the body,
incised ornament and white inlay.

132

KANTHAROS

Terracotta; ht. 8 cm.
Historical Museum of Lom, inv.
no. 10.
Background matte grey-brown,
ellipsoidal mouth, four nipples on
the most swollen part of the body,
low base at the back, incised
decoration and white inlay.

133

KANTHAROS

Terracotta; ht. 6 cm.
Historical Museum of Lom, inv.
no. 52.
Background dark brown or almost
black, polished.
Similar to previous item.

Two moulds in several parts. Pobit Kamak, Razgrad district. Late Bronze, 1600-1100 B.C.

134

THREE COMPONENTS OF STONE MOULD FOR AN AXE- SCEPTRE

a) *For the transverse part of the sceptre, spiral form, two parts; length 25 cm; width 16.5 cm.*
b) *Mould in two parts; length 9.5 cm; width 8.2 cm.*
c) *Mould in three parts; length 9.5 cm; width 8.2 cm.*

Archaeological Museum, Sofia, inv. no. 5086.
Bibl.: I. Venedikov, "Valčitranskoto sakrovište," in *Izkustvo*, 23, 1975, pp. 5-10.

135

136

MOULD FOR SWORD

AXE-SCEPTRE

a) *Two-part mould for sword.*
   Stone; length 41 cm.
District Museum of History, Razgrad,
inv. no. 1199 A, B.
Undocumented.

b) *Mould for haft of sword.*
   Stone; length 13.4 cm.
Departmental Museum of Razgrad,
inv. no. 1184 b.
Undocumented.

Stone; length 16.5 cm.
Pliska, Šumen district.
Late Bronze, 1600-1100 B.C.
Archaeological Museum, Plovdiv,
inv. no. 2144.
Undocumented.

137

AXE-SCEPTRE

Stone; length 15.3 cm.
Ljulin, Jambol district.
Late Bronze, 1600-1100 B.C.
Archaeological Museum, Sofia, inv.
no. 3500.
Bibl.: *Istoria na Balgarija*, I, Sofia,
1979, p. 94, fig. 5.

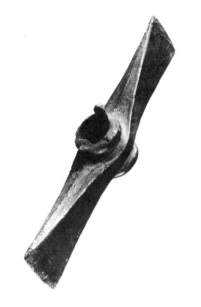

138

DOUBLE AXE

Bronze; length 24 cm.
Begunci, Plovdiv district.
Late Bronze, 1600-1100 B.C.
Archaeological Museum, Plovdiv,
inv. no. I-111.
Bibl.: *Istoria na Balgarija*, I, Sophia,
1979, p. 94; H. G. Buchholz,
"Doppeläxte und die frage der
Balkanbeziehungen des Agäischen
Kulturkreises," in *Ancient Bulgaria*,
1983, pp. 43-134, fig. 25f.

139

DOUBLE AXE

Bronze; length 19 cm.
Semerdžievo, Ruse district.
Late Bronze, 1600-1100 B.C.
Archaeological Museum, Sofia, inv.
no. 2852.
Bibl.: V. Mikov, *op. cit.*, p. 185, H. G.
Buchholz, *op. cit.*, p. 79, fig. 21a.

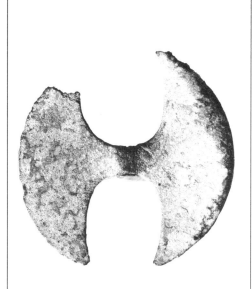

140

CULT AXE

Bronze; diam. 5 cm.
Semčinovo, Pazardžik district.
Late Bronze, 1600-1100 B.C.
Archaeological Museum, Sofia, inv.
no. 1802.
Two moon-shaped plaques joined
by a round part with hole in middle
for handle.
Bibl.: V. Mikov, *Predistoričeski*
selišta i nahodki v Balgarija, Sofia,
1933, p. 108, fig. 67; H. G. Buchholz,
op. cit., p. 69, fig. 17e.

141

LANCE TIP

Bronze; ht. 19.2 cm.
Saranci, near Sofia.
Late Bronze, 1600-1100 B.C.
Archaeological Museum, Sofia, inv.
no. 2755.
Bibl.: R. Popov, "Novootkriti
predistoričeski starini," in *BIAB*, 7,
1932-1933, p. 358, fig. 109.

142

SWORD

Bronze; length 85 cm.
Pavelsko, Smoljan district.
Late Bronze, 1600-1100. B.C.
Archaeological Museum, Plovdiv,
inv. no. 272.
Bibl.: D. Končev, *op. cit.*, p. 55.

143

RAPIER

Bronze; ht. 80 cm.
Dolno Levski, near Pazardžik.
Late Bronze, 1600-1100 B.C.
Archaeological Museum, Sofia, inv.
no. 616.
Mycenaean type.
Bibl.: V. Mikov, *Predistoričeski*
selišta i nahodki v Balgarija, Sofia,
1933, p. 107, no. 9, fig. 66; I.
Panajotov, "Bronze Rapiers, Swords
and Double Axes from Bulgaria," in
Thracia, 5, 1980, pp. 173-198.

THE VALČITRAN TREASURE, PLEVEN REGION (LATE BRONZE AGE, THIRTEENTH TO TWELFTH CENTURIES B.C.)

This treasure is one of the masterpieces of Thracian goldsmiths' work. Consisting of a large vessel, a triple receptacle, four cups and seven lids, it is the most important collection of gold objects ever found in Thrace, with a total weight of 12.5 kilograms.

Some archaeologists date it from the end of the Early Iron Age, but new finds of this period as well as objects discovered in Sofia and in Belogradec (Varna region) prove that in the Iron Age metal was not worked with such refinement. Besides, the conical-head rivets which hold the handles of the large vessel and the cups recall those found on Cretan and Mycenaean swords. The silver inlay on the lids is another argument for the Late Bronze Age. This treasure is distinguished by the simplicity of the shapes, and also by the sobriety of design which, on the big vessel, is limited to the grooved handles. There is a sense of restraint here which is not found in later objects. But the Thracian artist was also capable of creating complex works, as the triple receptacle shows: the electrum handle shaped like a trident, and the silver tubes which join the three hollow parts, prove that the caster worked as precisely as a goldsmith. The big lid reveals the same expertise: a bronze disc under the knob and a perforated cross reinforce the piece.

The treasure was originally much larger: the seven lids covered seven vessels which must all have been bigger than the single two-handled vessel that remains, which was not meant to have a lid.

The difference in quality between the pottery and the metalwork is evidence of the power of the nobility at the time, a nobility that had craftsmen at its disposal capable of satisfying its needs and its sophisticated taste. The treasure also shows how political power was linked to religious power, for a collection like this can only be ritual in nature. The number of large receptacles was probably greater than that of the small vessels, which are shaped more for pouring than for ablution. The cups were used to ladle the liquid from the large vessels and pour it into goblets during ritual ceremonies. The triple receptacle must have been used to mix three different liquids; its strange shape is another indication of the religious nature of the collection.

In its contents, the Valčitran treasure can be compared with another collection with an inscription which is a dedication to a Thracian divinity, Pyrmerulas; but this is a much later treasure, belonging to the period of the Roman Empire (no. 521).

Bibl.: V. Mikov, Zlatnoto sakrovište ot
Valčitran, *Sofia, 1958.*
I. Venedikov, "Valčitranskoto
sakrovište," in Izkustvo, *1975; L.*
Ognenova-Marinova, "Le trésor de
Valčitran: un jalon dans l'étude de la
religion thrace," in Pulpudeva, *2, 1978,*
pp. 240-244; V. Pingel, "Zum Schatzfund
von Valčitran in Nordbulgarien," in
Südosteuropa zwischen 1600-1000 v
Chr., *Berlin, 1982.*

144

TRIPLE RECEPTACLE

Gold; ht. 5.3 cm; width 23.9 cm; wt. 1190 g.
Valčitran, near Pleven.
Archaeological Museum, Sofia, inv. no. 3203.
Three hollow parts decorated with fishbone grooves. These parts are joined by two tubes through which the liquid flowed, and are attached to a trident-shaped handle. Niello decoration on handle.

145

TWO-HANDLED VESSEL

Gold; ht. 22.4 cm; wt. 4395 g.
Valčitran, near Pleven.
Archaeological Museum, Sofia, inv. no. 3192.
In two parts, silver solder. Large handles, vertically grooved and flat, are attached to the bulge by means of three rivets with conical heads.

146

LID

Gold; ht. 12.6 cm; diam. 36 cm; wt. 1755 g.
Valčitran, near Pleven.
Archaeological Museum, Sofia, inv. no. 3197.
At the base of the spherical knob, three concentric circles in relief around which extend inlaid silver geometrical motifs.

147

LID

Gold; ht. 12.6 cm; diam. 37 cm; wt. 1850 g.
Valčitran, near Pleven.
Archaeological Museum, Sofia, inv. no. 3196.
Similar to preceding lid.

148

LID

Gold; ht. 11.5 cm; diam. 21.5 cm; wt. 658 g.
Valčitran, near Pleven.
Archaeological Museum, Sofia, inv. no. 3198.
At base of knob in relief, three beaded concentric circles.

149

LID

Gold; ht. 3.4 cm; diam. 21.5 cm; wt. 374 g.
Valčitran, near Pleven.
Archaeological Museum, Sofia, inv. no. 3200.
Similar to preceding lid; lacks knob.

150

LID

Gold; ht. 11.6 cm; diam. 21.6 cm; wt. 462 g.
Valčitran, near Pleven.
Archaeological Museum, Sofia, inv. no. 3199.
Similar to preceding lid but partially preserved.

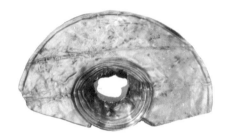

151

LID

Gold; ht. 3.1 cm; diam. 21.6 cm; wt. 297 g.
Valčitran, near Pleven.
Archaeological Museum, Sofia, inv. no. 3202.
Broken; part of knob and lid missing.

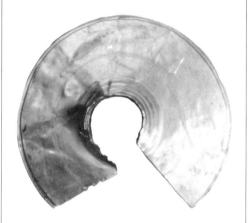

152

LID

Gold; ht. 4.8 cm; diam. 21.6 cm; wt. 300 g.
Valčitran, near Pleven.
Archaeological Museum, Sofia, inv. no. 3201.
Broken and partially preserved.

153

DRINKING VESSEL

Gold; tot. ht. 18.3 cm; diam. of opening 16.2 cm; wt. 919 g.
Valčitran, near Pleven.
Archaeological Museum, Sofia, inv. no. 3193.
Hemispherical bulge; large flat handle, vertically grooved and striated, ending in three festoons and attached to the bulge by three rivets with conical heads.

154

DRINKING VESSEL

Gold; tot. ht. 8.9 cm; diam. of opening 8.8 cm; wt. 123 g.
Valčitran, near Pleven.
Archaeological Museum, Sofia, inv. no. 3204.
Similar to preceding; three horizontal grooves around the opening.

155

DRINKING VESSEL

Gold; tot. ht. 8.9 cm; diam. of opening 4.9 cm; wt. 132 g.
Valčitran, near Pleven.
Archaeological Museum, Sofia, inv. no. 3195.
Similar to preceding vessel.

156

DRINKING VESSEL

Gold; tot. ht. 8.2 cm; diam. of opening 4.5 cm; wt. 130 g.
Valčitran, near Pleven.
Archaeological Museum, Sofia, inv. no. 3194.
Similar to preceding vessel.

157

EARRINGS

Gold; diam. 2.5 cm; wt. 26.13 g.
Vidin.
15ᵗʰ-11ᵗʰ cent. B.C.
District Museum of History, Vidin, inv. no. 102.
Triangular cross-section; intended to be suspended from ears by means of small rings.
Undocumented.

158

EARRINGS

Gold; diam. 1.8 cm; ht. 4.9 cm.
Čomakovci, near Vraca.
12ᵗʰ-11ᵗʰ cent. B.C.
Archaeological Museum, Sofia, inv. no. 6093.
Similar to preceding earrings.
Undocumented.

THRACE AND GEOMETRIC ART IN THE EARLY IRON AGE (TWELFTH TO SIXTH CENTURIES B.C.)

We know little about Thrace in the Early Iron Age, the era of megalithic building and geometric art. Myths and legends have not handed down to us the name of a single king or leader, nor the details of any event whatsoever. All that has survived are burial mounds, the number of which seems to have risen steeply at that time.

No matter how the migrations before and during the twelfth century B.C. took place, one thing is certain: the further towards the southeast, the greater were the waves of migration. All these movements went from Europe to Asia via Thrace. Thus the Thracian people went through difficult times at this period, and a majority of the inhabitants must have left the great plains to take refuge in the mountainous regions of the Sakar and the Strandža, in the eastern part of the Rhodope and the Balkans. After these migrations, there appeared in the southeastern territories great stone tombs, the dolmens, built of huge slabs, one or two serving as walls and another as the ceiling for a burial chamber from 2 to 2.6 metres long. Sometimes an entrance passage (dromos) and an antechamber come before the burial chamber, which is often covered by a tumulus. Again in the southeast one finds tombs cut out of the rock. All these tombs were apparently reserved for the nobles of the tribe. Pillaged in antiquity and up to modern times, the dolmens and rock-cut tombs contain nothing but pottery. However, richer archaeological discoveries have been made in northwestern Thrace, where the output of craftsmen was also kept only for the aristocracy. In women's tombs fibulae are mostly found, and in men's, weapons and horse trappings.

As in Greece, the Thracian pottery of this period uses the technique and decorative repertoire of the preceding epoch, but the workmanship is simpler, sometimes even clumsy. The ornamental motifs which predominate are circles with a dot in the centre, circles joined by tangents, triangles and other geometric figures, meanders or spirals. This decoration is generally incised, often coloured in white, sometimes also in relief. The filigree technique as well is inferior to that of earlier epochs. In the eastern part of Thrace the fibulae take on the styles of the Ionian islands, and in the west, those of continental Greece and Macedonia.

The bronze animal figurines characteristic of this era also imitate, in the west, Greek and Macedonian models, while in the east, where they are rare, they have some elements in common with those of Asia Minor. Among these figurines should be mentioned the statuette of a stag from the Sevlievo region, the symmetrical antlers of which end in a stylized bird head, rather summarily executed, a motif that will reappear in Thracian art and which is found among the Scythians.

Certain royal insignia known in Asia Minor also appear as eastern influences. In the first place we should mention the iron sceptre, the bronze upper part of which is in the shape of an axe decorated with animal heads or figures. But while in the Orient all axes had a wooden handle, in Thrace some of them became amulets. As for the animals, they are those that were found in Thrace: rams, bulls, goats, stags, horses, birds, etc. This kind of axe is widespread far into the northwest, and is found even in the Hallstatt necropolis. Other kingly insignia of this period, which Homer attributes to Caria and Lydia, are headstalls decorated with appliques: they are found throughout the northern part of the Balkan peninsula. Made of bronze, the appliques are shaped like small crosses, discs or rosettes; the only one with animal decoration is the Sofronievo headstall (no. 193).

Jewellery of the period is represented by several pairs of earrings in the form of open rings, and by bracelets (no. 172). Though we have little evidence of toreutics, the objects we have are particularly significant, such as the gold vessel from Kazičene in the Sofia region (no. 161), which goes back to the years 1000 to 700 B.C.: its simple ornamentation (deep, irregularly spaced grooving) recalls that of the pottery, but is as heavy and clumsy as the shape. This is particularly curious since usually it is the decoration on pottery that is considered to be an imitation of metalwork.

Treasure of Sofia

(tenth to eighth

centuries B.C.)

Bibl.: M. Stančeva, "Trakijski zlaten sad ot Sofia," in MPK, 1973, 3, pp. 3-5; A. Fol, "Simvolično pogrebenie ot Kazičene, Sofijsko," in Izkustvo, 3-4, 1975, pp. 11-13.

159

VESSEL

Copper, ht. 24 cm; diam. of mouth 34 cm; diam. of bulge 43 cm. Kazičene, near Sofia. Historical Museum of Sofia, inv. no. 3012.

160

VESSEL

Terracotta; ht. 22.6 cm; diam. of mouth 29 cm; diam. of bulge 32.6 cm. Kazičene, near Sofia. Historical Museum of Sofia, inv. no. 3013.

161

162

163

RECEPTACLE

*Gold; ht. 14.5 cm; diam. of mouth
24 cm.
Kazičene, near Sofia.
Historical Museum of Sofia, inv.
no. 3014.
Near opening, horizontal grooves
decorated with hatching, then
stippled in semicircles with centre
indicated; bulge decorated with
spaced vertical grooves; at the
bottom of the receptacle, concentric
circles and half-spheres in relief,
stippled volutes.*

RECEPTACLE

*Gold; ht. 6.5 cm; diam. 11.4 cm;
thickness 0.1 cm; wt. 77.4 g;
23.65 carats.
Belene, Pleven district.
12th-10th cent. B.C.
District Museum of History, Pleven,
inv. no. 3898.
Hemispherical form; cylindrical neck
with two horizontal grooves, the
lower one decorated with oblique
scoring. Bottom is marked with a
round furrow from which extend
twelve shallow radial grooves
leading to bosses in the most
swollen part of the receptacle.*

BASIN

*Terracotta; ht. 33 cm.
Široko pole, near Kardžali.
Beginning of Early Iron Age, 11th-8th
cent. B.C.
Archaeological Museum, Sofia, inv.
no. 2952.
Conical form, row of white triangles
inlaid around mouth and on the
three legs which terminate in summary feet.
Bibl.: V. Mikov, "Proizhodat na
kupolnite grobnici v Trakia," in BIAB,
19, 1955, p. 29, fig. 6.*

164

KANTHAROS

Terracotta; ht. 12 cm.
Krivodol, near Vraca.
Beginning of Early Iron Age.
Archaeological Museum, Sofia, inv.
no. 3256.
Vertically grooved bulge; at base of
neck and around mouth, undulating
lines incised.
Bibl.: V. Mikov, "Materiali ot
želiaznata epoha," in BIAB, 21, 1957,
p. 295, fig. 1.

165

CULT AXE

Bronze; ht. 12.5 cm.
Teteven.
10th-8th cent. B.C.
Archaeological Museum, Sofia, inv.
no. 745.
Back is decorated with three animal
heads: a bull, a goat and a ram.
Bibl.: A. Milčev, "Trako-kimerijski
nahodki v balgarskite zemi," in BIAB,
19, 1955, p. 359, fig. 2.

166

CULT AXE

Bronze; ht. 10.6 cm.
Origin unknown.
10th-7th cent. B.C.
Archaeological Museum, Sofia, inv.
no. 744.
Rounded blade perforated with two
holes; the heel is decorated with
three animal heads: goat, bull and
ram.
Bibl.: A. Milčev, op. cit., p. 359, no. 1,
fig. 1.

167

CULT AXE

Bronze; ht. 7.7 cm.
Stara Zagora.
10th-7th cent. B.C.
District Museum of History, Stara Zagora, inv. no. C3-225.
Heel is decorated with heads of bull, griffin and stag.
Bibl.: D. Nikolov, *Musée départemental historique de Stara Zagora*, Sofia, 1965, p. 132, fig. 24.

168

CULT AXE

Bronze; ht. 3.5 cm.
Kameno pole, near Vraca.
10th-7th cent. B.C.
District Museum of History, Vraca, inv. no. A 732.
Rounded blade with perforation (cf. no. 166 in which there are two holes); back is decorated with two animal heads: horse and ram.
Bibl.: B. Nikolov, "Trakijski pametnici vav Vrăcansko," in *BIAB*, 28, 1965, p. 170, fig. 10 b.

169

AXE-AMULET

Bronze; ht. 9.4 cm.
Monastery of Rila.
8th-7th cent. B.C.
Ecclesiastical Historical and Archaeological Museum, Sofia, inv. no. 6929.
Small rectangular blade; back is formed of two affrontee bird heads, with hooked beak and protuberant eye; ring between the two heads.
Bibl.: I. Venedikov, "Nahodki ot rannoželiaznata epoha," in *IVAC*, 14, 1963, p. 22, fig. 8; G. Kitov, "Trakijski simvolični sekiri i amuleti s izobraženija na životni," in *Arheologija*, 2, 1979, pp. 13-19.

170

STAG FIGURINE

Bronze; ht. 3.5 cm; length 4.3 cm.
Orjahovo, near Mihajlovgrad.
8ᵗʰ-7ᵗʰ cent. B.C.
Collection of the University of Sofia,
inv. no. M-1.
Summarily executed; with ring.
Bibl.: A. Milčev, "Trako-kimerijski
nahodki v balgarskite zemi," in *BIAB*,
19, 1955, p. 364, fig. 8.

171

STAG FIGURINE

Bronze; ht. 16 cm.
Sevlievo.
10ᵗʰ-7ᵗʰ cent. B.C.
Archaeological Museum, Sofia, inv.
no. 747.
Front legs and tip of right back leg
missing. Shoulder and thighs freely
executed, other parts of body
reduced to geometrical forms: trian-
gular head, round eye, prismatic
neck and body; symmetrical antlers
end in a stylized bird's head.
Bibl.: A. Milčev, *op. cit.*, p. 364, fig. 9;
L. Ognenova-Marinova, "Sur
l'origine de la statuette en bronze de
Sevlievo," in *Pulpudeva*, 1, 1976,
pp. 132-134.

172

173

174

BRACELET

Bronze; diam. 20.1 cm.
Ruska Bjala, near Vraca.
8th-7th cent. B.C.
Archaeological Museum, Sofia, inv.
no. 737.
Bracelet with slightly enlarged,
overlapping ends; engraved geo-
metric decoration.
Bibl.: R. Popov, "Grobni nahodki ot
hallštattskata epoha," in *Revue de
l'Académie bulgare des sciences*, 16,
1918, p. 109, no. 3, pl. IV, 2.

FIBULA

Bronze; width 14.5 cm.
Vidin.
8th-7th cent. B.C.
Archaeological Museum, Sofia, inv.
no. 120.
Bibl.: R. Popov, "Grobni nahodki ot
hallštattskata epoha," in *Revue de
l'Académie bulgare des sciences*, 16,
1918, p. 106, no. 2, pl. 1, 2; D.
Gergova, "Razvitie na fibulite v
Trakija prez staroželjaznata epoha,"
in *Vekove*, 1977, 1, pp. 47-57; D.
Gergova-Domaradska, "Some
Remarks on the Origin and
Development of the Double-looped
Fibulae in Thrace," in *Actes du IIe
CITh.*, 1980, I, pp. 199-202.

FIBULA

Bronze; width 7 cm.
Hvojna, near Smoljan.
8th-7th cent. B.C.
Archaeological Museum, Sofia, inv.
no. 264.
Thick, hollow arch decorated with
vertical ribs; back flat; foot rectan-
gular; on the pin, a movable bead.
Bibl.: R. Popov, "Hallštattski i
latenski fibuli ot razni nahodišta v
Balgarija," in *Revue de l'Académie
bulgare des sciences*, 6, 1913, p. 148.

175

FIBULA

Bronze; length 5.6 cm.
Bednjakovo, near Stara Zagora.
7ᵗʰ-6ᵗʰ cent. B.C.
Archaeological Museum, Sofia, inv.
no. 643.
Bow decorated with a central ball
and three tori.
Bibl.: R. Popov, op. cit., p. 150,
no. 10.

176

FIBULA

Bronze; length 13.1 cm.
Carevec, near Vraca.
7ᵗʰ-6ᵗʰ cent. B.C.
Archaeological Museum, Sofia, inv.
no. 1942.
Similar to preceding fibula.
Bibl.: R. Popov, "Predistoričeski
izsledvania vav Vračanskoto pole,"
in BIAB, 2, 1923-1924, p. 118,
fig. 53 A.

177

BELT BUCKLE

Bronze; width 9 cm.
Near Vidin.
8ᵗʰ-7ᵗʰ cent. B.C.
Archaeological Museum, Sofia, inv.
nos. 124 and 125.
Pierced plaque terminating in a ring;
decorated with lozenges and
triangles with engraved ornaments
on the anterior face: concentric
circles with a central dot and striated
bands.
Bibl.: R. Popov, "Grobni nahodki ot
hallštattskata epoha," in Revue de
l'Académie bulgare des sciences, 16,
1918, p. 108, no. 7, table III, fig. 1.

178

BELT

Bronze; length 26.7 cm.
Gumoštnik, Loveč district, Burial
mound no. 18.
8ᵗʰ-7ᵗʰ cent. B.C.
District Museum of History, Loveč,
inv. no. 1166.
Composed of four parts, similar to
no. 177.
Bibl.: G. Kitov, et al., Trakite v
Loveški okrag, Sofia, 1980, p. 15.

179

THREE BELT APPLIQUES

Bronze; width 6 cm.
Moravica, near Vidin.
8ᵗʰ-7ᵗʰ cent. B.C.
Archaeological Museum, Sofia, inv.
no. 657.
Similar to preceding, in three parts.
Bibl.: R. Popov, op. cit., p. 109, no. 2,
pl. IV, 1 A-C.

180

HAIRPIN

Bronze; ht. 12 cm; width 8.5 cm.
Daržanica, Vidin district.
7ᵗʰ-6ᵗʰ cent. B.C.
Archaeological Museum, Sofia, inv.
no. 3093.
Pin terminating at the top in the form
of an eight.
Bibl.: V. Mikov, "Nahodka ot
Daržanica, Vidinsko," in BIAB, 12,
1939, p. 142, fig. 150.

181

TORQUE

Bronze; diam. 15.4 cm.
Daržanica, Vidin district.
7th-6th cent. B.C.
Archaeological Museum, Sofia, inv.
no. 3092.
Round, solid bronze, the ends
widening into trapezoidal form.
Decorated with short grooves.
Bibl.: V. Mikov, *op. cit.*, p. 142.

182

TWO BRACELETS

Bronze; diam. 7.6 and 8 cm.
Daržanica, Vidin district.
7th-6th cent. B.C.
Archaeological Museum, Sofia, inv.
no. 3091.
Double wire wound into four spirals
around which is a smaller twisted
ring.
Bibl.: V. Mikov, *op. cit.*, p. 142.

183

BIT

Bronze; length 14.3 cm.
Origin unknown.
7th cent. B.C.
Archaeological Museum, Sofia, inv.
no. 2156.
Bibl.: I. Venedikov, "Trakijskata juzda,"
in *BIAB*, 21, 1957, p. 156, no. 5, fig. 5.

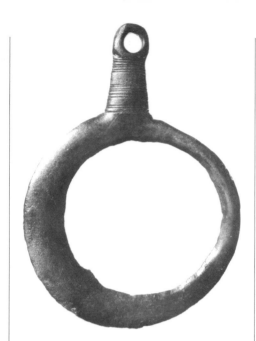

184

COMPONENTS OF HEADSTALL: THIRTY-NINE RINGS

Bronze; diam. 5 cm.
Jasen, near Vidin.
7th-6th cent. B.C.
Archaeological Museum, Sofia, inv.
no. 1825.

Bibl.: R. Popov, "Materiali za
proučvane na hallštattskata i
latenska kulturi v Balgarija," in
GNAM, 1921, p. 161, fig. 150.

Treasure from
Barzica, Varna
District.
Consists of two
earrings and four
belts. Eleventh to
seventh centuries
B.C.
Archaeological
Museum, Sofia.

Bibl.: D. Gergova, "Proizhod, harakter i datirovka na sakrovišteto ot selo Barzica (Šeremet)," in Arheologija, 20, 1983, fasc. 3, 4, pp. 6-15.

185

TWO EARRINGS

Gold; ht. 10.5 cm and 11.1 cm; width 6 cm and 6.5 cm; tot. wt. 40 g.
Inv. no. 2113.
Bow-shaped. Decorated with hemispherical bosses surrounded by S-shaped stippling and by five smaller bosses toward the ends.

186

BELT

Gold; diam. 23.5 cm; thickness 0.55 cm; wt. 211 g.
Inv. no. 2114.
Solid round wire, ends hammered into triangles with rounded corners and holes in the middle. Decorated with incised lines.

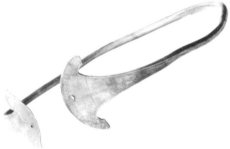

187

188

BELT

*Silver; diam. 29.5 cm; thickness
0.8 cm; wt. 465 g.
Inv. no. 2115.
Solid round wire, ends worked in the
form of loops. At the edge of the
loops a single volute is preserved,
the rest having been broken or lost.*

*Decorated with engraved striations
forming areas of netting, zigzags and
a schematic drawing of an aquatic
bird in geometric style.*

BELT

*Silver; diam. 25.5 cm; thickness
0.85 cm; wt. 470 g.
Inv. no. 2116.
Solid round wire, ends worked in
form of loops ending in volutes of
which only one is preserved. The
edges are decorated with engraved
striations forming netting, zigzags,
lozenges and a schematic drawing of
an aquatic bird in geometric style.*

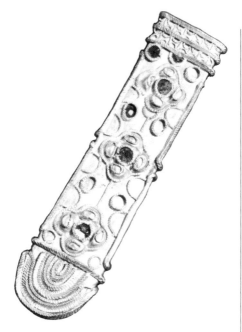

189

BELT

*Silver; diam. 21.5-25.5 cm; thickness
0.8 cm; wt. 315 g.
Inv. no. 2117.
Solid round wire, ends hammered,
round with holes, decorated with
several rows of stippling.*

190

ORNAMENTAL SHEATH

*Gold; ht. 20.1 cm.
Belogradec, near Varna.
8th-7th cent. B.C.
Archaeological Museum, Sofia, inv.
no. 2865.
Decorated in relief with incrustation
of amber, of which only a few stones
are preserved; at the ends, braided
decorations.
Bibl.: G. Tončeva, "Za rannoto
trakijsko iuvelirno izkustvo," in
Izkustvo, 1974, 4, p. 26.*

191

DAGGER

*Iron; length 42 cm.
Belogradec, near Varna.
8th-7th cent. B.C.
Archaeological Museum, Sofia, inv.
no. 2866.
Blade with gilded central rib.
Discovered with no. 190.
Bibl.: see no. 190.*

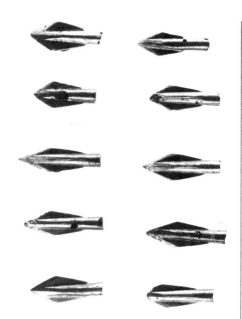

192

TEN ARROWHEADS

Bronze; length 3.5 cm; width 1.2 cm;
thickness 0.6 cm.
Belogradec, Varna district.
8th-7th cent. B.C.
Archaeological Museum, Sofia, inv.
no. K P6436.
Two broad arms forming an
elongated trapeze, sharp point.
Discovered with nos. 190, 191.
Bibl.: see no. 190.

193

HEADSTALL

Bronze; ht. 7 cm.
Sofronievo, near Vraca.
6th cent. B.C.
District Museum of History, Vraca,
inv. no. A-757.
In form of winged disc framed by
modelled ornaments: spirals and
triangles. At the peak, a bull's head
modelled in the round; in the lower
part, a button. On the surface of the
disc and of the button, engraved
decoration: spirals and circles with a
central dot. On the back, a ring.
Bibl.: B. Nikolov, "Trakijski pametnici
vav Vračansko," in BIAB, 28, 1965,
p. 169, fig. 8.

194

PHIALE

*Bronze; ht. 4 cm; diam. 17 cm.
Sofronievo, near Vraca.
6th cent. B.C.
District Museum of History, Vraca,
inv. no. A-747.
Two concentric circles around the
omphalos (central button).
Bibl.: B. Nikolov, op. cit., p. 176,
no. 24, fig. 5 A-B.*

195

CULT FIGURE

*Ceramic; ht. 23 cm; length 35 cm;
width 10 cm.
Burial mound at Junacite, Pazardžik
district.
11th-8th cent. B.C.
District Museum of History,
Pazardžik, inv. no. 3872.
Curved part of an altar terminating in
a zoomorphic figure with engraved
S-shaped decoration and, at the
neck, a human figure in position of
adoration.
Bibl.: R. Katinčarov, N. Merpert et al.,
Ploskata mogila pri s. Junacite,
pazardžiski okrag, Sofia, 1987.*

196

VOTIVE FIGURINE OF HORSE

*Stone; ht. 23 cm.
Dorkovo, Pazardžik district.
6th-4th cent. B.C.
District Museum of History,
Pazardžik, inv. no. 285.
The body is broken. Head and neck
are decorated with engraved circles
joined by tangential lines. At the
base is engraved a schematic
human figure in position of adoration. The halter is in relief.
Bibl.: B. Hänsel, "Plastik der
jungeren Bronzezeit und der alteren
Eisenzeit aus Bulgarien," in
Germania, 41, 1969.*

THRACIAN ART IN THE SECOND IRON AGE (525-280 B.C.)

In the middle of the sixth century B.C. Thrace underwent an expansion to which numerous burial mounds bear witness. The culture was then at its zenith, but at the same time was undergoing profound changes.

The Greeks established a large number of colonies on the Thracian coast: they built fortresses, temples, theatres and luxurious houses, sculpted statues and reliefs, manufactured vessels of bronze, gold and silver, and imported valuable fabrics and gold jewellery by means of which, under oriental influence, they introduced filigree. A rich Thracian, therefore, could easily buy products of Greek workmanship, either in the coastal cities or from the great centres of continental Greece. Along with these products, Greek coinage began to appear in Thracian markets.

The coast of Asia Minor passed at this time into the control of the Achaemenian Persians, who held power there until the coming of Alexander the Great. All the Greek cities of the coast, whether in Asia Minor or in Thrace, then changed to the Persian monetary system. Thrace could not remain outside the sphere of influence of this great oriental power. Contacts with the East were also furthered through the Greek colonies on its territory.

In the fifth and fourth centuries B.C. a flourishing trade sprang up between the interior of Thrace and the Asia Minor city of Cyzicus on the Propontis, Apollonia on the European coast of the Black Sea, Parion and Thracian Chersonesus on the Hellespont: all the treasures found in Thrace dating from this period contain coins from these cities only.

At the end of the fourth century B.C. we see the importation of large quantities of Greek works and at the same time, the creation of many typically Thracian works showing oriental influence.

THE DUVANLI BURIAL MOUNDS

Of the numerous burial mounds around the village of Duvanli in the Plovdiv region (central Bulgaria), about fifty have been excavated up to the present. They belong to different periods between the end of the sixth to the first century B.C. Five of them have made Duvanli a mecca of Thracian archaeology: the objects found in them are worthy of a place in the greatest museums. These are the richest, and also the oldest, of the burial mounds, dating from the end of the sixth and the fifth centuries B.C.

The three graves of women discovered in the burial mounds called Mušovica mogila (the oldest), Arabadžijskata mogila, and Kukova mogila, have yielded magnificent gold head ornaments made by Greek workshops in Thrace, breast-plate plaques of unusual design, torques and heavy bracelets, all evidence of luxury and wealth. The two other burial mounds named Goljamata mogila and Bašova mogila, which are later, contain tombs of men. In all these tombs there were a great number of bronze vessels, and, in the men's graves, cuirasses and helmets. Where the modern village of Duvanli stands was in antiquity part of the territory of the Thracian tribe of the Bessoi.

Bibl.: B. Filov, Nadgrobnite mogili pri Duvanli, *Sofia, 1934; D. E. Strong,* Greek and Roman Gold and Silver Plate, *London, 1966; A. Oliver, ed.,* Silver for the Gods: 800 Years of Greek and Roman Silver, *Toledo, 1977; Z. H. Archibald, "Some Aspects of the Hellenic Impact on Thrace," in* Ancient Bulgaria, *Nottingham, 1983; B. Deppert-Lippitz,* Griechischer Goldschmuck, *Mainz, 1985; H. Luschey, "Thrakein als ein Ort der Begegnung der Kelten mit iranischen Metallkunst," in* Beiträge sur Altertumskunde Kleinasiens, Festschrift für Kurt Bittel, *Mainz, 1983.*

Treasure from the burial mound known as "Mušovica mogila."
Duvanli, near Plovdiv.
Late sixth century B.C.
Archaeological Museum, Plovdiv.

This burial mound is almost contemporary with the campaign of Darius against the Scythians. Mušovica was undoubtedly the starting point for the rich Thracian treasures. All the objects found there are of gold and silver. The breastplate (no. 197), the fibula (no. 198), and the phiale inspired by Persian models (no. 203) may be classified as local products, while jewellery such as the earrings (nos. 199 and 200) came from Greek workshops in Thrace.

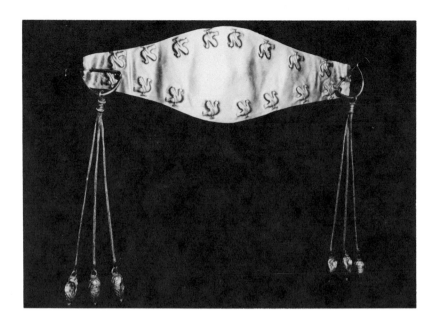

197

PECTORAL

Gold; length 25.9 cm; wt. 65.5 g.
Archaeological Museum, Plovdiv,
inv. no. 1531.
Hexagonal form; edge decorated
with sixteen stylized birds; at either
end, a fibula allowing the pectoral to
be attached to the garment. From
these fibulae are suspended, on
either side, three chains terminating
in acorn-shaped pendants.
Bibl.: *Duvanli*, pp. 84-85, nos. 1 and
3, pl. II/3.

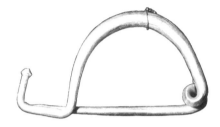

198

THRACIAN-TYPE FIBULA

Gold; ht. 4.9 cm; wt. 13.1 g.
Archaeological Museum, Plovdiv,
inv. no. 1532.
Bibl.: *Duvanli*, p. 84, no. 2, fig. 107/1.

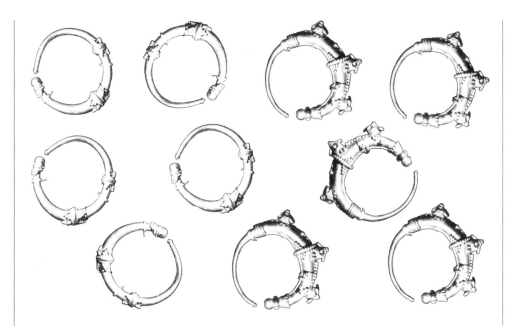

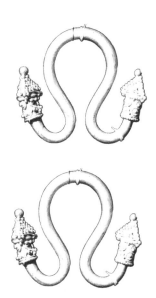

199

200

TEN EARRINGS

PENDANT EARRINGS

Gold; ht. 2.7 and 3.2 cm; wt. 7.3 and 9.9 g.
Archaeological Museum, Plovdiv, inv. no. 1537.
Open rings of which the enlarged part is decorated with rosettes and granulated lozenges.

Bibl.: *Duvanli*, p. 88, no. 6, fig. 109; B. Deppert-Lippitz, *op. cit.*, p. 126, fig. 77.

Gold; ht. 3.6 cm; wt. 26.05 and 26.4 g.
Archaeological Museum, Plovdiv, inv. no. 1538.
Round in section; extremities granulated and cylindrical, surmounted by a pyramid terminating in a gold bead; these pendants were attached to the ears by means of small rings.
Bibl.: *Duvanli*, p. 84, no. 7, fig. 109.

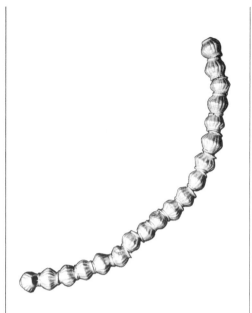

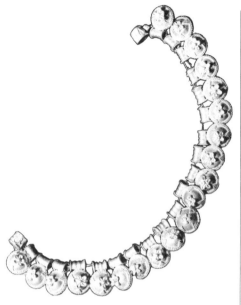

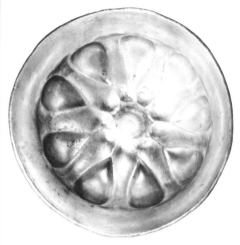

201

NECKLACE

Gold; wt. 11.5 g.
Archaeological Museum, Plovdiv,
inv. no. 1535.
Composed of sixteen grooved
beads.
Bibl.: *Duvanli*, p. 85, no. 5, fig. 108;
B. Deppert-Lippitz, *op. cit.*, p. 122,
fig. 70.

202

NECKLACE

Gold; wt. 79.6 g.
Archaeological Museum, Plovdiv,
inv. nos. 1534 and 1536.
Composed of nineteen cylindrical,
grooved beads; beneath each bead,
a disc decorated with a rosette and
milling.
Bibl.: *Duvanli*, p. 85, no. 4, fig. 108.

203

PHIALE

Silver; ht. 4.6 cm; diam. 11.7 cm.
Archaeological Museum, Plovdiv,
inv. no. 1539.
In the bottom, repoussé decoration:
almond-shaped swellings arranged
in a rosette.
Bibl.: *Duvanli*, p. 89, no. 8, fig. 110;
D. E. Strong, *op. cit.*, p. 77;
H. Luschey, *Metallkunst*, A1, fig. 4.1.

Treasure from the burial mound known as "Kukova mogila." Duvanli, near Plovdiv. Early fifth century B.C.

The treasure from this burial mound dates from the first decades of the fifth century B.C., from the period when the Thracian territories between the Rhodopes and the Aegean were under the domination of the Persians, who were preparing for their campaign against the Greeks. An offering, undoubtedly royal, accompanied the woman buried in this tomb: a gold amphora (no. 204), the work of an Achaemenian master. Was it a token of peace between the Bessoi and the Persian armies that occupied the neighbouring territory? We cannot be sure. In this tomb there were found necklaces and earrings (nos. 208 and 209) resembling those of Mušovica, and also two bracelets and a torque (nos. 206 and 207) which in their solidity and barbaric style prove the existence of contacts between the local goldsmiths and those of Chalkis in Macedonia. Among local products may be included the breast-plate (no. 205) and the silver phiale (no. 210). Such a mixture of local, Greek, Macedonian and Persian shapes was possible only in Thrace.

204

AMPHORA

Silver; partially gilded; ht. 27 cm; diam. of mouth 13.4 cm.
Archaeological Museum, Sofia, inv. no. 6137.
Decorated with palmettes and lotus alternating on the shoulder and upper part of the bulge; the lower part is vertically grooved; between neck and shoulder, a row of eggs and darts; between shoulder and bulge, a braid; handles in the form of horned lions, heads turned toward the back; a projection on one handle starts at the back of the lion.
Bibl.: *Duvanli*, pp. 46-50, pl. IIIe, fig. 55-59; P. Amandry, "Toreutique achéménide," in *AK*, 2, 1959, pp. 39-43; H. Luschey, *Metallkunst*, A2, fig. 4.2, pl. 59, 2.

205

PECTORAL

Gold; length 23.4 cm; wt. 50.1 g.
Archaeological Museum, Plovdiv, inv. no. 1266.
Ellipsoidal form; at either end, an attachment hole; over the entire surface, repoussé decoration: dots, beads and semicircles.
Bibl.: *Duvanli*, p. 41, no. 1, pl. I/1.

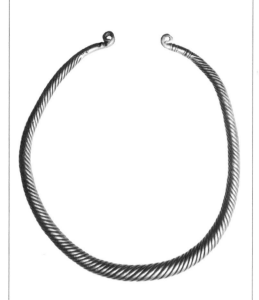

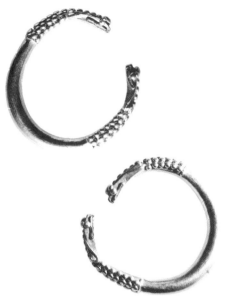

206

TORQUE

Gold; diam. 13.3 cm; wt. 350 g.
Archaeological Museum, Plovdiv,
inv. no. 1271.
Twisted; end in form of ring.
Bibl.: *Duvanli*, p. 44, no. 8, fig. 50.

207

TWO BRACELETS

Gold; diam. 9 cm; wt. 257.1 and
298.25 g.
Archaeological Museum, Sofia, inv.
nos. 6128 and 6189.
Extremities in form of snake:
filigreed decoration around the eyes
and mouth, granulated scales.
Bibl.: *Duvanli*, p. 44, no. 9, fig. 51-52;
cf. silver bracelets from Chalkis, P.
Amandry, *Stathatos* III, nos. 114-119,
pl. 21-22, pp. 51-52.

208

PENDANT EARRINGS

Gold; ht. 4.5 cm; wt. 20.1 and
18.25 g.
Archaeological Museum, Sofia, inv.
nos. 6134 and 6190.
At either end, a granulated pyramid
(one pyramid missing).
Bibl.: *Duvanli*, p. 44, no. 7, fig. 49,
1-2; B. Deppert-Lippitz, *op. cit.*,
p. 130, fig. 79.

209

210

SEVEN EARRINGS

Gold; diam. 2.5 cm; wt. 5.6 to 6.2 g.
Archaeological Museum, Sofia, inv.
nos. 6130, 6131 and 6191.
Archaeological Museum, Plovdiv,
inv. no. 1270.

Ring-shaped, becoming thinner at
ends, wrapped in twisted gold wire;
the enlarged part is decorated with
rows of beads.
Bibl.: *Duvanli*, p. 44, no. 5, fig. 48-50.

PHIALE

Silver; ht. 6.6 cm; diam. 26 cm; wt.
120 g.
Archaeological Museum, Plovdiv,
inv. no. 1275.
With omphalos (central button).
Bibl.: *Duvanli*, p. 51, no. 15, fig. 60;
D. E. Strong, *op. cit.*, p. 77; H.
Luschey, *Metallkunst*, A3, fig. 4, 3,
pl. 60, 4.

Treasure from "Arabadžiskata mogila" burial mound. Duvanli, near Plovdiv. End of the first half of the fifth century B.C. Archaeological Museum, Plovdiv.

These grave goods include a locally executed pectoral (no. 211) and Greek jewels (nos. 212-214) similar to those of the oldest Duvanli burial mound.

211

PECTORAL

Gold; length 16.5 cm; wt. 16.75 g.
Archaeological Museum, Plovdiv, inv. no. 1645.
Hexagonal form; attachment hole at either end; repoussé decoration: circles, dots and summary motif depicting a tree of life.
Bibl.: *Duvanli*, pp. 131-132, no. 2, fig. 153.

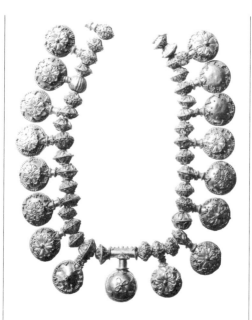

212

NECKLACE

Gold; wt. 54.7 g.
Archaeological Museum, Plovdiv, inv. no. 1646.
Composed of filigreed gold beads from which are suspended seventeen spheres decorated with rosettes and granulations.
Bibl.: *Duvanli*, p. 132, nos. 3-4, fig. 154.

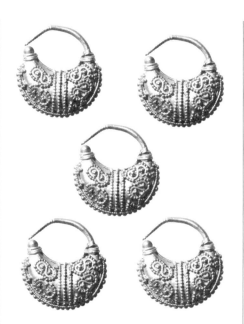

Treasure from the burial mound known as "Goljamata mogila." Duvanli, near Plovdiv. Middle of fifth century B.C. Archaeological Museum, Plovdiv.

This burial mound covered the oldest man's tomb found at Duvanli. The gold breast-plate plaques (nos. 215 and 216) were made in local workshops. The grave goods also included a large number of objects of Greek manufacture, among which were two magnificent silver kantharoi.

213

FIVE EARRINGS

Gold; width 2.4 to 2.5 cm; wt. 31.35 g.
Archaeological Museum, Plovdiv, inv. no. 1647.
In form of wineskin; decorated with spirals and milled triangles.
Bibl.: *Duvanli*, p. 133, nos. 5-6, fig. 155/3-7; B. Deppert-Lippitz, *op. cit.*, p. 149, fig. 98.

214

TWO PENDANT EARRINGS

Gold; ht. 2.8 and 3 cm; wt. 12.9 and 12.75 g.
Archaeological Museum, Plovdiv, inv. nos. 1641-1642.
In form of spirals terminating in a pyramid; milled decoration.
Bibl.: *Duvanli*, p. 133, no. 6, fig. 155/1-2; B. Deppert-Lippitz, *op. cit.*, p. 130, fig. 80.

215

PECTORAL

Gold; width 17.5 cm; wt. 28 g.
Archaeological Museum, Plovdiv,
inv. no. 1644.
Edged with a row of short parallel
lines, then with small bosses
surrounded by circles joined by
stippled lines; in the field, five
bosses surrounded by short
repoussé lines; attachment hole at
either end.
Bibl.: *Duvanli*, p. 105, no. 3,
fig. 131/1.

216

PECTORAL

Gold; width 38.5 cm; wt. 86.95 g.
Archaeological Museum, Plovdiv,
inv. no. 1643.
Edged with dots and rosettes; entire
surface decorated with rosettes in
various sizes; in the centre, three
quadrangular motifs edged with
dots; attachment hole at either end.
Bibl.: *Duvanli*, p. 105, no. 2,
fig. 131/2.

217

KANTHAROS

Silver (with gilding); ht. with
handles, 25.5 cm; wt. 1073 g.
Archaeological Museum, Plovdiv,
inv. no. 1634.
Decorated with groups of two
figures, engraved and gilded. On
one side, Dionysos to whom a
Bacchante is offering a doe. On the
other side, a Satyr and a Bacchante
are dancing, holding thyrsi. At points
where handles are attached to
mouth are appliqued heads of Seleni
crowned with ivy.
Bibl.: *Duvanli*, pp. 106-110, no. 4,
pl. VII; Z. H. Szymanska, "Greek or
Thracian? Some Problems on
Identifying Sources of Metal Work,"
in *DITK*, 1984, p. 106; J. Dörig, *Jdl*,
80, 1965, pp. 250-260, fig. 93-94; R.
Ross Holloway, N. Nabers, "Le
canthare d'argent de Roscigno
(Monte Pruno, Salerne)," in *Aurifex*,
1, 1980, p. 67, fig. 8.

204

AMPHORA (DETAIL)

This silver item, partially gilt, comes from the treasure of Kukova Mogila and dates from the fifth century B.C. It is particularly interesting because of the handles shaped like horned lions with their heads turned backwards.

341

DRINKING VESSEL

The lip of this cup is decorated with two handles with satyr's heads. In the centre, a relief showing a hind attacked by a griffin.

506

APPLIQUE

Depiction of the fight between Herakles and the Nemean Lion, surrounded by two lions, two lion-griffins and two winged lions.

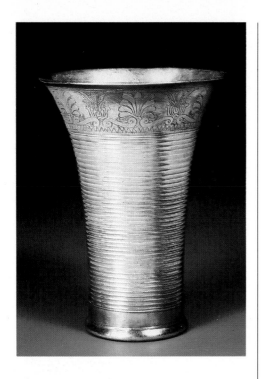

275

GOBLET

Under the rim is an engraved decoration of lotus flowers and palmettes. Horizontal grooves cover most of the surface of the goblet, with a smooth band near the foot.

212

NECKLACE

Openwork gold beads and spheres decorated with rosettes and stippling.

528-531

FOUR RINGS

The rings are grooved, and the settings decorated with spirals and blue stones.

214

TWO EARRINGS

Spirals decorated with small beads, with the ends finishing in a pyramid.

426

RHYTON

This drinking vessel is in the shape of an Amazon's head. The liquid pours through the open mouth of the lion on the medallion at her neck. The Amazon wears a helmet decorated with two griffins and engraved plant motifs. The handle bears a winged sphinx.

422

RHYTON

The lower part of this rhyton from the Panagjurište Treasure ends in a protoma of a goat depicted in a very realistic manner. The pouring hole is between the two front feet of the animal. Around the neck of the vessel are Hera, Artemis, Apollo and Nike: the name of each divinity is engraved beside the head.

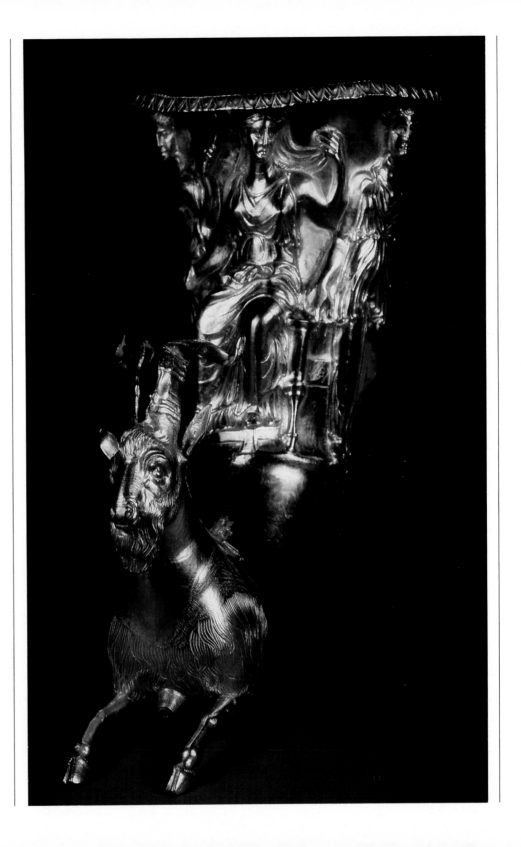

362

RHYTON

The decoration on this silver rhyton in the shape of a hind's head depicts a silenus carrying a kantharos on his shoulder and flanked by two satyrs.

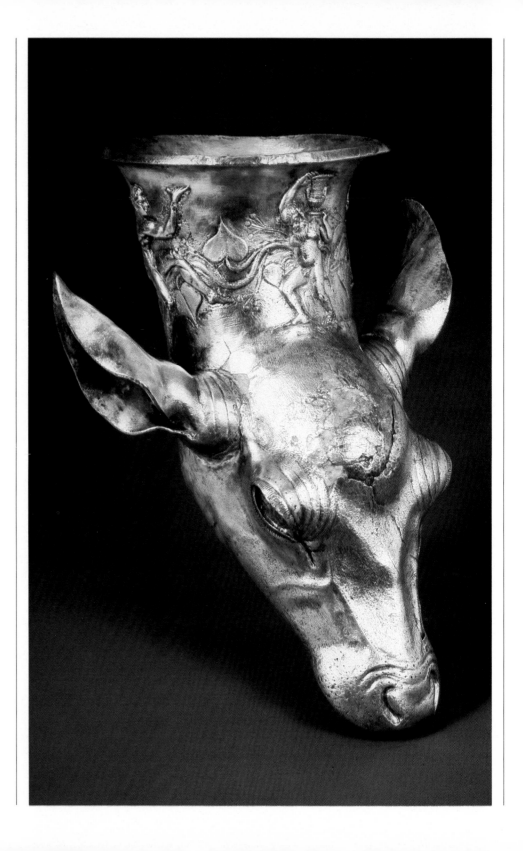

CUP

*Terracotta with incised ornaments and
white inlay work.
This cup, dating from the Late Bronze Age, was
discovered at Izvor, district of Plovdiv.*

532-546

RING AND NECKLACE

*These two items of jewellery from the
Nikolaevo Treasure illustrate the quality
of work of the Thracian artisans
during the Roman era.*

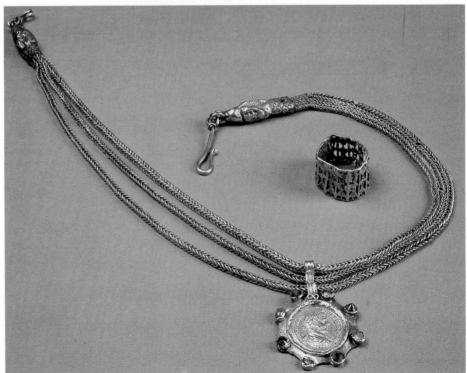

40

DRINKING VESSEL

Neolithic terracotta with white inlay on a red background, decorations in black paint.

508

CUP

Composed of two bodies, one inserted inside the other, and decorated on the outside with moulded reliefs.

330

APPLIQUE

Shows a horseman armed with a spear and riding a stallion. Behind the horseman, there is the head of a woman.

338

RHYTON

The mouth of this drinking vessel is decorated with beads, egg and dart design, and ivy tendrils. It finishes in a protoma of a galloping horse. The liquid is poured through the mouth of a lion's head, which is placed between the horse's hooves.

220

RHYTON (DETAIL)

The horseshoes, mane and harness are gilded. The liquid pours through a hole between the hooves.

325

APPLIQUE

Uneven in shape, bordered with egg and dart design, showing a horseman attacked by a bear and trampling down a wolf.

221

PHIALE

Silver gilt. Around the omphalos, there are bands with palmettes alternating with lotus flowers (on the inside) and laurel leaves (on the outside). The rest of the vessel shows a scene of four quadrigae; in each of them, there is a driver and a soldier.

Following pages

505

TWO HELMET MASKS

The one on the left shows a beardless bronze face with hair of iron.
The one on the right is similar to number 505, but the face is in silver (this object is not in the exhibition).

ERICH LESSING
MAGNUM

421

PHIALE

The decoration, in repoussé work, is arranged in concentric circles; first, a row of acorns, then three rows of Negro heads. The spaces between the rows are filled with palmette ornamentation. On the inside, an inscription records the weight in two measuring systems: in Lampsaque staters, and in drachmas (not seen in the photograph).

58

MODEL OF A SANCTUARY

Terracotta. A sort of chimney may be seen on either side of the double-sloped roof.

5

ANTHROPOMORPHIC DRINKING VESSEL

The decoration on this vessel is a rough depiction of a human face. Terracotta covered with a beige glaze.

590

DECADRACHMA OF THE DERONIANS

The obverse of this silver coin shows a man in a chariot pulled by an ox. A solar symbol can be seen above the ox.

428

RHYTON

In the shape of an Amazon's head, wearing a necklace. In the middle of the necklace is a lion's head, the mouth of which is the hole for pouring. The handle ends in a wingless sphinx.

144-156

THE VALČITRAN TREASURE

One of the masterpieces of Thracian goldsmiths' work. Consisting of a large drinking vessel, a triple receptacle, four cups and seven lids, it is the most important collection of gold objects ever found in Thrace, with a total weight of 12.5 kilograms.

BREAST-PLATE

*Extremely stylized depiction of a lion,
the mane composed of lozenges.*

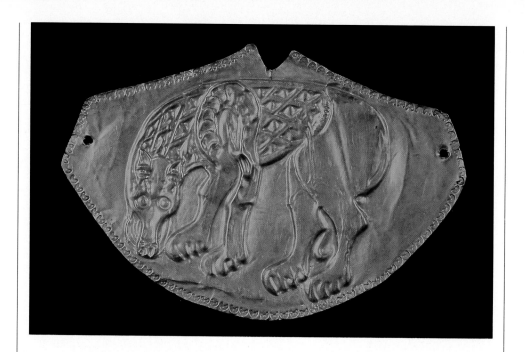

453

TWO EARRINGS

*Each is composed of an open ring
ending in a figure of Pegasus, with a
pendant shaped like an amphora.*

89-93-97-99-102

ITEMS FROM THE TREASURE OF VARNA

*More than three thousand objects of
14-carat gold, with a total weight of
over 5.6 kilograms were discovered in
the necropolis of Varna. They provide
valuable evidence of the perfectly
organized society which inhabited the
Balkan peninsula at the end of the
Bronze Age.
The photograph shows a sceptre
made up of several pieces, necklace
plaques bearing the heads of horned
animals, small appliques and other
ornaments.*

57

FLAT IDOL

On this image of a female figure dating from the Neolithic period, the parts of the body are rendered schematically by holes and incised lines. The greaves are of copper.

52

RITUAL SCENE

These terracotta figurines represent a model of an open-air sanctuary, with priestesses, altars, tables, chairs and ritual receptacles.

253

APPLIQUE

This bronze applique bears a stylized animal, with the head turned around and the feet turned backwards.

171

FIGURINE OF A STAG

The forefeet and the ends of the hind feet are missing.
The shoulders and haunches are treated freely, but the
other parts of the body are reduced to geometric shapes.
The antlers end in a stylized bird's head.

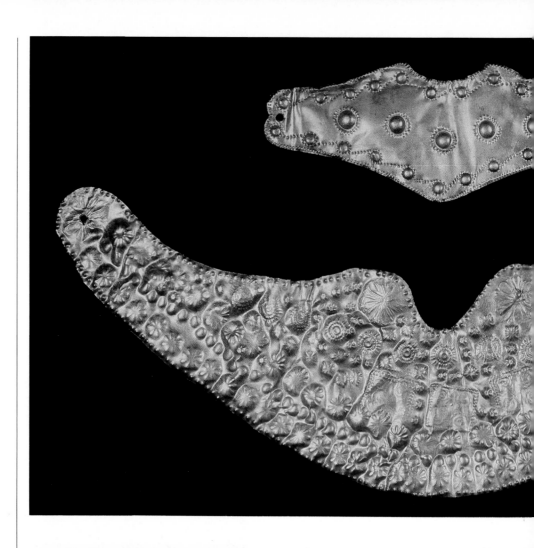

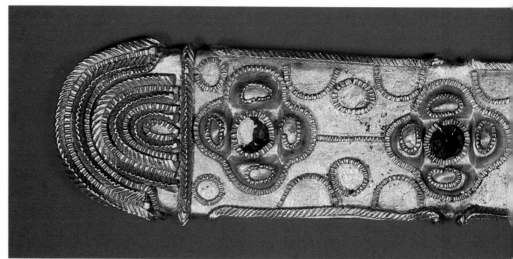

190

OUTER CASING OF A SCABBARD

Relief work with amber inlay. Only a few stones are left.

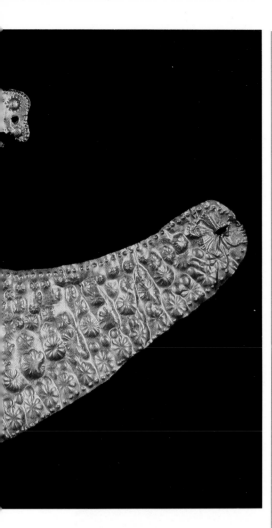

215-216

TWO BREAST-PLATES

*The smaller is bordered by a series of lines, then with
small bosses surrounded and linked by stippled lines. The
centre is decorated with five bigger bosses surrounded by
small lines in repoussé.
The entire surface of the larger breast-plate is decorated
with rosettes and quadrangular motifs.*

207

TWO BRACELETS

*The tips are shaped like snakes, the eyes and mouths of
which are decorated in openwork.*

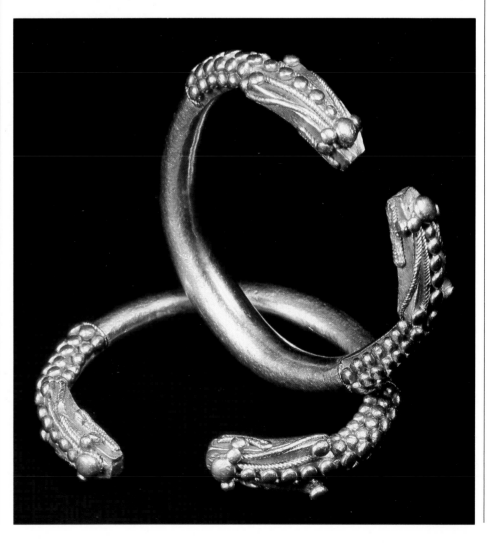

CHEEK-GUARD OF A HELMET

*This cheek-guard, which was fastened to
the helmet by a hinge, is decorated with
the figure of a nude Herakles. In his right hand
he holds a club, and in his left hand a bow.
Also seen is the skin of a lion
hanging from his left arm.*

624-626

ROGOZEN TREASURE

*Discovered by great luck in the territory once
held by the Thracian tribe of Triballoi, this
extraordinary group of silver objects,
assembled between the fifth and sixth centuries, represents one of the
most important archaeological
discoveries ever made in Bulgaria.
The decorations on these pieces present us
with a wide selection of Thracian mythological
images, unrivalled in number to
this day. The vases bear inscriptions
and signs giving the
names of Thracian
kings and cities,
as well as, for the first
time, the name of the artisan:
Disloias.*

420

AMPHORA-RHYTON

*On the bulge, a complete scene in relief:
five warriors attack the entrance to a palace,
where an old man is hiding. Some brandish
a short sword, one blows a
trumpet. All are nude: only on their
shoulders do they wear a chlamys,
which leaves the rest of the body uncovered. On the other side of the door,
a young man speaks with an old man.*

420

AMPHORA RHYTON (DETAIL)

*One of the two centaurs forming the
handles of this remarkable example of
goldsmiths' work.*

526

SMALL BOWL

This object represents a gift made to the Thracian Horseman by a Romanized Greek. The inscription is in Greek.

565

CHARIOT ORNAMENT

A depiction of Herakles wearing the skin of the Nemean Lion.

350

JUG-RHYTON

The mouthpiece and base of the neck are decorated with egg and dart motifs, while the upper part of the bowl is encircled with gadroons.

Treasure from the burial mound known as "Bašova mogila." Duvanli, near Plovdiv. Late fifth to early fourth century B.C. Archaeological Museum, Plovdiv.

Among these grave goods, the gold breast-plate depicting a lion (no. 218) was made by a local craftsman inspired by Achaemenian models which he adapted to his own taste. The jug and the rhyton (nos. 219 and 220) are Greek products from the Propontis, heavily influenced by Persian art. The tomb seems to be from the time of the Peloponnesian Wars.

218

PECTORAL

Gold; length 13.9 cm; width 13.8 cm; wt. 19.6 g.
Archaeological Museum, Plovdiv, inv. no. 1514.
Semicircular; decorated with double axes along the border; in the field, highly stylized lion: mane composed of lozenges, wrinkles on cheeks; attachment hole at either end.
Bibl.: *Duvanli*, p. 62, no. 1, pl. II, 1.

219

JUG

Silver; ht. 8.6 cm; diam. 8.3 cm; wt. 236 g.
Archaeological Museum, Plovdiv, inv. no. 1518.
Vertically grooved bulge; two volutes at the upper attachment point of handle; on neck, Greek inscription: ΔΑΔΑΛΕΜΕ.
Bibl.: *Duvanli*, p. 67, no. 5, fig. 84;
Z. H. Szymanska, *op. cit.*, p. 107;
D. E. Strong, *op. cit.*, p. 84, pl. 17B.

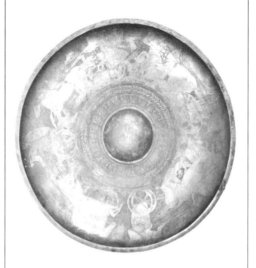

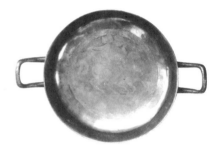

220

221

222

RHYTON

Silver; ht. 20.6 cm.
Archaeological Museum, Plovdiv,
inv. no. 1517.
Lip decorated with beads and egg
and dart; on the neck, band of
alternating palmettes and lotus
blossoms and row of small incised
circles; vertically grooved bulge
terminating in a ring of beads;
extremity in form of horse protoma,
of which hooves, mane and harness
are gilded; between horse's legs,
hole for spout; interior of rhyton
bears Greek inscription:
ΔΑΔΑΛΕΜΕ.
Bibl.: *Duvanli*, p. 67, no. 4, pl. VI and
fig. 83; Z. H. Szymanska, *op. cit.*,
p. 106; D. E. Strong, *op. cit.*, p. 86,
pl. 20A; H. Luschey, *Metallkunst*, C6.

PHIALE

Silver (with gilding); ht. 3 cm; diam.
20.5 cm; wt. 428 g.
Archaeological Museum, Plovdiv,
inv. no. 1515.
Around the omphalos are two bands
wherein palmettes alternate with
lotus blossoms (on the inside) and
laurel leaves (on the outside). The
rest consists of a scene depicting
four quadrigae in each of which is a
driver and a soldier. The figures are
gilded. Below the mouth is a Greek
inscription: ΔΑΔΑΛΕΜΕ.
Bibl.: *Duvanli*, pp. 63-66, no. 2, pl. IV;
D. E. Strong, *op. cit.*, pp. 74, 80,
pl. 15B.

KYLIX (CUP)

Silver (with gilding); ht. 3 cm; diam.
13 cm; wt. 220 g.
Archaeological Museum, Plovdiv,
inv. no. 1516.
Inside the receptacle, a wreath of
laurel leaves forms a gilded frame
surrounding the gilded image of
Hesperia on horseback. Inside,
beneath the mouth, is engraved the
Greek inscription: ΔΑΔΑΛΕΜΕ.
Bibl.: *Duvanli*, pp. 66-67, no. 3,
fig. 81.

ISOLATED OR ACCIDENTAL FINDS.
END OF THE SIXTH AND BEGINNING OF THE FIFTH CENTURIES B.C.

Many objects from different burial mounds and from accidental finds add to our knowledge of the magnificent style of life led by the Thracian nobility at the end of the sixth and the beginning of the fifth centuries B.C. Finds from this period have been made at Čelopek, Ruec, Pastuša, Sadovec, Staroselo, Červenkova mogila near Brezovo, Mazračevo, Daskal Atanasovo, Ezerovo, and Skrebatno. Thus we can be sure that the military gear (breast-plates and helmets) and the jewellery (rings, bracelets, torques, and earrings) found at Duvanli were common all over Thrace.

The same objects are found in all these tombs: changes only came about at the end of the fifth and the beginning of the fourth centuries, when hydriae and helmets disappeared, to be replaced by other vessels and another sort of military gear.

Among accidental finds which are difficult to date with certainty should be mentioned two items of particular importance: the Garčinovo matrix (no. 233), and the Loveč belt (no. 247). The bronze matrix was used to decorate silver goblets. It is true that no vessel in this style has yet been found in Bulgaria; but in another part of Thrace, in present-day Rumania, the Adjighiol treasure includes a silver goblet with decoration similar to that produced by this mould: the main motif is a stag, whose antlers are shaped into animal heads.

The Loveč belt (no. 247) has a kind of ornamentation often found on gold breast-plates from Anatolia: a symmetrical composition with hunting scenes arranged on both sides of a plant motif influenced by oriental design and symbolizing the tree of life.

223

PHIALE

Gold; ht. 3 cm; diam. 14.5 cm; wt. 809.5 g.
Daskal Atanasovo, near Stara Zagora.
5th cent. B.C.
District Museum of History, Stara Zagora, inv. no. II C3-1132.
Repoussé pattern of alternating leaves and lotus buds.
Bibl.: D. Nikolov, "Zlatni fiali ot s. Daskal Atanasovo, Starozagorskos" in *Izsledvania v pamet na K. Skorpil*, Sofia, 1961, pp. 367-368, fig. 1.

224

MEDALLION

*Gold; diam. 4.5 cm; wt. 22.96 g.
Pazardžik.
6th cent. B.C.
Archaeological Museum, Sofia, inv.
no. 4175.
Round, vertically grooved frame,
inside it the perforated figure of a
two-bodied sphinx.*
Bibl.: B. Filov, *L'art antique en
Bulgarie*, Sofia, 1925, p. 15, fig. 10.

225

BRACELET

*Gold; diam. 8.4 cm; wt. 17.65 g.
Skrebatno, near Blagoevgrad.
5th cent. B.C.
Archaeological Museum, Sovia, inv.
no. 3168.*

*Twisted; extremities flattened and
broader, decorated with a border of
small dots; two holes at either end.*
Bibl.: V. Mikov, "Trakijski nakitni
predmeti ot V i IV vek pr. n. e.," in
BIAB, 17, 1950, p. 151, fig. 89.

226

BRACELET

Gold; diam. 10 cm; wt. 41.5 g.
Skrebatno, near Blagoevgrad.
5th cent. B.C.
Archaeological Museum, Sofia, inv.
no. 3167.
Twisted, extremities in form of
spirals.
Bibl.: V. Mikov, *op. cit.*, p. 151,
fig. 89.

227

EARRING

Gold; diam. 3.4 cm; wt. 11.72 g.
Mazračevo, near Kjustendil.
5th cent. B.C.
Archaeological Museum, Sofia, inv.
no. 7945.
Terminating in the form of snake
protoma: granulations grouped in
triangles to suggest scales.
Bibl.: *Tr. Izk.*, p. 372, no. 178.

228

PECTORAL

Gold; ht. 13.5 cm; width 3.7 cm; wt.
30.7 g.
Northeastern Bulgaria, discovery site
unknown.
5th cent. B.C.
Archaeological Museum, Sofia.
Form hexagonal, decorated with
repoussé dots.
Undocumented.

229

PECTORAL

*Gold; width 17 cm; wt. 40.84 g.
Staro Selo, near Sliven.
Second quarter of 5th cent. B.C.
Archaeological Museum, Sofia, inv.
no. 8123.
Discoveries in the burial mound at
Staro Selo include, in addition to the
pectoral, a hydria and a basin in
bronze, a silver goblet, a large
quantity of pottery and the oldest
Thracian seal currently known. The
pectoral, ellipsoidal in form, has a
smooth narrow border, then a
decoration of lotus blossoms
alternating with a decorative motif
depicting Thracian-style pendant
earrings; in the centre, a highly
stylized tree of life; at either end, an
attachment hole near which is a
summarily executed palmette.*
Bibl.: I. Venedikov, "Nahodkata do
Staro Selo, Slivensko," in *BIAB*,
27, 1964, p. 77, no. 1, fig. 1.

230

PECTORAL

*Gold; width 17.5 cm; wt. 19.8 g.
"Červenkova mogila" burial mound
near Brezovo, Plovdiv district.
Second half of 5th cent. B.C.
Archaeological Museum, Plovdiv,
inv. no. 1809.
This burial mound has yielded
particularly rich grave goods,
notably some Attic vases from the
5th cent. B.C. The pectoral, ellipsoidal
in form, is bordered with decorative
motifs in the form of scales, which,
at regular intervals, form triangles.*
Bibl.: I. Velkov, "Mogilni grobni
nahodišta ot Brezovo," in *BIAB*, 8,
1934, p. 5, fig. 2.

231

232

PECTORAL

Gold; width 16.8 cm; wt. 28.1 g.
Ezerovo, near Plovdiv.
Late 5th cent. B.C.
Archaeological Museum, Sofia, inv.
no. 5218.
The grave goods discovered at
Ezerovo also included ring (no. 232)
and a large number of terracotta
objects and bronze vessels. The

pectoral is in the form of an irregular
hexagon, the lower part longer than
the upper. Border of dots in relief; in
the field, rows of circles; attachment
hole at either end.
Bibl.: B. Filov, "Zlaten prasten s
trakijski nadpis," in *BIAB*, 3, 1911,
no. 167, p. 206, no. 2, pl. III, 1.

RING

Gold; diam. 2.7 cm; wt. 31.3 g.
Ezerovo, near Plovdiv.
Late 5th cent. B.C.
Archaeological Museum, Sofia, inv.
no. 5217.
On the swivelling bezel, fastened to
the ring by means of hinges,
inscription in the Thracian language,
in Greek letters:

> *ΡΟΛΙΣΤΕΝΕΑΣΝ*
> *ΕΡΕΝΕΑΤΙΛ*
> *ΤΕΑΝΗΣΚΟΑ*
> *ΡΑΖΕΑΔΟΜ*
> *ΕΑΝΤΙΛΕΖΥ*
> *ΠΤΑΜΙΗΕ*
> *ΡΑΖ*

and, beside it: ΗΛΤΑ
Bibl.: B. Filov, *op. cit.*, p. 203, pl. III.

233

234

MATRIX

Bronze; length 29 cm.
Garčinovo, near Targovište.
5th cent. B.C.
District Museum of History, Šumen,
inv. no. 23.
Intended for stamping goblets. The
central motif of the decoration
depicts a stag, head back, legs
folded under the body, the shoulder
a stylized bird's head, tips of antlers
representing heads of animals. The
stag is being attacked by a small
lion. Behind the stag, a winged lion-
griffin with a single horn and, on
either side, heads of birds. In front of
the stag, a bird with hooked beak
whose talons also form birds' heads.

On the lower frieze can be seen from
left to right a lion, lion-griffin and a
horned lion-griffin turned to the left,
and three lions and a stag turned to
the right. These images are
remarkably similar to animal motifs
in Scythian art.
Bibl.: N. Fettich, *Der Skythische Fund*
von Gartschinovo, Budapest, 1934,
pl. I-IV; A. Farkas, "Style and Subject
Matter in Native Thracian Art," in
MMJ, 16, 1982, p. 37; S. Kolkowna,
"Outils d'orfèvres au nord et à
l'ouest de la mer Noire," in *Aurifex 1*,
1980, p. 110.

MATRIX

Bronze; ht. 4.8 cm; width 5 cm.
Kubrat, Razgrad district.
5th-4th cent. B.C.
District Museum of History, Razgrad,
inv. no. 3719.
Irregular round outline. Winged
anthropo-zoomorphic figure in relief,
human head in profile with Phrygian
cap. A broad wing covers the horse
protoma with raised tail. On the
shoulders, a slain animal (dog or
wolf) which the creature is holding
by the back leg and the neck.
Bibl.: T. Ivanov, "Trakijski bronzov
relief," in *Izkustvo*, 1982, 3, pp. 33-35.

235

MATRIX

*Bronze; length 7.4 cm; width 5.7 cm;
thickness 1.3 cm.
Gorsko Ablanovo, Targovište
district.
5th-4th cent. B.C.
District Museum of History,
Targovište, inv. no. 3553.
Similar to mould from Kubrat.*
Bibl.: M. Krasteva, "Bronzova
matrica ot G. Ablanovo,
Targovištko," in *Izkustvo*, 1983, 4,
pp. 45-47.

236

MATRIX

*Bronze; length 3.9 cm; width 3.2 cm;
thickness 1.1 cm.
Bozvelijsko, Varna district.
4th -3rd cent. B.C.
Varna Museum of Art and History,
inv. no. ll-2709.
Irregular rectangular outline, a boar
in relief running toward the right
being attacked by a dog which has
bitten its right front leg.*
Bibl.: A. Minčev, "Dve trakijski
bronzovi aplikacii ot Varnenskija
musej," in *Izkustvo*, 26, 5, 1976,
pp. 25-27, fig. 1.

237

238

MATRIX

*Bronze; length 4.1 cm; width 2.9 cm;
thickness 1 cm.*
Bozvelijsko, Varna district.
4ᵗʰ -3ʳᵈ cent. B.C.
*Varna Museum of Art and History,
inv. no. II-2710.*
*Irregular rectangular outline. A bear
in relief turned toward the left is
being attacked by a dog which has
bitten its back.*
*Found at the same time as preceding
matrix. Both were used for making
appliques from precious metals.*
Bibl.: A. Minčev, *op. cit.*, pp. 27-29,
fig. 2.

FRAGMENT OF RECEPTACLE DECORATED
WITH A STAG IN RELIEF

*Terracotta; ht. 12.3 cm; width
15.2 cm; thickness 2.2 cm.*
*Gorna Manastririca (Borovo), Ruse
district.*
5ᵗʰ-4ᵗʰ cent. B.C.
*Archaeological Museum, Sofia, inv.
no. 380.*

Fragment of a thick-walled
receptacle, grey-brown after firing.
Stag in relief, head turned to the
right and back, legs folded under the
body.
Bibl.: *Tr. Izk.*, p. 386, no. 312.

239

HELMET

Bronze; ht. 27 cm; width 23 cm.
Čelopek, Sofia district.
6th-5th cent. B.C.
National History Museum, Sofia, inv.
no. 17393.
Corinthian-type with eyebrows in
relief. At peak of skull-piece, four
symmetrical holes for attaching a
crest.
Undocumented.

240

HELMET

Bronze; ht. 21 cm.
Origin unknown.
Second half of 5th cent. B.C.
Archaeological Museum, Sofia, inv.
no. 4013.
Part of helmet and cheek-guards
missing; across the skull-piece,
griffin in relief.
Bibl.: Tr. Izk., p. 378, no. 243.

241

HELMET CHEEK-GUARD

Bronze; ht. 14.5 cm.
Garlo, Sofia district.
5th cent. B.C.
Archaeological Museum, Sofia, inv.
no. 6650.
Formerly attached to helmet by
means of a hinge. Decorated with
relief figure of Herakles, naked,
young, head turned back, walking to
the left. On his shoulder, a quiver
with arrows. Right hand holds a
club, the left, a bow; a lionskin hangs
from the same arm.
Bibl.: I. Velkov, in BIAB, 12, 1930,
p. 434.

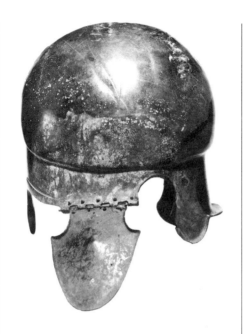

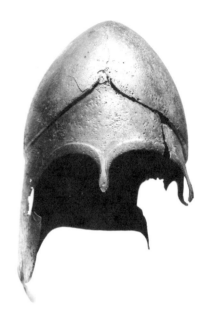

242

HELMET

Bronze; ht. 21 cm.
Sborište, near Sliven.
5th cent. B.C.
District Historical Museum of
Nova Zagora, inv. no. 1152.
Eyebrows are indicated; helmet has
a nose-protector and cheek-guards
attached by means of hinges.
Bibl.: N. Kojčev, "Materiali ot grobni
nahodki ot Novozagorsko," in *BIAB*,
19, 1955, p. 56, no. 3, fig. 4-A-B.

243

HELMET

Bronze; ht. 17 cm.
Peruštica, near Plovdiv.
Early 5th cent. B.C.
Archaeological Museum, Sofia, inv.
no. 2445.
Bibl.: G. Seure, "Chars thrace," in
BCH, 49, 1925, p. 436, no. 90, fig. 11;
for this type of helmet known as
"Thracian" or "Phrygian," cf.
specimen in Ioannina Museum (inv.
no. 6419), *Alexander the Great*,
Thessaloniki, 1980, p. 54.

244

HELMET

Bronze; ht. 30 cm.
Sadovec.
5th cent. B.C.
Archaeological Museum, Sofia, inv.
no. 6756.
With rounded cheek-guards, one of
which is missing.
Bibl.: I. Velkov and C. Danov,
"Novootkriti starini," in *BIAB*, 12,
1938, p. 440, fig. 232; V. Dimova, D.
Ivanov, "Antike Helme," in *Thracia*,
3, 1974, p. 139.

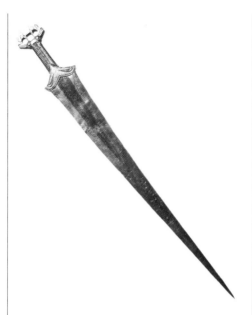

245

SWORD

Iron; length 73 cm; width 8.3 cm.
Agatovo, Gabrovo district.
5th -4th cent. B.C.
Historical Museum of Sevlievo, inv.
no. 613.
In form of double-edged wedge
broadening like a heart above the
hilt, which terminates in two
perforated griffin heads.
Bibl.: A. Milčev, N. Kovačev,
"Neobnarodvani pametnici ot
Sevlievsko," in *Arheologija*, 1967, 2,
p. 40, fig. 2.

246

BREAST-PLATE

Bronze; preserved ht. 25 cm.
Ruec, near Targovište.
450-400 B.C.
Archaeological Museum, Sofia, inv.
no. 6168.
A cut-stone tomb in the burial
mound at Ruec contained interesting
grave goods. Aside from the cuirass,
discoveries included a bronze hydria
and fragments of red-figured Greek
pottery. The cuirass presents a motif
of stylized muscles on front and
back. There is also a semicircular
section for protecting the abdomen.

Bibl.: I. Belkov, "Novi mogilni
nahodki," in *BIAB*, 5, 1928-1929,
p. 39, fig. 53-54; L. Ognenova, "Les
cuirasses de bronze trouvées en
Thrace," in *BCH*, 85, 1961, II,
pp. 519-522, fig. 14.

247

BELT

Silver gilt; length 31 cm.
Loveč, near Stara Zagora.
5th-4th cent. B.C.
Archaeological Museum, Sofia, inv.
no. 6617.
Rectangular plaque with hook at
either end. Significant decoration: in
the centre, three lotus blossoms

between two boars; on either side, a
knight; beneath the horses on one
side, a helmet, on the other side, a
dog; at either end, an archer with
one knee on the ground.
Bibl.: I. Velkov, "Srebaren kolan ot s.
Loveč, Starozagorsko," in *BIAB*, 8,
1934, pp. 18-33.

The only group of burial mounds from this period to have been discovered and systematically excavated is that of Mezek. In other cases the objects came from accidental finds, which made it impossible to carry out archaeological research. It is important to note that, despite the existence of the Odrysian kingdom, rich discoveries have been made further north on both sides of the Balkans. These must be attributed to tribes which either had broken away from this kingdom, or had never been under its domination. The crisis through which the Odrysian kingdom passed at the end of the fifth and beginning of the fourth centuries B.C. is clearly apparent in the archaeological remains.

Another interesting fact which emerges from these remains is the widespread use of bronze and silver harness appliques. Although some archaeologists explain this by the Scythian presence, it should be emphasized that such pieces are rarely found in southeast Thrace, the land nearest to Asia Minor, nor in the northeast, in the region closest to the Scythians. Strange though it may seem, it is in fact in northwestern Thrace that most of these appliques have been found. Incidentally, phialae and silver vessels were also widespread, and buckler ornaments appeared at the same time.

These objects are decorated with animalist motifs in a style close to that of the Scythians, but preserving certain purely Achaemenian characteristics. Unlike during the geometric epoch, the animals most often shown from this time on were the lion, the bear, the wolf, the griffin, and the lion-griffin, and other imaginary beasts with snakes' bodies entirely foreign to earlier Thracian art. The human figure also appears: in some compositions the principal place is occupied by a god in the form of a horseman. So although the animalist motifs, so complex as to render interpretation often difficult, resemble the Scythian works of art, certain traits show the originality of Thracian art.

Animalist decoration was of course not unique to Scythian and Thracian art. The Greeks who occupied the coastal cities of Thrace also introduced, under Achaemenian influence, a number of oriental elements in toreutics. At the same period there appeared in Thrace rhyta (drinking vessels) in the shape of human or animal heads, as well as much jewellery in the animalist style from Greek workshops: heads of lions, bulls, or horned lions. Greek craftsmen at this period tended towards increasing stylization, as did the Thracian craftsmen: the muscles, and the wrinkles around the eyes and muzzle were treated in a conventional manner.

In brief, objects of this period show an oriental influence which was to grow until the time of the campaigns of Alexander the Great in Asia.

Treasure from "Srednata mogila" burial mound. Near Mezek, Haskovo area. Late fifth to early fourth centuries B.C. Archaeological Museum, Sofia.

248

HEADSTALL

Silver; ht. 4 cm.
Archaeological Museum, Sofia, inv. no. 6800.
In form of lion's head in full round between two goats' heads; lion's mane indicated by semicircles; behind the head, a round opening for the bridle.
Bibl.: I. Velkov, "Razkopki okolo Mezek i gara Svilengrad," in *BIAB*, 11, 1937, p. 134, fig. 124-125; compare with Rumanian finds at Agighiol and Craïova, D. Berciu, *Arta traco-getica*, Bucharest, 1969; also Peretu, E. Moscalu, P. Voievozeanu, "Le tombeau princier gète et le trésor de Peretu," in *Actes du II CITh*, 1976, pp. 383-390.

249

THREE APPLIQUES

Silver; ht. 5 cm.
Archaeological Museum, Sofia, inv.
nos. 6797-6799.
Three-branched cross decorated
with lions' heads: lower jaw not
depicted, wrinkles on cheeks;
concentric circles with centre;
hanger on back.
Bibl.: I. Velkov, op. cit., p. 134,
fig. 123.

250

PHIALE

Silver; ht. 4.5 cm; diam. 13 cm.
Mezek, Haskovo district.
Late fifth to early fourth centuries
B.C.
Archaeological Museum, Sofia, inv.
no. 6796.
Surrounding the amphorae is a
many-leaved rosette of radial
grooves. Beneath the mouth a band
of gadroons.
Bibl.: I. Velkov, op. cit., p. 134, no. 1,
fig. 122.

Treasure of Brezovo,

near Plovdiv.

Late fifth to early

fourth centuries B.C.

Archaeological

Museum, Sofia.

These objects were found in a burial mound. The most important is a collection of horse trappings, but there were also discovered vessels like those from the burial mound named Srednata mogila, near Mezek. Very similar horse trappings have been found in the great Scythian tomb of Tolstaja mogila in the Ukraine (cf. A. P. Mancevič, Zolotoj nagrudnik iz Tolstoj mogily," in *Thracia*, 5, 1980, pp. 97-120.)

Elements of horse trappings.

251

HEADSTALL

Silver; ht. 4.7 cm.
Archaeological Museum, Sofia, inv. no. 1712.
Formed of two lions' heads placed one above the other; the upper head is in full round (wrinkles on cheeks behind which mane is indicated by two semicircles); lower head, in relief, is seen from above; lower jaw is missing.
Bibl.: *Duvanli*, p. 28, no. 4, fig. 6.

252

TWO APPLIQUES

Silver-plated bronze; ht. 6.1-6.3 cm.
Archaeological Museum, Sofia, inv. no. 1712.
Perforated in form of cross whose branches, arranged around an omphalos (central button) are joined by spirals and circles reminiscent of animal motifs.
Bibl.: *Duvanli*, p. 28, no. 5, fig. 7.

253

TWO APPLIQUES

Bronze; ht. 5 cm.
Archaeological Museum, Sofia, inv. no. 1712.
In form of animal, head turned, legs folded; shoulders and hindquarters highly stylized.
Bibl.: *Duvanli*, p. 29, no. 6, fig. 8.

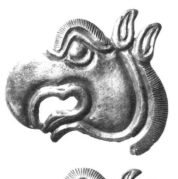

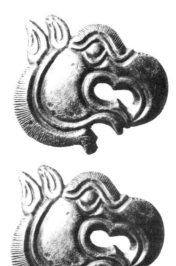

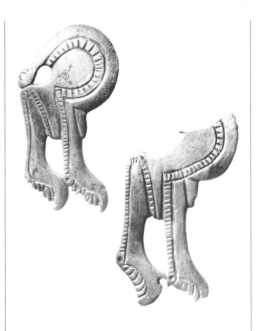

254

255

TWO PAIRS OF APPLIQUES

Silver; ht. 4.5 and 4.8 cm.
Archaeological Museum, Sofia, inv.
no. 1712.

In form of griffin's head, beak open,
mane indicated by semicircular band
of engraved striations.
Bibl.: *Duvanli*, p. 27, no. 2, fig. 2-3.

TWO APPLIQUES

Silver; ht. 7.2 cm.
Archaeological Museum, Sofia, inv.
no. 1712.
In form of lion's paws emerging
from shoulder of animal; claws
curved and pointed.
Bibl.: *Duvanli*, p. 27, no. 3, fig. 4-5.

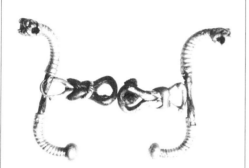

256

BIT

Silver; ht. 18 cm.
Archaeological Museum, Sofia, inv.
no. 1712.
One of the branches, which form an
S, terminates in a lion's head, the
other in a button.
Bibl.: *Duvanli*, p. 29, nos. 7-8,
fig. 9-12.

257

TWO PHIALAE

Silver; ht. 2.1 and 2.3 cm; diam. 8.7
and 10.1 cm; wt. 110.5 and 124.4 g.
Archaeological Museum, Sofia, inv.
no. 1709.
Bibl.: *Duvanli*, p. 31, no. 10,
fig. 14-15.

258

RING

Gold; diam. 2.5 cm; wt. 14.75 g.
Archaeological Museum, Sofia, inv.
no. 1579.
On the bezel, summarily executed
decoration depicts a horseman
making his way toward a woman
who holds a rhyton. Both figures are
dressed.
Bibl.: *Duvanli*, p. 24, no. 1, fig. 1.

Treasure of Raduvene, near Loveč.

Fifth to fourth centuries B.C.

Archaeological Museum, Sofia.

This treasure was an accidental discovery. The collection of objects below has been dated by the style.

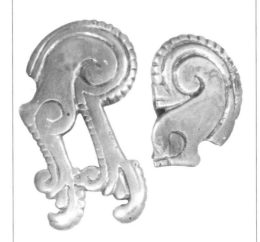

259

TWO APPLIQUES FROM HORSE TRAPPINGS

Silver; width 4 cm; wt. 24.5 g.
Archaeological Museum, Sofia, inv. nos. 5201-5202.
In form of lion's paws emerging from shoulder of animal (cf. no. 255); lower part of one applique is missing.
Bibl.: *Duvanli*, p. 54, no. 54, fig. 56.

260

ARYBALLO

Silver; ht. 14.5 cm; diam. 7 cm; wt. 340.7 g.
Archaeological Museum, Sofia, inv. no. 5199.
Undecorated; notched lip.
Bibl.: *Duvanli*, p. 54, no. 50, fig. 55; P. Meyers, "Three Silver Objects from Thrace, a Technical Examination," in *MMJ*, 16, 1982, p. 52, fig. 4; compare form with vessel from Kul-Oba, V. Schiltz, *Or des Scythes*, Paris, 1975, no. 91.

261

PHIALE

Silver; diam. 13 cm.
Archaeological Museum, Sofia, inv.
no. 5195.
With omphalos (central button);
undecorated.
Bibl.: *Duvanli*, pp. 52-54, no. 49,
fig. 53 and 54.

262

PHIALE

Silver; diam. 10 cm.
Archaeological Museum, Sofia, inv.
no. 5193.

With omphalos; part of base
missing.
Bibl.: cf. no. 261.

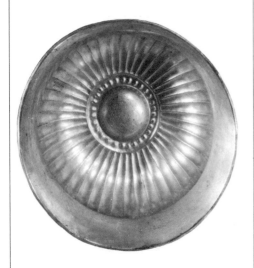

263

PHIALE

*Silver; diam. 12.4 cm.
Archaeological Museum, Sofia, inv.
no. 5192.
Omphalos surrounded by beads;
gadrooned base.*
Bibl.: cf. no. 261.

264

PHIALE

*Silver; diam. 12.4 cm.
Archaeological Museum, Sofia, inv.
no. 5196.
With omphalos; undecorated; small
hole on the side.*
Bibl.: cf. no. 261.

265

PHIALE

*Silver; diam. 19.5 cm.
Archaeological Museum, Sofia, inv.
no. 5189.
Gadrooned; around omphalos,
sawtooth and bead decoration.*
Bibl.: cf. no. 261.

266

PHIALE

Silver; diam. 10.5 cm.
Archaeological Museum, Sofia, inv.
no. 5190.
With omphalos; slightly dented
gadrooned base.
Bibl.: cf. no. 261.

267

PHIALE

Silver; diam. 10.5 cm.
Archaeological Museum, Sofia, inv.
no. 5191.
With omphalos; gadrooned base.
Bibl.: cf. no. 261.

268

PHIALE

Silver; diam. 11.9 cm.
Archaeological Museum, Sofia, inv.
no. 5197.
With omphalos; undecorated.
Bibl.: cf. no. 261.

269

PHIALE

Silver; diam. 8.8 cm.
Gradnica, near Gabrovo.
4ᵗʰ cent. B.C.
Collection of University of Sofia, inv. no. CY-1.
Around the omphalos, decoration of grooves and olive-shaped motifs along a smooth band.
Bibl.: D. P. Dimitzov, "Trakijska grobna nahodka ot s. Dalboki Starozagozsko," in *RP*, IV, 1949, p. 228, fig. 27-28.

Elements of horse trappings from Bukjovci, near Vraca. Late fifth to early fourth centuries B.C. Archaeological Museum, Sofia.

Bibl.: I. Velkov, H. Danov, "Novootkriti starini," in BIAB, *12, 1938, no. 5, and pp. 7-8, fig. 227-228.*

270

HEADSTALL

Silver; ht. 3.8 cm.
Archaeological Museum, Sofia, inv. no. 6698.
In form of falcon's head with hooked beak and protruding eye; lower part of the object is decorated with a palmette; behind the falcon's head, a round opening for the bridle.

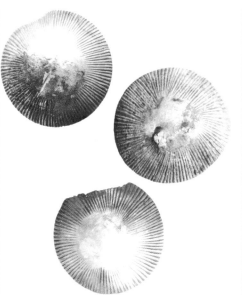

271

APPLIQUE

Silver; ht. 2.8 cm.
Archaeological Museum, Sofia, inv.
no. 6700.
Decorated with two lotus blossoms,
joined; hanger on back.

272

THREE APPLIQUES

Silver; ht. 5.8 cm.
Archaeological Museum, Sofia, inv.
no. 6701 a, b, c.
Round, hanger on back.

273

PHIALE

Silver; ht. 5.5 cm; diam. 13 cm.
Late 5th-early 4th cent. B.C.
Archaeological Museum, Sofia, inv.
no. 6697.
Around the omphalos, decorated
with repoussé grooves; on the
shoulder, frieze of engraved
festoons, then a row of egg and dart.
Bibl.: I. Velkov and C. Danov, op. cit.,
p. 436, nos. 3-4, fig. 225-226.

274

PHIALE

Silver; ht. 7 cm; diam. 17.7 cm.
Late 5th-early 4th cent. B.C.
Archaeological Museum, Sofia, inv.
no. 6696.
Grooves on the phiale are
surmounted by three fillets and a
row of egg and dart.

275

GOBLET

Silver, traces of gilt; ht. 12.2 cm.
Late 5th-early 4th cent. B.C.
Archaeological Museum, Sofia, inv.
no. 6694.
On lip, engraved and gilded
decoration of alternating lotus
blossoms and palmettes. Body of
vase is covered with horizontal
grooves except for a smooth band
above the foot.
Bibl.: I. Velkov, H. Danov, op. cit.,
p. 435, no. 1; D. E. Strong, Greek and
Roman Gold and Silver Plate,
London, 1966, p. 85.

276

JUG

Silver; ht. 8.6 cm.
Late 5th-early 4th cent. B.C.
Archaeological Museum, Sofia, inv.
no. 6695.
Body of jug is covered with vertical
grooves broken by an undecorated
horizontal band. Along the band,
and at base of neck, a row of beads;
curved handle with lower extremity
in the form of a palmette.
Bibl.: I. Velkov, H. Danov, op. cit.,
p. 436, no. 2, fig. 224.

Elements of horse

trappings from

Teteven.

Late fifth and early

fourth centuries B.C.

Municipal Historical

Museum of Teteven.

Bibl.: T. Gerasimov, "Dve nahodki sas skitski bronzovi ukrasi ot Severna Balgarija," in BIAB, 17, 1950, pp. 254-255.

277

HEADSTALL

Bronze; ht. 5.5 cm.
Municipal Historical Museum of Teteven, inv. no. A-20.
In form of highly stylized griffin head surrounded by mane; behind the head, a round opening for the bridle.

278

TWO APPLIQUES

Bronze; diam. 4 cm.
Municipal Historical Museum of Teteven, inv. nos. A-21 and A-22.
Irregular form; decoration depicts a group of griffins attacking a highly stylized lion; hanger on back.

279

APPLIQUE

Bronze; diam. 4 cm.
Municipal Historical Museum of
Teteven, inv. no. A-23.
Round, undecorated; hanger on
back.

Elements of horse trappings from Orizovo, near Stara Zagora.

Late fifth and early fourth centuries B.C.

Archaeological Museum, Plovdiv.

Bronze vases have also been discovered in this burial mound.
Bibl.: D. Čončev, "Antično mogilno pogrebenie pri Orizovo," in GPM, I, 1948, pp. 21-22, nos. 4-6, fig. 8-10.

280

HEADSTALL

Bronze; ht. 3 cm.
Archaeological Museum, Plovdiv,
inv. no. 2582.
In form of three-dimensional griffin
head: hooked beak, large round
eyes, semicircles engraved on
cheeks; beneath head, round
opening for the bridle.

Elements of horse trappings from Lazar Stanevo, near Loveč. Late fifth century B.C.

Bibl.: G. Kitov et al., Trakite v Loveški okrag, Sofia, 1980, p. 9-10, G. Kitov, "Konskoe snarjaženie vo Frakii," in Actes du II CITh, I, Bucharest, 1980, pp. 295-300.

281

TWO APPLIQUES

Bronze; ht. 5 cm.
Archaeological Museum, Plovdiv, inv. nos. 2583-2584.
Decorated with a griffin and another unidentified animal, stylized shoulder in form of horse's head; hanger on back.

282

APPLIQUE

Bronze; ht. 5 cm.
Archaeological Museum, Plovdiv, inv. no. 2585.
In form of griffin protoma; hanger on back.

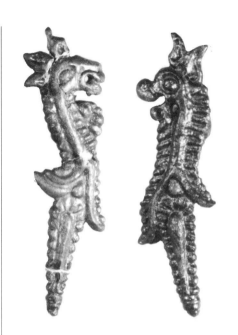

283

HEADSTALL

Silver; ht. 3.3 cm; width 5 cm.
Lazar Stanevo, near Loveč.
District Museum of History, Loveč,
inv. no. 137.

284

TWO CHEEK-GUARDS

Silver; ht. 9.8 cm.
Lazar Stanevo, near Loveč.
District Museum of History, Loveč,
inv. nos. 142-143.

285

TWO CHEEK-GUARDS

Silver; ht. 5.8 and 4.3 cm.
Lazar Stanevo, near Loveč.
District Museum of History, Loveč,
inv. nos. 1010-1011.

286

TWO APPLIQUES

Antimony bronze; diam. 6 cm.
Lazar Stanevo, near Loveč.
District Museum of History, Loveč,
inv. nos. 1008-1009.
Round, perforated. From the central
part, forming a circle in relief and a
concentric circle, radiate fifteen
tangential grooves ending in a
volute.
Bibl.: G. Kitov *et al., Trakite v Loveški*
okrag, Sofia, 1980, p. 9.

287

APPLIQUE IN FORM OF DOE

Bronze; ht. 3.5 cm; width 5.3 cm.
Lazar Stanevo, near Loveč.
District Museum of History, Loveč,
inv. no. 899.

Bibl.: G. Kitov, *et al., op. cit.,* p. 9,
fig. 3.

288

APPLIQUE IN FORM OF DOG

Bronze; ht. 6.4 cm.
Lazar Stanevo, near Loveč.
Archaeological Museum, Sofia, inv.
no. 8401.
Undocumented.

289

HEADSTALL

Silver; ht. 7.4 cm.
Sveštari, near Razgrad.
End of 5th cent. B.C.
Archaeological Museum, Sofia, inv.
no. 3159.
Ellipsoidal in shape. The upper part
is ornamented with a round boss of
a man's head, the hair indicated by
small engraved polygons; beneath
the head, a hole for the bridle. The
lower part is decorated with a lion's
head in relief, shown as if seen from
above; the mane is indicated by
triangles, the lower jaw not shown.
On each side of the head, a bird;
above, grooves in a fan shape
resembling birds' tails.
Bibl.: Tr. Izk., p. 380, no. 257.

Horse trappings

from Bednjakovo,

near Stara Zagora.

Fourth century B.C.

Archaeological

Museum, Sofia.

In addition to these appliques, an Attic
vase with red figures was also found in
this burial mound.
Bibl.: Duvanli, pp. 49-50, nos. 44-46,
fig. 47-51.

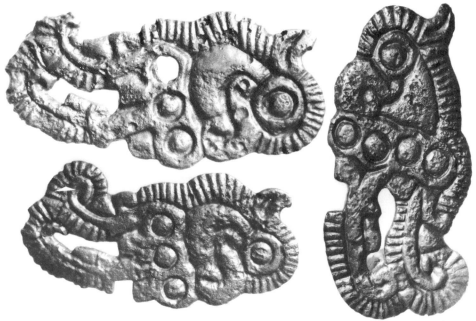

290

HEADSTALL

Bronze; ht. 3 cm.
Archaeological Museum, Sofia, inv. no. 4235.
Upper part depicts an animal head in full round; the rather careless execution makes it impossible to identify the animal, which vaguely resembles a hare. Behind the head, a round opening for the bridle; the lower part is decorated with a summarily executed palmette.

291

THREE APPLIQUES

Bronze; ht. 5.8 cm.
Archaeological Museum, Sofia, inv. no. 4235.
In form of griffin protoma; eyes are clearly drawn, ears erect; paws reminiscent of a lion's. On two of the appliques the decorative motif is oriented toward the left, the third toward the right, as can be seen from the griffin's ear. Hanger on back.

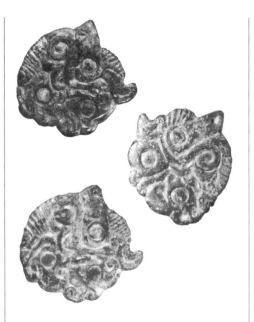

292

THREE APPLIQUES

Bronze; ht. 3.8 cm.
Archaeological Museum, Sofia, inv.
no. 4235.
In form of animal's head; hanger on
back.

293

SKYPHOS

Silver, partially gilded; ht. 8.9 cm.
Strelča, near Pazardžik.
4th cent. B.C.
Archaeological Museum, Sofia, inv.
no. 8432.
Bibl.: G. Kitov, "Skifosat ot Strelča,"
in *Izkustvo*, 1979, 3, pp. 27-31.

294

PECTORAL

Gold; ht. 8.3 cm; width 20.8 cm.
Strelča, near Pazardžik.
4th cent. B.C.
Archaeological Museum, Sofia, inv.
no. 8431.
Bibl.: G. Kitov, *Trakijskite mogili Kraj*
Strelča, Sofia, 1979, p. 15, fig. 17.

295

VESSEL

Silver; ht. 11 cm.
Strelča, near Pazardžik.
4ᵗʰ cent. B.C.
Archaeological Museum, Plovdiv,
inv. no. 3356.
In middle and at base of neck, row of
egg and dart.
Bibl.: G. Kitov, op. cit., p. 16, fig. 18.

296

PECTORAL

Gold; width 9.8 cm.
Goljam Željazna, near Sofia.
4ᵗʰ cent. B.C.
Archaeological Museum, Sofia, inv.
no. 3235.
Lozenge-shaped, decorated with
beads.
Bibl.: V. Mikov, "Trakijski nakitni
predmeti ot V i IV vek," in BIAB, 17,
1950, pp. 147-148, fig. 85.

297

PECTORAL

Gold; width 13.5 cm; wt. 7.62 g.
Vojnicite, near Stara Zagora.
4ᵗʰ cent. B.C.
Archaeological Museum, Sofia, inv.
no. 3110.
The partially preserved pectoral,
ellipsoidal in form, has a border of
dots in relief, then a decoration in
which Thracian-type "pendant
earrings" alternate with circles with
a central dot. In the field, small
bosses surrounded by dots.
Bibl.: Tr. Izk., p. 337, no. 229-A.

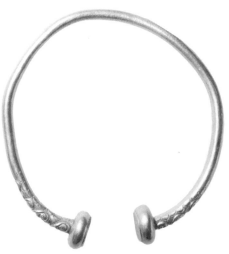

298

PECTORAL

Gold; width 12.7 cm; wt. 11.50 g.
Opalčenec, near Plovdiv.
4ᵗʰ cent. B.C.
Archaeological Museum, Plovdiv,
inv. no. 1383.
Ellipsoidal in form; on the border,
eleven motifs in form of double
concentric circle; in centre, four
figures of women arranged in a
cross; all are identical and dressed in
the same manner: a long chiton and
mantle covering the head; at either
end of the pectoral, attachment hole.
Bibl.: B. Djakovič, "Trakijskata
grobnica pri selo Opalčenec," in
GNBP, 1930, p. 187, fig. 1.

299

BRACELET

Gold; diam. 8 cm; wt. 24.48 g.
Ajtos, Burgas district.
4ᵗʰ cent. B.C.
Archaeological Museum, Sofia, inv.
no. 8099.
Fashioned like a snake coiled into a
spiral, head and tail summarily
executed.
Bibl.: *Tr. Izk.*, p. 379, no. 252.

300

TORQUE

Gold; diam. 14.5 cm; wt. 430 g.
4ᵗʰ cent. B.C.
Archaeological Museum, Sofia, inv.
no. 3242.
The ends, decorated with plant
motifs, terminate in plugs. This is the
only torque of its type discovered in
Thrace.
Bibl.: *Tr. Izk.*, p. 379, no. 154.

301

EXTREMITY OF A TORQUE

Gold; width 3.7 cm; wt. 9.45 g.
Gerlovo, near Šumen.
Late 4th-early 3rd cent. B.C.
Archaeological Museum, Sofia, inv.
no. 5753.
Cylindrical element decorated with
spirals and palmettes terminating in
a (hollow) ram's head.
Bibl.: *Tr. Izk.*, p. 373, no. 193.

302

RING

Gold; diam. 2.85 cm; wt. 11.8 g.
Gložene, near Loveč.
4th cent. B.C.
Archaeological Museum, Sofia, inv.
no. 7955.
On the bezel a summarily executed
horse before a bearded man holding
a horn in his right hand.
Bibl.: *Tr. Izk.*, p. 375, no. 208.

303

RING

Gold; diam. 2.6 cm; wt. 18 g.
Origin unknown.
4th cent. B.C.
Archaeological Museum, Sofia, inv.
no. 8398.
On the bezel, ellipsoidal in form, a
horseman turned toward the right.
The man, with a pointed beard, is
wearing a chlamys which drifts
behind him. The muscles of the
horse are indicated; the tail forms a
right angle; the head is represented
by two spheres and the hooves by
balls.
Bibl.: *Tr. Izk.*, p. 375, no. 207.

304

305

306

EARRING

Gold; ht. 2.1 cm; wt. 1.94 g.
Rankovci, near Blagoevgrad.
4th cent. B.C.
Archaeological Museum, Sofia, inv.
no. 5742.
Lower part, in form of askos, is
hollow. Row of beads in the centre,
at either end and at the base of the
ring.
Bibl.: *Tr. Izk.*, p. 373, no. 189.

PAIR OF EARRINGS

Gold; diam. 1.5 cm; wt. 2.5 g.
Madara, near Šumen.
4th cent. B.C.
Archaeological Museum, Sofia, inv.
nos. 6819-6820.
In form of twisted ring terminating in
a lion's head decorated with milling.
Bibl.: R. Popov, Migila no. 1. *Sbornik
Madara*, 1, 1934, p. 253, fig. 218.

TWO BRACELETS

Silver; width 4.5 cm.
Granitovo, near Šumen.
4th cent. B.C.
Archaeological Museum, Sofia, inv.
no. 4036 a-b.
Pointed extremities decorated with
three grooves and with incisions.
Bibl.: A. Dimitrova, "Srebarno
sakrovište ot selo Vladinja,
Loveško," in *BIAB*, 29, 1966,
pp. 119-121, nos. 6-7, fig. 8-9.

Treasure of Vladinja, near Loveč.
Fourth century B.C.
Archaeological Museum, Sofia.

307

TWO BRACELETS

Silver; width 3.5 and 3.8 cm.
Near Lom.
4th cent. B.C.
Municipal Historical Museum of Lom, inv. no. 20199.
Decorated with grooves and incised ornaments.
Bibl.: A. Dimitrova, *op. cit.*,
pp. 121-122, nos. 8-9, fig. 10-11.

308

TWO FIBULAE

Silver; ht. 6.5 cm.
Near Lom.
4th cent. B.C.
Municipal Historical Museum of Lom, inv. no. 20200.
Bow decorated with twelve cruciform motifs; one extremity, leaf-shaped, is decorated with bucrania (decorative motif in shape of oxen head).
Bibl.: A. Dimitrova, *op. cit.*, p. 117,
no. 4, fig. 4-5.

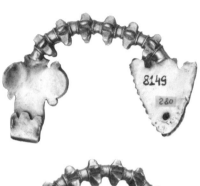

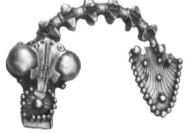

309

PHIALE

Silver; ht. 3.5 cm; diam. 10.5 cm.
Early 4th cent. B.C.
Archaeological Museum, Sofia, inv.
no. 8150.
A cross whose branches are
decorated with scales surrounds the
omphalos.
Bibl.: A. Dimitrova, *op. cit.*, p. 123,
no. 11, fig. 15-16.

310

BRACELET

Silver; length 28.5 cm; width 4.5 cm.
4th cent. B.C.
Archaeological Museum, Sofia, inv.
no. 8151.
Open and thinner at the ends;
decorated with grooves and
engraved ornaments.
Bibl.: A. Dimitrova, *op. cit.*, p. 118,
no. 5, fig. 6-7.

311

TWO FIBULAE

Silver; ht. 6.6 and 6 cm; width 4.7
and 8 cm.
4th cent. B.C.
Archaeological Museum, Sofia, inv.
nos. 8148-8149.
Same type as fibulae from Bukjovci;
pins are missing.
Bibl.: A. Dimitrova, *op. cit.*, p. 115,
nos. 1-2, fig. 2 A-B.

Second treasure
from Bukjovci, near
Vraca.
Fourth century B.C.
Archaeological
Museum, Sofia.

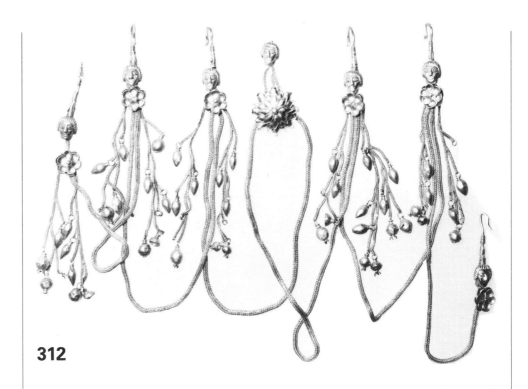

312

PARURE

Silver.
Archaeological Museum, Sofia, inv.
no. 2558-A.
Includes five fibulae (a sixth is
missing) decorated with palmettes
and rosettes. Each fibula is attached
by means of a hook to a drop
composed of two motifs: a man's
head and a rosette from which
chains descend; the latter terminate
in tassels of which the extremity is in
the shape of a poppy pistil. A
broader chain joins the six drops; in
the centre, a large rosette and a
head.
Bibl.: R. Popov, "Srebarno
sakrovište ot S. Bukjovci," in *GNAM*,
Sofia, 1922-1925, p. 18, fig. 2-10; B.
Deppert-Lippitz, *op. cit.*, p. 198.

313

SMALL VASE

Silver; ht. 6.4 cm.
Archaeological Museum, Sofia, inv.
no. 2558-b.
Undecorated.
Bibl.: R. Popov, *op. cit.*, p. 8, fig. 11.

314

JUG

Silver; ht. 9 cm.
Archaeological Museum, Sofia, inv.
no. 2558-B.
A large part of the mouth is missing;
the lower part of the bulge is
gadrooned; at the upper attachment
point the handle terminates in
volutes, at the lower, in a palmette.
Bibl.: R. Popov, *op. cit.*, p. 8, fig. 12.

RICH TOMBS FROM THE FOURTH CENTURY B.C.

The great discoveries at Letnica, Alexandrovo, and Braničevo contain many similar objects. This enables us to consider these objects contemporary with them. The grave goods of the "Mogilanskata mogila" of Vraca can also be attributed to this same period.

Everywhere, but particularly at Vraca and at Braničevo, there have been found silver phialae with the names of the Thracian kings Kotys I (383-359) and Amatokos (359-351), on whose orders they had been made to be offered to the personages buried in these tombs.

**Treasure of Letnica,
near Loveč.
400-350 B.C.
District Museum of
History, Loveč.**

This treasure, found in a bronze vessel, was an accidental discovery. It consists of a bit, a headstall, and small pierced silver plaques, part of a harness. Each applique has a ring at the back to enable it to be fixed on to the harness. The pierced plaques recall other finds of this type. What is new about this treasure are the numerous square or rectangular plaques showing scenes of everyday life or of imaginary animals. These are the work of another artist; in their original realism can be seen a strong oriental influence.
Bibl.: I. Venedikov and P. Pavlov, *Sakrovišteto ot Letnica*, Sophia, 1974, pp. 5-40, fig. 1-40.

315

HEADSTALL

*Silver gilt; ht. 5 cm.
District Museum of History, Loveč, inv. no. 593.
Lion attacking a bull, which lies prostrate, with paws extended; beneath the lion, a round opening for the bridle.*

316

TWO APPLIQUES

*Silver gilt; ht. 7 cm.
District Museum of History, Loveč, inv. no. 606.
Triangular in form: branches start at a central omphalos and terminate in griffin heads with hooked beaks; behind the animal's eye, a semi-circle indicating the beginning of the mane; border of short parallel lines.*

317

APPLIQUE

Silver gilt; diam. 7 cm.
District Museum of History, Loveč,
inv. no. 591.
Circular in form, depicting eight
heads of horses, of which ears,
mane and details of harness
indicated; all heads are in profile, the
eye full-face.

318

APPLIQUE

Silver gilt; ht. 5 cm.
District Museum of History, Loveč,
inv. no. 605.
Rectangular in form, bordered on
three sides by a row of egg and dart;
on the first side, a woman with long
hair, wearing a long robe and
holding a patera in her right hand;
before the woman, a three-headed
serpent.

319

APPLIQUE

Silver gilt; ht. 5 cm.
District Museum of History, Loveč,
inv. no. 604.
Two women and a man in a
rectangular frame. The man is sitting
on a cushion and has pulled up his
garment. His long hair is pulled into
a quiff at the top of the head, and he
has a beard and moustache. The
woman, sitting on his knees, has
pulled her garment up in front. The
image represents the sacred
marriage of two divinities. The man
and woman are embracing. Behind

320

321

them, another woman, wearing a long robe, holds a branch in her right hand, while her left hand rests on a vase. The breasts of the two women are represented by small circles; the head of each figure is in profile, the eye full-face.
Bibl.: I. Marazov, "Hierogamijata ot Letnica," in *Arheologija*, 4, 1976, pp. 1-13.

APPLIQUE

Silver gilt; ht. 4.5 cm.
District Museum of History, Loveč, inv. no. 582.
Square in form; broken egg and dart border (cf. preceding no.); wolf attacking a doe: the animals' coats are indicated, the local artist having paid particular attention to providing a detailed depiction of the muscles.

APPLIQUE

Silver gilt; ht. 6 cm.
District Museum of History, Loveč, inv. no. 581.
Rectangular in form; egg and dart border broken in several places; two bears wrestling, standing on their hind legs; heads highly stylized, tails indicated by spirals, fur indicated by wisps.

322

APPLIQUE

Silver gilt; ht. 5 cm.
District Museum of History, Loveč,
inv. no. 580.
Rectangular; bordered by a row of
egg and dart; griffin with outspread
wings attacking an elk whose legs
are folded under the body.

323

APPLIQUE

Silver gilt; ht. 5 cm.
District Museum of History, Loveč,
inv. no. 583.
Rectangular in form; bordered by
egg and dart on two sides; Nereid
astride a hippocampus; the Nymph
wears a long robe; the breasts are
represented by two small circles; the
face is in profile, the eye full-face.

324

APPLIQUE

Silver gilt; ht. 5 cm.
District Museum of History, Loveč,
inv. no. 589.
Rectangular in form, horseman
holding a phiale in the left hand;
long hair, short beard; he wears a
coat of mail and rides a stallion of
which only the harness and saddle
are indicated.

325

APPLIQUE

Silver gilt; ht. 5 cm.
District Museum of History, Loveč,
inv. no. 590.
Irregular form; bordered by a row of
egg and dart broken by figures; a
horseman attacked by a bear and
walking over a wolf. The horseman,
riding a stallion, brandishes a lance
in his right hand and holds the reins
in his left; he wears a coat of mail
and greaves.

326

APPLIQUE

Silver gilt; ht. 4.5 cm.
District Museum of History, Loveč,
inv. no. 584.
Irregular form; horseman
brandishing a lance; behind him, a
horse's head.

327

TWO APPLIQUES

Silver gilt; ht. 5 cm.
District Museum of History, Loveč,
inv. nos. 587-588.
Rectangular; horseman with a short
beard wearing a coat of mail and
brandishing a lance in his left hand;
behind him, a man's head.

328

APPLIQUE

Silver gilt; ht. 4.5 cm.
District Museum of History, Loveč,
inv. no. 585.
Rectangular; horseman, hair pulled
into a quiff at top of head and
wearing a coat of mail; riding a
stallion, he brandishes a lance in his
right hand and holds the reins with
his left; behind him, a bow. The
plaque includes a border of egg and
dart broken by the lance, the horse's
hooves, and the bow, and also by
the horse's tail and the horseman's
head, which project outside the
frame.

329

APPLIQUE

Silver gilt; ht. 4.2 cm.
District Museum of History, Loveč,
inv. no. 586.
Analogous to preceding. Lance and
horse's tail project outside frame;
behind the horseman, a horse's
head fills the empty space in the
corner of the plaque.

330

APPLIQUE

Silver; ht. 4.5 cm.
District Museum of History, Loveč,
inv. no. 583 A.
Similar to preceding, but there is a
woman's head behind the
horseman.

331

APPLIQUE

Silver gilt; ht. 7 cm.
District Museum of History, Loveč,
inv. no. 592.
Openwork plaque, irregular in form.
it depicts the struggle between a lion
and a griffin which clutch at one
another, standing on their hind legs.
Two snakes take part in the combat
and stand erect behind them. The
tension of the struggle is masterfully
rendered, although the artist is not
yet free of conventions and still
restricts himself to the local style,
notably in depicting the animals'
heads.

332

FOUR APPLIQUES

Silver gilt; ht. 2.8 cm.
District Museum of History, Loveč,
inv. no. 594.
Irregular form, perforated; two
eagles before two griffins.

333

RECEPTACLE FROM THE
TREASURE OF LETNICA

Bronze; ht. 20 cm; diam. 37 cm.
Letnica, Loveč district.
4th cent. B.C.
District Museum of History, Loveč,
inv. no. 601.
Hemispherical form. Lip cut so as to
receive a lid (missing). Opposite the
flat part around the mouth, two
anchor-shaped appliques with, on
top, semicircles to which circular
rings are attached.
Restoration of part of receptacle and
of ringed appliques.

Treasure of Alexandrovo, near Loveč.

Early fourth century B.C.

334

PHIALE

*Silver; diam. 13.5 cm; wt. 133.7 g.
Alexandrovo, near Loveč.
Early 4th cent. B.C.
Archaeological Museum, Sofia, inv.
no. 2241.
Gadrooned, inscription on neck in
Greek characters with the name of
king Kotys: ΚΟΤΥΟΣ ΕΓ ΓΗΙΣΤΩΝ.*
Bibl.: *Duvanli*, pp. 180-181, fig. 202;
D. E. Strong, *Greek and Roman Gold
and Silver Plate*, London, 1966, p. 77,
pl. 16A; H. Luschey, *Metallkunst*,
B10.

335

PHIALE

*Silver; diam. 12.2 cm; wt. 123.4 g.
Alexandrovo, near Loveč.
Early 4th cent. B.C.
Archaeological Museum, Sofia, inv.
no. 2242.
Similar to preceding, but omphalos
is gilded; same inscription.*
Bibl.: *Duvanli*, p. 185, fig. 203; D. E.
Strong, *op. cit.*, p. 77.

336

PHIALE

*Silver; diam. 12.52 cm; wt. 133.2 g.
Alexandrovo, near Loveč.
Early 4th cent. B.C.
Archaeological Museum, Sofia, inv.
no. 2243.
Undecorated.*
Bibl.: *Duvanli*, p. 185, fig. 204; D. E.
Strong, *op. cit.*, p. 77.

337

PROTOMA OF PEGASUS

Gold; ht. 14.8 cm; wt. 449.2 g.
*Vazovo, Razgrad district (near
Sveštari).*
4th cent. B.C.
*District Museum of History, Razgrad,
inv. no. 1409.*
*Galloping horse, muscles of body
standing out. The head is treated
realistically; between the ears is a
horn. Opening for the bit. Halter and
reins are indicated in stippling.
Feathered wings in relief are
attached to body (partially
preserved).*
Bibl.: M. Gabrovski, S. Kalojanov,
"Protome na Pegas," in *Vekove*, 9,
1980, 3, pp. 77-82, fig. 1.

**Treasure of Borovo,
near Ruse.
First half of fourth
century B.C.
District Museum of
History, Ruse.**

Discovered at the end of December 1974,
this treasure consists of a magnificent
set of five drinking vessels: three rhyta
ending in protomae of a horse, a bull
and a sphinx, a great two-handled cup,
in the centre of which is depicted a doe
attacked by a griffin, and a silver jug-
rhyton the bulge of which shows scenes
from the mysteries of Dionysos. The
worship of the latter is also referred to
on two of the rhyta by means of decorative ivy wreaths, and on the handles of
the cup by satyrs' heads.

Bibl.: D. Ivanov, "Srebarnoto sakrovište
ot s. Borovo," in Izkustvo, 25, 1975, 3-4,
pp. 14-21; D. Ivanov, "Le trésor de
Borovo," in Actes du II CITh., 1, 1980,
pp. 391-404; I. Marazov, Ritonite v
drevna Trakija, Sofia, 1978; I. Marazov,
"Les rhytons thraces (IVe-IIIe siècle avant
J.-C.)," in Pulpudeva, 1, 1976,
pp. 206-212.

338

RHYTON

Silver; ht. 20.2 cm.
Inv. no. II-357.
*Body of vessel is grooved; around
mouth, bead and egg and dart
decoration; beneath, in a band
bounded by two wavy incised lines,
branches of ivy. The rhyton
terminates in a partially gilded
galloping horse protoma; between
horse's legs, a lion's head, from the
mouth of which liquid flows; on the
horse's belly, in Greek characters,
name of king Kotys: ΚΟΤΥΟΣ ΕΓ
ΒΕΟΥ.*
Bibl.: cf. rhyton from Poltava: I.
Marazov, "Za data i proishoda na
poltavskija riton s protome na kon ot
Ermitaža," in *Arheologija*, 15, 1973,
pp. 1-10; and the rhyton recently
found in the Caucasus:
K. Dneprovskij and N. Lopatin,
"Sokrovišča kurganov Adygei," in
Sovetskij muzej, 4, 1986, p. 62.

339

340

341

RHYTON

Silver; ht. 20.2 cm.
District Museum of History, Ruse,
inv. no. II-358.
Vertical grooves on body; egg and
dart decoration around mouth;
beneath, gilded band of two
branches of ivy in relief. Lower part
terminates in a partially gilded
sphinx protoma. Spout is between
the animal's feet. On the belly,
inscription in Greek: ΚΟΤΥΟΣ ΕΓ
ΒΕΟΥ.
Bibl.: H. Luschey, *Metallkunst*, B 13.

RHYTON

Silver; ht. 16.5 cm.
District Museum of History, Ruse,
inv. no. II-359.
Horizontal grooves on body;
palmette on lower part.
The rhyton terminates in a partially
gilded bull protoma. The spout is
between the feet.
Bibl.: Z. H. Szymanska, "Greek or
Thracian? Some Problems of
Identifying Sources of Metal Work,"
in *DITK*, 1984, p. 108; H. Luschey,
Metallkunst, B 13.

CUP

Silver; diam. 29 cm.
District Museum of History, Ruse,
inv. no. II-360.
Edge decorated with gilded egg and
dart, broken by two handles with
heads of Satyrs in relief; centre,
gilded depiction, in relief, of a doe
being attacked by a griffin.

342

JUG-RHYTON

Silver; ht. 18.2 cm.
Inv. no. II-361.
Jug is richly decorated: two bands in relief depicting scenes from the cult of Dionysos, with Dionysos, Ariane and Herakles. Around the spout, swans in relief. Handle is missing. On the neck, inscription in Greek: ΚΟΤΥΟΣ ΕΓ ΒΕΟΥ.
Bibl.: A. Minčev, "The Pitcher-Rhyton: A Special Feature of Thracian Rhyta," in *Pulpudeva*, 3, 1980, p. 179, fig. 5-6; H. Luschey, *Metallkunst*, B 14; I. Marazov, "Kaničkata riton ot Borovo i kultat kam kabirite," in *Izkustvo*, 5, 1986, pp. 46-52.

Treasure of Vraca from burial mound known as "Mogilanskata mogila."
380-350 B.C.
District Museum of History, Vraca.

Three tombs have been found in this burial mound, of which one was pillaged in antiquity. Another contained only two small vessels, one of gold, the other of silver. In the richest tomb were found the skeletons of a man, a woman, and three horses. The woman was wearing earrings and a gold crown (no. 345). One horse wore richly ornamented trappings, while the other two were harnessed to a chariot. In the same tomb there were two small vessels and four phialae, together with a cnemis (greave) of remarkable workmanship which is too fragile to be moved.

Bibl.: I. Venedikov, Sakrovišteto ot Vraca, Sofia, 1975.

343

VESSEL WITH ONE HANDLE

Silver gilt; ht. 8 cm; diam. 7 cm.
District Museum of History, Vraca, inv. no. B-392.
Grooved bulge, undecorated neck.
Bibl.: B. Nikolov, "Grobnica III ot Mogilanskata Mogila," in *Arheologija*, 1967, 1, p. 16, fig. 4.

344

345

VASE WITH ONE HANDLE

TWO EARRINGS

Gold; ht. 9 cm; wt. 240 g.
District Museum of History, Vraca,
inv. no. B-391.
Decorated with egg and dart on rim
of mouth and on base, frieze of
palmettes between neck and bulge;
on the latter, a symmetrical
composition depicting, back to back,
two winged quadrigae with four-
spoked wheels. Each chariot is
driven by Apollo, beardless and
wearing a short-sleeved tunic,
depicted in profile, except for the eye
which is seen full-face. Handle in
Gordian knot; on the side opposite
the handle, a palmette separates the
two chariots on the bulge.
Bibl.: B. Nikolov, *op. cit.*, pp. 16-17,
fig. 5-6; Z. H. Szymanska, "Greek or
Thracian? Some Problems of
Identifying Sources of Metal Work,"
in *DITK*, 1984, p. 107.

Gold; ht. 7.5 cm; wt. 37 g.
District Museum of History, Vraca,
inv. no. B-60.
Upper part in form of disc bordered
with a row of beads and decorated
with spirals and rosettes; lower part
in form of crescent surmounted by a
siren and bordered with rosettes
from which are suspended chains
ending in tassels.

Bibl.: I. Venedikov, "Novootkrito
trakijsko mogilno pogrebenie vav
Vraca," in *Arheologija*, 1, 1966, p. 12,
fig. 2.

346

PHIALE

Silver; ht. 4.5 cm; diam. 12.5 cm.
District Museum of History, Vraca,
inv. no. B-68.
Undecorated; bears a stippled Greek
inscription: ΚΟΤΥΟΣ ΕΓ ΒΕΟΥ.
Bibl.: I. Venedikov, *op. cit.*, p. 12,
fig. 8; H. Luschey, *Metallkunst*, B15.

347

PHIALE

Silver; ht. 4.5 cm; diam. 12.5 cm.
District Museum of History, Vraca,
inv. no. B-69.
Undecorated; same inscription.
Bibl.: I. Venedikov, *op. cit.*, p. 12.

348

PHIALE

Silver; ht. 4.5 cm; diam. 10 cm.
District Museum of History, Vraca,
inv. no. B-70.
On the omphalos, head of Aphrodite
in profile (gilded).
Bibl.: I. Venedikov, *op. cit.*, p. 12;
H. Luschey, *Metallkunst*, B16.

349

THIRTY-SEVEN SMALL
ROUND APPLIQUES

Gold; diam. 2 cm.
District Museum of History, Vraca,
inv. no. B-63.
In form of rosettes.
Bibl.: I. Venedikov, *op. cit.*, p. 12.

350

JUG-RHYTON

Silver, partially gilded; ht. 16.5 cm;
diam. 9 cm.
District Museum of History, Vraca,
inv. no. B-67.
Egg and dart decoration around
mouth and at base of neck,
gadroons on upper part of bulge.
Bibl.: I. Venedikov, *op. cit.*, p. 12,
fig. 7; A. Minčev, *op. cit.*, p. 179,
fig. 8-9.

351

VASE-RHYTON

Silver; ht. 14 cm; diam. 6 cm.
District Museum of History, Vraca,
inv. no. B-66.
In form of pine cone.
Bibl.: I. Venedikov, *op. cit.*, p. 12;
A. Minčev, *op. cit.*, p. 179, fig. 6-7;
H. Luschey, *Metallkunst*, A 17.

**Elements of harness
from treasure of
Vraca.**

352

353

354

HEADSTALL

*Silver; ht. 6.5 cm.
District Museum of History, Vraca,
inv. no. B-41.
Lion's head in full round, fan-shaped
mane; beneath the animal's head, a
round opening for the bridle.*
Bibl.: I. Venedikov, *op. cit.*, p. 12,
fig. 5; cf. for the whole, comparison
with Thraco-Getae finds from
Rumania: D. Berciu, *Arta traco-
getica*, Bucharest, 1969.

TWO APPLIQUES

*Silver; ht. 10 cm.
District Museum of History, Vraca,
inv. nos. B-30,31.
Irregular form; lion attacking a bull
in a rather unnatural position; heads
highly stylized, teeth indicated; the
lion's mane is emphasized by a
decoration of scales, spirals and
engraved striations; the bull's horns
resemble those of a goat. On the
back, a hanger.*
Bibl.: I. Venedikov, *op. cit.*, p. 12,
fig. 6.

TWO APPLIQUES

*Silver; diam. 7 cm.
District Museum of History, Vraca,
inv. nos. B-36,37.
Round, perforated, bordered by a
row of short incised lines; in the
centre, omphalos bordered by
incised lines and surrounded by
three heads of monsters with open
mouths, alternating with other
fantastic animals that suggest
lizards.*
Bibl.: I. Venedikov, *op. cit.*, p. 12.

355

356

TWO APPLIQUES

Silver; ht. 8.5 cm.
District Museum of History, Vraca,
inv. nos. B-38,39.
Perforated, irregular in form; border
of short parallel lines in relief; in the
field, fantastic animal suggesting a
lizard and three animals' heads; on
the back, hanger.

FOUR APPLIQUES

Silver; ht. 7 cm.
District Museum of History, Vraca,
inv. nos. B-32-35.

In form of swastika the branches of
which terminate in a griffin's head:
hooked beak, large round eye.

357

BIT

Silver; ht. 18 cm.
District Museum of History, Vraca,
inv. no. B-29.
Central part is an iron chain.

358

EIGHTY CYLINDRICAL ELEMENTS

Silver; ht. 1 cm.
District Museum of History, Vraca,
inv. no. B-44.

359

TWELVE SMALL HEADS

Silver.
District Museum of History, Vraca,
inv. no. B-42.

Treasure from Rozovec, near Plovdiv. Early fourth century B.C. Archaeological Museum, Sofia.

This treasure was discovered in a domed tomb, under a burial mound.

360

PHIALE

Silver; ht. 6.7 cm; diam. 10 cm; wt. 164 g.
Braničevo, near Šumen.
Second half of 4th cent. B.C.
District Museum of History, Šumen, inv. no. 408.
With omphalos; lower part decorated with scale-shaped motifs; neck undecorated.
Bibl.: C. Dremsizova, *Nadgrobna mogila pri s. Braničevo*, Sofia, 1960, p. 451, fig. 6; H. Luschey, *Metallkunst*, B20.

361

VESSEL

Silver; ht. 15.3 cm; diam. 8.8 cm; wt. 214 g.
Archaeological Museum, Sofia, inv. no. b-39.
Bulge decorated with broad leaves; rows of egg and dart at base of neck.
Bibl.: *Duvanli*, p. 170, no. 3, pl. XI/I; H. Luschey, *Metallkunst*, B19.

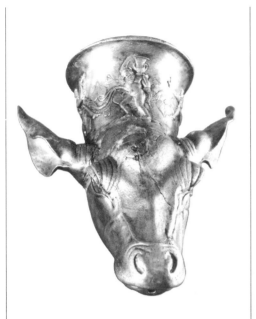

362

RHYTON

Silver; ht. 11.2 cm; diam. 9 cm; wt. 49.5 g.
Archaeological Museum, Sofia, inv. no. b-49.
In form of doe's head; neck decorated with a wreath of ivy leaves; in the centre, Silenus carrying a kanatharos on his shoulder and surrounded by two Satyrs.
Bibl.: *Duvanli*, pp. 167-169, no. 3, pl. X; D. E. Strong, *Greek and Roman Gold and Silver Plate*, London, 1966, p. 87, pl. 20B; L. Byvanck-Quarles van Ufford, "Remarques sur les relations entre l'Ionie grecque, la Thrace et l'Italie," in *BABesch*, 41, 1966, p. 38, fig. 1; H. Luschey, *Metallkunst*, C 18.

363

SHIELD APPLIQUE

Silver; ht. 21.8 cm.
Archaeological Museum, Sofia, inv. no. b-37.
Oblong form.
Bibl.: *Duvanli*, p. 169, no. 2, fig. 185.

364

EIGHT SHIELD APPLIQUES

Silver; diam. 8 cm.
Archaeological Museum, Sofia, inv. no. b-36.
Round, with omphalos.
Bibl.: *Duvanli*, p. 169, no. 1, fig. 184.

Treasure from

Varbica, near

Šumen.

Second half of

fourth century B.C.

Archaeological

Museum, Sofia.

Besides the phiale and the jug shown here, rich grave goods were found at Varbica, notably an iron breastplate inlaid with silver very like the Mezek breastplate.

365

PHIALE

Silver; ht. 8.7 cm; diam. 9.7 cm; wt. 168.5 g.
Archaeological Museum, Sofia, inv. no. 51.
Narrow and deep; on the neck, engraved and gilded ivy wreath; hexagonal bottom decorated with gadroons; beneath the base, a rosette.
Bibl.: *Duvanli*, p. 173, no. 3, fig. 188, 189; D. E. Strong, *op. cit.*, p. 101, fig. 23B.

366

VESSEL WITH ONE HANDLE

Silver; ht. 17.8 cm; diam. 9.6 cm; wt. 380 g.
Archaeological Museum, Sofia, inv. no. 51.
Decorated with a frieze of laurel leaves and a row of egg and dart. The handle, in Gordian knot, terminates at the upper attachment point in volutes, at the lower attachment point in spirals.
Bibl.: *Duvanli*, p. 174, no. 4, pl. XI, 2.

**Treasure from burial
mound known as
"Maltepe mogila."
Near Mezek,
Haskovo area.
350-300 B.C.
Archaeological
Museum, Sofia.**

This treasure comes from a great domed
tomb in which were found the graves of
a man and two women, and ornaments
from a chariot. A total length of 32
metres, the tomb consists of a long
entrance passage (dromos), two antechambers and a burial chamber. The
latter, circular in shape with a beehive
dome, held the tomb of the man in
whose honour the monument was built.
Near him was found an iron breastplate
inlaid with silver. The burnt bones of two
women were found under a thin layer of
earth separating the double floor of the
two antechambers. The tomb contained
magnificent gold jewellery. Near each of
the women was found a tetradrachma of
Alexander the Great (336-323), which
enables us to date these graves as being
somewhat later than that of the man.

367

TWO APPLIQUES

*Gold; ht. 3.4 cm; wt. 6.55 and 6.9 g.
Archaeological Museum, Sofia, inv.
no. 6452.
Irregular form; decorated with
highly stylized plant motifs; on the
back, a hanger.*
Bibl.: B. Filov, "Kupolnite grobnici
pri Mezek," in *BIAB*, 11, 1937,
pp. 30-31, fig. 27-28.

368

FOUR APPLIQUES

*Gold; diam. 2.2, 2.7 and 2.8 cm; wt.
9.35 to 9.95 g.
Archaeological Museum, Sofia, inv.
no. 6453.
Circular form; decorated with a triple
rosette; on the back, a hanger.*
Bibl.: B. Filov, *op. cit.*, p. 31, nos. 2-3,
fig. 29.

369

NECKLACE

Gold; length 38 cm; wt. 6.5 g.
Archaeological Museum, Sofia, inv.
no. 6249.
In form of chain terminating at either
end in a lion's head.
Bibl.; B. Filov, *op. cit.*, p. 77, no. 3,
fig. 84, 4.

370

NECKLACE

Gold; wt. 27.15 g.
Archaeological Museum, Sofia, inv.
nos. 6426-6428.
Composed of twelve hollow spheres
and of two elements elongated at
either end; in the centre, a vase-
shaped pendant; the entire piece is
richly decorated in filigree-work.
Bibl.: B. Filov, *op. cit.*, pp. 76-77,
nos. 1-2, fig. 84, 1-2.

371

FIVE EARRINGS

Gold; diam. 2.2 and 2 cm; wt. 6.4,
6.55, 4.1 and 4.19 g.
Archaeological Museum, Sofia, inv.
nos. 6441 and 6442.
In form of twisted ring; one
extremity, broader than the other, is
decorated with spiral motifs and
terminates in a lion's head.
Bibl.: B. Filov, *op. cit.*, p. 77, nos. 5-7,
fig. 30, 1-5; for the type, cf. *Les*
ors hellénistiques de Tarente, Paris,
1986-1987, p. 140, nos. 114-117;
E. Coche de La Ferté, *Les bijoux*
antiques, Paris, 1956, p. 59,
pl. XVII, 1.

372

TWENTY-EIGHT BUTTONS

Gold; width 1.1 cm; wt. 22.9 g.
Archaeological Museum, Sofia, inv.
no. 6433.
In form of knot; a small ring allowed
them to be attached to garment.
Bibl.: B. Filov, op. cit., p. 34, no. 7,
fig. 32.

373

DOOR APPLIQUE FROM THE MALTEPE BURIAL MOUND

Bronze; ht. 4.7 cm; diam. 11 cm.
Mezek, near Haskovo.
Circa 350 B.C.
Archaeological Museum, Sofia, inv.
no. 6405.
Round, decorated with a head of
Zeus.
Bibl.: B. Filov, op. cit., p. 53.

374

DOOR KNOB APPLIQUE FROM THE MALTEPE BURIAL MOUND

Bronze; ht. 4.4 cm; diam. 11 cm.
Mezek, near Haskovo.
Circa 350 B.C.
Archaeological Museum, Sofia, inv.
no. 6406.
Round, decorated with a lion's head
with a movable ring in its mouth.
Bibl.: B. Filov, op. cit., p. 53.

Lukovit Treasure.

End of the fourth

century B.C.

Archaeological

Museum, Sofia.

This treasure must have been buried during the Macedonian domination of Thrace, perhaps in the time of Alexander the Great when he crossed the territory of the Triballoi. It consists of three small jugs, nine phialae, and a large number of silver appliques decorated with animal motifs and pictures of horsemen. The collection must have belonged to a prince of the Triballoi in northern Bulgaria, and can be dated from the end of the fourth century B.C.

Bibl.: D. Dimitrov, "Materialna kultura i izkustvoto na trakite prez rannata elinistična epoha IV-III vek pr. n.e.," in Découvertes archéologiques en Bulgarie, *Sofia, 1957, pp. 64-67, fig. 1-3; A. Mantsévitch, "Origine des objets de toreutique d'époque scythe," in* Aurifex, *1980, pp. 80-105.*

375

HEADSTALL

*Silver; ht. 10 cm; wt. 67 g.
Archaeological Museum, Sofia, inv. no. 8212.
Ellipsoidal in form; decoration partially gilded, suggesting a lion's mane; in the centre, a griffin's head in full round.*

376

HEADSTALL

*Silver gilt; width 5.2 cm; wt. 41.5 g.
Archaeological Museum, Sofia, inv. no. 8203.
Lion's head in full round; above and below, decoration in form of palmette.*

377

TWO APPLIQUES

Silver; width 7.5 and 6.6 cm; wt. 38 and 38.7 g.
Archaeological Museum, Sofia, inv. nos. 8213-8214.
Irregular form; horseman armed with lance, attacking a lion; some sections are gilded.

378

TWO APPLIQUES

Silver; length 8.7 cm; width 4.9 cm; wt. 102 g.
Archaeological Museum, Sofia, inv. nos. 8215-8216.
Lion with gilded mane attacking a stag whose legs are folded under the body.

379

TWO APPLIQUES

Silver; length 10.3 cm; wt. 31.5 g.
Archaeological Museum, Sofia, inv. nos. 8197-8198.
Two griffins face to face, legs folded under body; upper parts of the two animals are joined by a single tail, which is that of a bird.

380

TWO APPLIQUES

*Silver gilt; length 8.7 cm; width
4.9 cm; wt. 32 g.
Archaeological Museum, Sofia, inv.
nos. 8204-8205.
Animal decoration, difficult to
identify, surrounded by rosettes and
spirals.*

381

FOUR APPLIQUES

*Silver; length 10.3 cm; width 9.8 cm;
wt. 34.6 g.
Archaeological Museum, Sofia, inv.
nos. 8193-8196.*

*Swastika form, with branches
starting from an omphalos and
terminating in a griffin's head.*

382

TWO ROUND APPLIQUES

Silver; diam. 9.3 and 9.4 cm; wt. 59.1 and 49 g.
Archaeological Museum, Sofia, inv. nos. 8208-8209.
Undecorated.

383

ROUND APPLIQUE

Silver gilt; diam. 3.9 cm; wt. 19.2 g.
Archaeological Museum, Sofia, inv. no. 8201.
In form of rosette.

384

TWO ROUND APPLIQUES

Silver; diam. 4.7 cm; wt. 24.2 g.
Archaeological Museum, Sofia, inv. nos. 8210-8211.
In centre, gilded rosette.

385

PHIALE

Silver; ht. 6.8 cm; diam. 7.8 cm; wt. 68.6 g.
Archaeological Museum, Sofia, inv. no. 8219.
Undecorated.

386

PHIALE

Silver; ht. 5.6 cm; diam. 5.4 cm; wt. 35.1 g.
Archaeological Museum, Sofia, inv. no. 8220.
Similar to preceding.

387

PHIALE

Silver; ht. 4.2 cm; diam. 12.5 cm; wt. 122.3 g.
Archaeological Museum, Sofia, inv. no. 7990.
Similar to preceding.

388

PHIALE

Silver; ht. 6 cm; diam. 7.7 cm; wt. 94.5 g.
Archaeological Museum, Sofia, inv. no. 8006.
Similar to preceding.

389

PHIALE

Silver; ht. 4.5 cm; diam. 10.7 cm; wt. 70.2 g.
Archaeological Museum, Sofia, inv. no. 8223.
Grooved bottom.

390

PHIALE

Silver; ht. 5.1 cm; diam. 10.6 cm; wt. 70.7 g.
Archaeological Museum, Sofia, inv. no. 8222.
Similar to preceding.

391

PHIALE

Silver; ht. 7 cm; diam. 8.6 cm; wt. 99.7 g.
Archaeological Museum, Sofia, inv. no. 8226.
Decorated with alternating heads of women and palmettes.

392

PHIALE

Silver; ht. 4.5 cm; diam. 14.4 cm; wt. 176.2 g.
Archaeological Museum, Sofia, inv. no. 8225.
Decorated with alternating almonds and palmettes.

393

PHIALE

Silver; ht. 2.8 cm; diam. 13 cm; wt. 71.8 g.
Archaeological Museum, Sofia, inv. no. 8224.
Decorated with motifs in form of almonds and lotus blossoms.

394

SMALL JUG

Silver; ht. 13.9 cm.
Archaeological Museum, Sofia, inv.
no. 8212.
Decorated with beads around the
mouth and on the bulge, volutes at
upper attachment point of the
handle and with a palmette at lower
attachment point.

395

SMALL JUG

Silver; ht. 15.3 cm; diam. 6 cm; wt.
157.7 g.
Archaeological Museum, Sofia, inv.
no. 8217.
Similar to preceding.

396

SMALL JUG

Silver; ht. 14.1 cm; diam. 5.3 cm.
Archaeological Museum, Sofia, inv.
no. 7937.
Similar to preceding, but with egg
and dart decoration.

397

SMALL JUG

Silver; ht. 13.3 cm; wt. 140.8 g.
Archaeological Museum, Sofia, inv.
no. 8472.
At base of neck, a band in relief with
vertical striations. Decorated with a
branch from the tip of which, at
regular intervals, emerge leaves
similar to ivy, beneath a five-petalled
corolla. The lower part is decorated
with grooves bordered with
meanders, with oblique notches.
Bibl.: G. Kitov, "Novopostapila
trakijska aplikacija ot Lukovit," in
Izkustvo, 5, 1987, fig. 3.

398

PHIALE

Silver; ht. 5 cm; wt. 96.7 g.
Archaeological Museum, Sofia, inv.
no. 8473.
Neck is higher than body.
Undecorated.
Bibl.: G. Kitov, *op. cit.*, fig. 4.

Harness ornaments forming part of the Lukovit treasure.

399

HEADSTALL

Silver; ht. 10.3 cm.
Archaeological Museum, Sofia, inv. no. 8005.
Decorated with two griffins face to face, manes indicated by short incised lines; at the top, a griffin head in full round; on the back, a hanger.

400

THREE ROUND APPLIQUES

Silver; diam. 9.4 cm.
Archaeological Museum, Sofia, inv. nos. 8205-8207.
Undecorated; on the back, a hanger.

401

TWO APPLIQUES

Silver gilt; diam. 3.5 cm.
Archaeological Museum, Sofia, inv.
nos. 8199-8200.
In form of rosette; in centre,
engraved decoration.

402

APPLIQUE

Silver gilt; diam. 2.2 cm.
Archaeological Museum, Sofia, inv.
no. 8202.

403

TWO APPLIQUES

Silver gilt; ht. 2.4 cm.
Archaeological Museum, Sofia, inv.
no. 8232.
In form of sphinx.

404

TWO APPLIQUES

Silver gilt; ht. 2.4 cm.
Archaeological Museum, Sofia, inv.
no. 8232.
In form of griffin.

405

TWENTY-SIX HARNESS ORNAMENTS

Silver; diam. 2 cm.
Archaeological Museum, Sofia, inv.
no. 8229.
Hemispherical; undecorated.

406

SIXTEEN HARNESS ORNAMENTS

Silver; ht. 1.3 cm.
Archaeological Museum, Sofia, inv.
no. 8230.
In form of lion's head.

407

SEVEN HARNESS
ORNAMENTS

Silver; ht. 2.6 cm.
Archaeological Museum, Sofia, inv.
no. 8231.
In form of human head.

408

EXTREMITY OF WHIP

Silver gilt; ht. 5.3 cm.
Archaeological Museum, Sofia, inv.
no. 8227.
In form of head of dog holding ring
in its mouth.

409

TWO HARNESS ORNAMENTS

Silver; diam. 2.6 cm.
Archaeological Museum, Sofia, inv.
no. 8240 a-b.
In form of rosette; in centre, open
cylindrical tube.

410

NINETY-FIVE TUBULAR ELEMENTS

Silver; width 1.9 to 3 cm.
Archaeological Museum, Sofia, inv. no. 8237.

411

PENDANT EARRING

Gold; ht. 10.1 cm; wt. 27.39 g.
Bojana, near Sofia.
Late 4ᵗʰ cent. B.C.
Archaeological Museum, Sofia, inv. no. 2887.
In form of open ring terminating in a three-sided pyramid, decorated with milled work comprising geometrical motifs; at the tip, two spheres joined by three beads.
Bibl.: Tr. Izk, p. 373, no. 194.

412

413

PECTORAL

JUG

Gold; width 16.1 cm; wt. 6.79 g.
Skalica, near Jambol.
Second half of 4th cent. B.C.
Archaeological Museum, Sofia, inv.
no. 7946.
Oblong; two highly stylized trees of
life. Surface is covered with dots
comprising various motifs:
sawtooth, fishbone; attachment hole
at either end.

Bibl.: T. Ivanov, "Trakijsko mogilno
pogrebenie ot s. Skalica
Jambolsko," in *Arheologija*, 1960,
2, p. 41.

Silver; ht. 8 cm; diam. of mouth
6 cm.
Gornjane, near Blagoevgrad.
330-300 B.C.
Archaeological Museum, Sofia, inv.
no. 6764.
Pear-shaped; undecorated.
Bibl.: V. Mikov, "Grobna nahodka ot
Gorniane, Nervokopsko," in *BIAB*,
11, 1937, p. 209, no. 2, fig. 189.

414

RING

Silver; diam. 2.8 cm; length 4.3 cm.
Gornjane, near Blagoevgrad.
330-300 B.C.
Archaeological Museum, Sofia, inv.
no. 6765.
In form of a helical snake with flat
head.
Bibl.: V. Mikov, *op. cit.*, p. 209, no. 3,
fig. 191.

415

HELMET

Bronze; ht. 14 cm.
Brjastovec, near Burgas.
4th cent. B.C.
Archaeological Museum, Sofia, inv.
no. 3454.
Helmet is decorated with two horns.
The cheek-guards, which would
have been iron, are missing; only
the skull-piece remains.
Bibl.: I. Velkov, "Novi mogilni
nahodki," in *BIAB*, 5, 1928-1929,
p. 41, fig. 58.

416

TWO GREAVES

Bronze; ht. 42 cm.
Asenovgrad.
4th cent. B.C.
Archaeological Museum, Sofia, inv.
no. 7309.
They take on the shape of the leg; a
stamp has been affixed to the upper,
outer extremity.
Bibl.: T. Ivanov, "Predpazno
vaoraženie na trakiec ot
Asenovgrad," in *RP*, I, 1948, p. 102,
no. 1, fig. 71-72.

417

LANCE TIP

Iron; length 24 cm.
Jankovo, Šumen district.
4th cent. B.C.
National Museum of History, Sofia,
inv. no. 8872.
In form of elongated leaf, posterior
part broad and rounded, flat rib
running along the length. The leaf
terminates in a narrow socket.
Undocumented.

418

LANCE TIP

Iron; length 66 cm; width 5 cm.
Živovci, Mihajlovgrad district.
3rd cent. B.C.
Archaeological Museum, Sofia, inv.
no. 3263.
Tip is an elongated triangle with a rib
in the middle, followed by a long
four-edged socket which then
becomes cylindrical. Beside the edge
at the tip, four concentric circles in
relief with centre and four summarily
executed drawings of birds.

419

CURVED CUTLASS

Iron; length 39.2 cm; width 3.5 cm.
Near Sevlievo, Gabrovo district.
3rd cent. B.C.
Historical Museum of Sevlievo, inv.
no. 640.
Arched blade with a curve on the
outer edge, tip curved in the
opposite direction. Decorated with
two concentric circles. Hilt is
delimited by two round pieces and a
cylindrical ferrule.
Undocumented.

PANAGJURIŠTE TREASURE (END OF FOURTH TO BEGINNING OF FIFTH CENTURIES B.C.) ARCHAEOLOGICAL MUSEUM, PLOVDIV

This treasure is important not only for its weight in gold (6.1 kg), but also for the originality of its forms and ornamentation. It consists of a phiale and eight rhyta, one shaped like an amphora, the others like heads of women or animals. All these receptacles contain an orifice cut in the lower part for the liquid to flow out, which had to be plugged when filling the recipient. The amphora-rhyton had two openings so that two people could drink at once, and was possibly used for ceremonies of fraternization. The collection must have been made by several artists, and comes from the city of Lampsaque on the Asian coast of the Dardanelles: the inscriptions indicate the weight of certain recipients in staterae, the measuring unit of that city. The subjects depicted—an attack on a palace, the judgement of Paris, Bacchantes—belong to the Hellenistic repertoire. What is remarkable here is the way in which muscular tension, gestures and emotions are rendered.

Bibl.: I. Venedikov, Panagjurskoto sakrovište, Sofia, 1961; I. Venedikov, The Panagjurischte Gold Treasure, Sofia, 1961; K. Kolev, "Trakijskoto panagjurskoto sakrovište," in Trakija, 1976, 3, pp. 170-187; H. Hoffman, "The Date of the Panagurishte Treasure," in RM, 65, 1958, pp. 121-141; E. Simon, "Der Goldschatz von Panagjuriste—eine Schöpfung der Alexanderzeit," in AK, 3, 1960, pp. 3-27; N. Kontoleon, "The Gold Treasure of Panagurischte," in Balkan Studies, 3, 1962, pp. 185-200; M. Pfrommer (in Fr.), "Italien, Makedonien, Kleinasien," in JdI, 98, 1983; P. Zazoff, C. Höcker, and L. Schneider, "Zur Thrakischen Kunst im Frühhellenismus," in AA, 1985, pp. 595-643.

420

AMPHORA-RHYTON

Gold; ht. 28 cm; wt. 1695.25 g.
Archaeological Museum, Plovdiv,
inv. no. 3203.
On the foot, two figures separated
by a rosette: bearded Silenus
carrying a kanatharos and the child
Herakles smothering snakes. On
either side, two Negro heads, the
open mouths forming spouts.
Handles in the form of centaurs,
hands raised, front legs resting on
the mouth, of which the rim is
decorated with egg and dart and
with beads. At the base of the
(undecorated) neck, a row of egg
and dart. On the bulge, an entire
scene in relief: five warriors attack
the entrance to a palace in which an
old man is hiding. Some brandish a
short sword, one blows a trumpet.
All are nude, save for a chlamys on
the shoulders which leaves the body
uncovered. Details of weapons and

clothing are delicately engraved. On
the other side of the door, a young
man converses with an old man.
Above and below the figures, frieze
of palmettes. An inscription on the
neck indicates the weight of the
vessel in Greek figures and in staters
of the city of Lampsaque:
200 staters, 1/2 drachma and 1
obole.
Bibl.: K. Kolev, "Scènes thraces sur
l'amphore-rhyton du trésor d'or de
Panaguriste," in *Pulpudeva*, 1, 1976,
pp. 184-205; P. Amandry,
"Toreutique achéménide," in *AK*, 2,
1959, pp. 38-56; G. Roux, "Meurtre
dans un sanctuaire sur l'amphore de
Panaguriste," in *AK*, 7, 1964, p. 30;
H. E. del Medico, "À propos du
trésor de Panaguriste: un portrait
d'Alexandre par Lysippe," in *Persica*,
3, 1967-1968, p. 37; J. G. Griffith,
"The Siege Scene on the Gold
Amphora of the Panagjurischte
Treasure," in *JHS*, 94, 1974,
pp. 38-41; E. K. Borthwick, "The
Scene on the Panagjurishte
Amphora: a New Solution," in *JHS*,
96, 1976, pp. 148-151; M. Daumas,
"L'amphore de Panaguriste et les
Sept contre Thèbes," in *AK*, 21, 1978,
pp. 23-31; J. G. Griffith, "Some
Further Thoughts on the Amphora-
Rhyton from Panagjurischte," in
Actes du II CITh, 1980,1, pp. 405-412;
G. F. Hind, "The Scene on the Gold
Amphora of Panaguriste Once
More," in *Ancient Bulgaria*, 1983,
pp. 253-274.

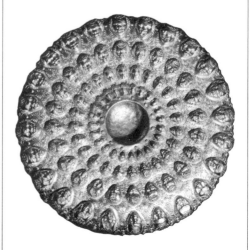

421

PHIALE

Gold; diam. 25 cm; wt. 845.7 g.
Archaeological Museum, Plovdiv,
inv. no. 3204.
Around the omphalos, executed
separately and welded to the silver,
the repoussé decoration is arranged
in concentric circles: first a row
of acorns, then three rows of
Negroes' heads. Between these
different motifs, a palmette
decoration covers the entire surface.
Inside, an inscription indicates the
weight in two systems of
measurement: in Lampsaque staters
and in drachmas.
Bibl.: D. E. Strong, *Greek and Roman
Gold and Silver Plate*, London, 1966,
p. 97; cf. Metropolitan phiale:
D. E. Strong, *op. cit.*, pl. 23A;
Kul-Oba phiale: V. Schiltz, *Or des
Scythes*, Paris, 1975, no. 94.

422

423

RHYTON

Gold; ht. 14 cm; wt. 439.05 g.
Archaeological Museum, Plovdiv,
inv. no. 3196.
No handle. Lower part terminates in
a very realistically treated goat
protoma. The spout is between the
front legs of the animal. On the rim
of the mouth, egg and dart and bead
decoration. On the neck, Hera,
Artemis, Apollo and Nike: the name
of each divinity is engraved near the
head.

RHYTON

Gold; ht. 13.5 cm; wt. 674.6 g.
Archaeological Museum, Plovdiv,
inv. no. 3197.
In form of stag's head. Spout is on
the animal's lower lip. Handle in
form of lion with front feet on rim of
mouth, decorated in egg and dart
and beads. On the neck, scene
representing the Judgement of
Paris: the names of Athena, Hera
and Aphrodite are engraved near
their heads.
Bibl.: D. E. Strong, *op. cit.*, p. 102,
pl. 23B.

424

RHYTON

*Gold; ht. 12.5 cm; wt. 505.5 g.
Archaeological Museum, Plovdiv,
inv. no. 3198.
Similar to preceding save for the
decoration on the neck, which
depicts, on one side, Herakles
battling the Ceryneian hind, on the
other, Theseus wrestling with the
bull at Marathon.*

425

RHYTON

*Gold; ht. 12.5 cm; wt. 505.5 g.
Archaeological Museum, Plovdiv,
inv. no. 3199.
In form of ram's head. The animal's
head is treated with great mastery;
the muzzle is smooth, the fleece
decoratively rendered by means of
small coupled circles. On the neck,
Dionysos and the nymph Eriope,
seated; on either side, dancing
bacchantes, bare-breasted. Handle
similar to that on no. 423.*

426

RHYTON

*Gold; ht. 20.5 cm; wt. 387.3 g.
Archaeological Museum, Plovdiv,
inv. no. 3202.
In form of Amazon's head; on the
neck, in the middle of a necklace,
medallion in form of lion's head
whose open mouth constitutes the
spout. Handle, square in section,
decorated with grooves and
terminating in a winged sphinx in
full round, front legs on the edge of
the mouth. The Amazon wears a
helmet decorated with two figurines
of griffins in relief and with engraved
plant motifs.*
Bibl.: K. Kolev, "Nouvelle opinion
sur les trois vases-rhytons à forme
de tête de femme du trésor thrace en
or de Panagjurishte," in *Pulpudeva*,
2, 1978, pp. 315-335.

427

RHYTON

Gold; ht. 14 cm; wt. 460.75 g.
Archaeological Museum, Plovdiv,
inv. no. 3200.
Handle, mouth and spout as in
preceding number, but neck is
undecorated and the Amazon is
bare-headed. The nape is covered
with a spangled hair net which
extends onto the temples by means
of a decorative strip, tied in a bow on
the forehead.
Bibl.: see no. 426; M. Pfrommer,
"Italien, Makedonien, Kleinasien," in
Jdl, 98, 1983.

428

RHYTON

Gold; ht. 22.5 cm; wt. 466.75 g.
Archaeological Museum, Plovdiv,
inv. no. 3201.
Similar to preceding, but wings of
sphinx are missing.

429

TWO APPLIQUES

Gold; ht. 6.3 cm; width 5.4 cm.
Panagjurište, Pazardžik district.
350-300 B.C.
Archaeological Museum, Sofia, inv.
no. 3557.
Form a griffin's head which must
have decorated the edge of an object
to which they would have been
fastened with gold nails. Spiral
ornament attached.
Bibl.: B. Filov, "Pametnici na
trakijskoto izkustvo," in *BIAB*, 6,
1916-1918.

430

TWO APPLIQUES FROM HORSE TRAPPINGS

Bronze; ht. 6.5 cm.
Panagjurište.
350-300 B.C.
Archaeological Museum, Sofia, inv.
no. 3569.
Two paws and shoulder of lion,
decorated with griffin heads.
Bibl.: *Duvanli*, pp. 44-45, nos. 29-30,
fig. 32-33.

431

TWO APPLIQUES FROM HORSE TRAPPINGS

Silver; diam. 8.6 cm.
Panagjurište.
350-300 B.C.
Archaeological Museum, Sofia, inv.
no. 3559.
Circular; Herakles wrestling the
Nemean lion; the hero squeezes in
his arms the neck of the animal,
which is trying to free itself. The
artisan has expressed the animal's
pain, the movement and tension of
its muscles. Traces of gilding.
Bibl.: *Duvanli*, p. 39, no. 22, pl. I/7.

432

TWO APPLIQUES FROM HORSE TRAPPINGS

Silver; ht. 5.5 cm.
Panagjurište.
350-300 B.C.
Archaeological Museum, Sofia, inv. no. 3553.
Square in form; crowned head of Apollo; traces of gilding.
Bibl.: *Duvanli*, p. 38, no. 21, pl. I/1-4.

433

CENTRAL APPLIQUE FROM SHIELD

Silver; ht. 32 cm.
Panagjurište.
350-300 B.C.
Archaeological Museum, Sofia, inv. no. 3555.
Oblong; border with a double row of repoussé beads; a central rosette on either side of which is depicted a griffin, then, on the upper extremity, Herakles and the Nemean lion. Near the lower extremity, a Silenus. Chest of both figures shown full-face, but legs, feet and head are in profile.
Bibl.: L. Ognenova, "Opit za rekonstrukcia na dva štita ot Trakia," in *BIAB*, 18, 1952, pp. 63-64, nos. 1-4, fig. 19-22 A-B; *Duvanli*, pp. 40-41, no. 23, fig. 25.

434

TWO SHIELD APPLIQUES

Silver; diam. 9.2 and 9.5 cm.
Panagjurište.
350-300 B.C.
Archaeological Museum, Sofia, inv. no. 3561.
Circular, bordered by a double row of beads; in the centre, four leaves bordered with dots around an omphalos.
Bibl.: *Duvanli*, p. 43, no. 25, fig. 28-29.

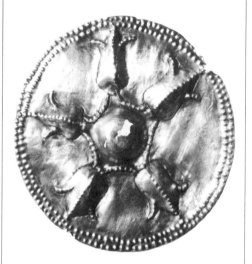

435

436

TWO SHIELD APPLIQUES

Silver; diam. 8 cm.
Panagjurište.
350-300 B.C.
Archaeological Museum, Sofia, inv.
no. 3561.
Circular, bordered with a double row
of beads; around the central
omphalos, two animals, a bird and a
palmette.
Bibl.: Duvanli, p. 43, no. 24,
fig. 26-27.

SHIELD APPLIQUE

Silver; diam. 8.6 cm.
Panagjurište.
350-300 B.C.
Archaeological Museum, Sofia, inv.
no. 3561.
Circular, bordered by a double row
of beads; around the central
omphalos, five lotus blossoms.
Bibl.: Duvanli, p. 44, no. 26, fig. 30.

Kralevo treasure.

First half of third

century B.C.

Found in 1979 during excavations of the Thracian burial mound near the village of Kralevo, department of Targovište. It consists of gold and silver jewellery and harness appliques. Besides the cinerary urn, which is a hydria of gilded terracotta, there have been found a funerary crown of gilded ceramic, a silver breastplate, an iron bit and strigil, pottery, notably an amphora from Thasos, and an axe-sceptre.

Bibl.: G. Ginev, Sakrovišteto ot Kralevo, Sofia, 1983.

437

438

SCEPTRE-AXE

Iron; length 17.2 cm; width 9 cm; thickness 0.9 to 1 cm.
District Museum of History, Targovište, inv. no. 2315.
Elongated trapezoid, the two sides of the curved blade are bow-shaped. Wide part sharpened, narrow part massive, cylindrical part with hole for hilt, continued by another massive cylindrical part with horizontal grooves terminating in a disc-shaped projection.
Bibl.: G. Ginev, *op. cit.*, p. 10, fig. 7.

PAIR OF EARRINGS

Gold; width 0.7 cm; diam. 1.4 cm; wt. 6.13 and 6.07 g.
District Museum of History, Targovište, inv. no. 2309.
Ring surrounded by twisted wire, the broad part terminating in a lion's head. Ornaments in relief are moulded and imitate filigree.
Bibl.: G. Ginev, *op. cit.*, p. 11, fig. 21-22; see no. 371.

439

PAIR OF BRACELETS

*Silver with gilding; diam. 6.8 cm; wt.
33.49 and 30.9 g.
District Museum of History,
Targovište, inv. no. 2310.
Plaque in form of snake coiled into a
spiral, head and tail in relief, with
incised scales next to them. Part of
tail of one snake missing.
Bibl.: G. Ginev, op. cit., p. 11,
fig. 17-18.*

440

HEADSTALL

*Gold; length 4.4 cm; ht. 2 cm; wt.
18.2 g.
District Museum of History,
Targovište, inv. no. 2304.
From the middle of the base projects
an eagle's head welded to the form
of a Beotian shield. The ornaments
on the base are in filigree and
consist of two palmettes with five
and seven leaves respectively, one
of them bearing traces of glass
paste.*

441

APPLIQUE

*Gold; diam. 3.5 to 3.7 cm; wt. 8.14 g.
District Museum of History,
Targovište, inv. no. 2305.
In form of rosette with fourteen
leaves of which seven are complete,
the others, constituting a second
row, being half visible. Filigree
borders and a transverse rib on all
leaves. In the centre, inside a circle, a
pyramid formed of four granules.
One granule at the tip of each leaf.
Traces of glass paste on the leaves
in the inner row.
Bibl.: G. Ginev, op. cit., p. 13,
fig. 30-31.*

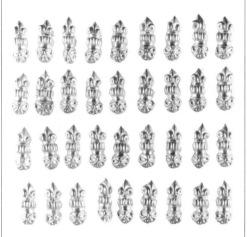

442

FOUR ROUND APPLIQUES

Gold; diam. 3.8 cm; wt. 20.1, 18.96, 17.78 and 14.85 g.
District Museum of History, Targovište, inv. nos. 2300-2303.
On a round plaque is welded an irregular half-sphere in high relief representing a bearded Herakles, full-face, the head covered with a lion's skin. The hero's wavy beard and moustache, as well as the lion's mane, are formed of incised lines. Band of egg and dart filled with multicoloured glass paste, ranging from thirty-three to thirty-five in number. Egg and dart and outer border are decorated with filigree.
Bibl.: G. Ginev, *op. cit.*, p. 15, fig. 28-29.

443

TWO RECTANGULAR APPLIQUES

Gold; length 4.6 cm; ht. 3.7 cm; wt. 24.67 and 25.95 g.
District Museum of History, Targovište, inv. nos. 2298-2299.
On a rectangular plaque is welded another, smaller plaque with a griffin in relief, the front leg raised. The griffins face one another on the two appliques. Parts of the wings are formed of horizontal lines in relief, and of strokes. Framed by a band of egg and dart with filigree border bearing traces of glass paste.
Bibl.: G. Ginev, *op. cit.*, p. 16, fig. 34-35.

444

THIRTY-SIX SMALL APPLIQUES

Gold; length 1.9 to 2.2 cm; width 0.7 to 0.9 cm; tot. wt. 36.36 g.
District Museum of History, Targovište, inv. no. 2306.
Elongated form divided into three parts, the first a lotus blossom, the middle with six transverse grooves and the third, a five-petalled rosette. Rings attached to the bottom of the hollow part.
Bibl.: G. Ginev, *op. cit.*, p. 18, fig. 15-38.

445

TWO APPLIQUES

*Gold; ht. 0.6 cm; diam. 1.1 cm; wt.
3.92 and 4.66 g.
District Museum of History,
Targovište, inv. no. 2307.
In form of trunk of low cone, with
broad flat base and vertical opening.
Undecorated.*
Bibl.: G. Ginev, *op. cit.*, p. 19,
fig. 36-37.

446

RING

*Gold; diam. 2.2 cm; wt. 9.65 g.
District Museum of History,
Targovište, inv. no. 2308.
Closed, made of round wire.*
Bibl.: G. Ginev, *op. cit.*, p. 19,
fig. 36-37.

**Parures from
Seuthopolis, near
Kazanlak.
Early third century
B.C.
Archaeological
Museum, Sofia.**

Bibl.: K. Žuglev, *"Razkopi i prooučvania
na mogila no 1—Koprinka,"* in Annuaire
de l'Université de Sofia, faculté
d'histoire et de philosophie, *11, 7, 1952,
2, pp. 241 and 251, fig. 29;* M.
Čičikova, Seuthopolis, *1970, no. 92.*

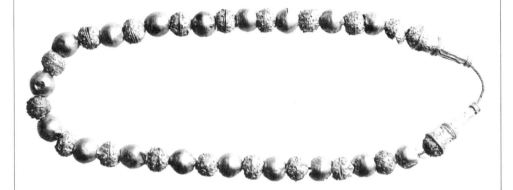

447

TWO EARRINGS

*Gold; diam. 1.7 and 1.8 cm; wt. 3.95
and 3.79 g.
Archaeological Museum, Sofia, inv.
no. 7852 a-b.
Twisted, terminating in a lion's head.
Bibl.: see no. 371.*

448

NECKLACE

*Gold.
Archaeological Museum, Sofia, inv.
no. 7853.*

*Composed of thirty-six round beads,
smooth beads alternating with
filigree beads; at either end, filigreed
spindle-shaped element.*

449

TWO SMALL FIBULAE

Gold; width 1.5 cm; wt. 1.03 g.
Archaeological Museum, Sofia, inv.
no. 7856.

450

PENDANT AND FOUR
ELEMENTS OF NECKLACE

Gold; ht. 3.6 cm; wt. 12.5 g.
Varna.
Early 3rd cent. B.C.
Archaeological Museum, Sofia, inv.
no. 2382.
The pyramid-shaped pendant bears
plant decorations with blue enamel
inlay.
Bibl.: T. Ivanov, "Trakijski mogilni
pogrebenija v Odessos i okolnostta
mu prez rannoelinističnata epoha,"
in IVAD, 10, 1956, p. 93, no. 2, pl. III/2.

451

TWO EARRINGS

Gold; diam. 4.8 cm; wt. 4.55 g.
Asenovgrad.
3rd cent. B.C.
Archaeological Museum, Sofia, inv.
no. 4232.
In form of open ring terminating at
one end in a hook, at the other in a
bull's head.
Bibl.; Tr. Izk, p. 372, no. 184.

Jewels from a necropolis near Nesebar.

452

453

NECKLACE

Gold; length 32 cm.
Nesebar.
3rd cent. B.C.
District Museum of History, Burgas, inv. no. 1334.
In form of chain; clasp, decorated with an amethyst inserted into an openwork cylindrical element, terminates in a lion's head to which are attached, on one side, a hook, on the other side, a ring.
Bibl.: I. Galabov, "Kamenni grobnici pri Nesebar," in BIAB, 19, 1955, p. 141, fig. 9, C.

TWO EARRINGS

Gold; diam. 2.7 cm; wt. 29 g.
Nesebar.
3rd cent. B.C.
District Museum of History, Burgas, inv. nos. 1332-1333.
In form of open ring terminating at one end in a figure of Pegasus; pendant in form of small lidded amphora; certain details of Pegasus and of pendant in filigree.
Bibl.: I. Galabov, op. cit., p. 141, fig. 15, A-B.

454

TWO EARRINGS

Gold; ht. 2.6 cm.
Nesebar.
3ʳᵈ cent. B.C.
Municipal Museum of Nesebar, inv.
nos. 369-370.
In form of open ring, twisted,
terminating at one end in the head of
a Maenad, crowned with enamelled
laurel leaves, the hair wrapped in a
band.
Bibl.: Ž. Čimbuleva, "Novootkrita
elinistična grobnica ot Nesebar," in
Arheologija, 1964, 4, p. 58, no. 3,
fig. 3.

455

ORNAMENTAL APPLIQUE

Gold; length 8.7 cm.
Nesebar.
3ʳᵈ cent. B.C.
District Museum of History, Burgas,
inv. no. 1301.
Ellipsoidal in form; delicate border in
relief; in the field, repoussé
decoration depicting a mythological
scene: in the centre, Cepheus and
Cassiopeia, at the extremities,
Perseus cutting off the Gorgon's
head and Andromeda trying to
escape from the monster; to
Andromeda's left, a small Eros. This
applique was fastened to a bronze
fibula.
Bibl.: I. Galabov, *op. cit.*, p. 144,
fig. 11.

456

ORNAMENTAL APPLIQUE

Gold; length 6.9 cm.
Nesebar.
3ʳᵈ cent. B.C.
District Museum of History, Burgas,
inv. no. 1343.
Ellipsoidal in form; decorated with a
Gorgon. This applique was fastened
to the garment by means of a fibula
and thus would have acted as a
pectoral, although there is no
attachment hole at the extremities.
Bibl.: I. Galabov, *op. cit.*, p. 144,
fig. 7-8, B.

457

458

ORNAMENTAL APPLIQUE

Gold; length 8.1 cm.
Nesebar.
Middle of 3rd cent. B.C.
District Museum of History, Burgas,
inv. no. 1335.
Ellipsoidal in form. Like the two
preceding appliques, it was attached
to a bronze fibula. The plant
decoration included inlaid stones, no
longer extant. The presence of two
wings suggests that in the centre,
the stone would have been
engraved to depict a Gorgon.
Bibl.: I. Galabov, *op. cit.*, p. 141,
fig. 9, B.

TWO PARURES

Gold; ht. 9 cm.
Nesebar.
Middle of 3rd cent. B.C.
District Museum of History, Burgas,
inv. nos. 1302-1303.
It is impossible to determine the
precise function of these objects, of
which the upper part terminates in
the form of a woman's head, the hair
encircled by a diadem. The entire
surface is covered with dots.
Bibl.: I. Galabov, *op. cit.*, p. 144,
fig. 10, C-D.

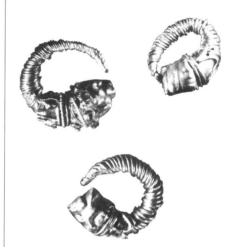

459

RING

Gold; length 6.1 cm.
Nesebar.
Middle of 3rd cent. B.C.
District Museum of History, Burgas,
inv. no. 1336.
Spiral in form, depicting a dragon. It
was decorated with six stones; only
one amethyst remains.
Bibl.: I. Galabov, op. cit., p. 142,
fig. 12-13; B. Deppert-Lippitz,
Griechischer Goldschmuck, Mainz,
1985, p. 273, fig. 209.

460

RING

Gold; length 4 cm.
Nesebar.
Middle of 3rd cent. B.C.
Municipal Museum of Nesebar, inv.
no. 3681.
In form of snake coiled in a spiral.
Bibl.: Ž. Čimbuleva, op. cit., p. 58,
fig. 2.

461

THREE EARRINGS

Gold.
Sveštari, Razgrad district.
Middle of 3rd cent. B.C.
District Museum of History, Razgrad,
inv. nos. 4185, 4186 and 3373.
Open ring formed of twisted wire, at
one extremity a lion's head
decorated with a jagged crown.
Undocumented.

462

PHIALE

Silver; ht. 5.5 cm; diam. 10.4 cm.
Sveštari, Razgrad district.
Middle of 3rd cent. B.C.
District Museum of History, Razgrad,
inv. no. KB 8723.
With omphalos, undecorated.
Undocumented.

463

FIGURE OF WOMAN

Limestone; ht. 41 cm.
Sveštari, Razgrad district.
Middle of 3rd cent. B.C.
District Museum of History, Razgrad,
inv. no. 8731.
Incomplete. Hair pulled back to nape.
Floor-length chiton, twice belted.
Slightly open arms hold the upper
part of the garment, right leg
forward. Traces of polychrome
decoration.

464

PHIALE

Silver; diam. 8.5 cm.
Priboi, near Pernik.
3rd-2nd cent. B.C.
Archaeological Museum, Sofia, inv.
no. 6755.
Interior smooth; on exterior,
background decorated with
concentric circles and bulge
decorated with gadroons and beads
arranged in a rosette. The phiale has
been melted.

Appliques from the harnessing of a chariot from burial mound near Mezek. Archaeological Museum, Sofia.

Although this burial mound dates from the second half of the fourth century B.C., the contents seem to belong to a later grave of the third century.

465

FIVE RINGS FROM REINS

Bronze; width 7.3 to 8.4 cm.
Archaeological Museum, Sofia, inv. nos. 6411-6412.
Lower part decorated with a highly stylized human head.
Bibl.: B. Filov, "Kupolnite grobnici pri Mezek," in *BIAB*, 11, 1937, p. 61, no. 30, fig. 69.

466

RECTANGULAR BUCKLE

Bronze; ht. 12 cm.
Archaeological Museum, Sofia, inv. no. 6418.
Bibl.: B. Filov, *op. cit.*, p. 65, no. 34, fig. 70.

467

TWO ORNAMENTS

Bronze; ht. 12.1 cm.
Archaeological Museum, Sofia, inv.
no. 6413.
In form of flower, with
anthropomorphic elements; back
flat; stem of one ornament is broken.
Bibl.: B. Filov, *op. cit.*, p. 61, no. 29,
fig. 23.

468

ROSETTE

Bronze, traces of silver; ht. 12.2 cm.
Archaeological Museum, Sofia, inv.
no. 6413.
Stem emerging from rosette, ends in
a stylized head.
Bibl.: B. Filov, *op. cit.*, p. 55, no. 15,
fig. 52.

469

ORNAMENT

Bronze; ht. 11.3 cm.
Archaeological Museum, Sofia, inv.
no. 6413.
Forked extremities are decorated
with an animal's head.
Bibl.: B. Filov, *op. cit.*, p. 55, no. 16,
fig. 53.

470

FIGURINE OF BOAR

Bronze; length 17.2 cm; ht. 8.1 cm.
Šeinovo, Stara Zagora district.
3rd-2nd cent. B.C.
Archaeological Museum, Sofia, inv.
no. 4017A.
Animal is on its feet, in a tranquil
pose. Body is well modelled, hair
indicated by means of stippled lines.
Bibl.: M. Domaradski, "Kelti i Traki,"
in *Izkustvo*, 1983, 4, pp. 37-42,
fig. 5-6.

471

RING

Silvered bronze; diam. 2.6 cm; width
0.6 to 1.3 cm.
Ognjanovo, Sofia district.
3rd-2nd cent. B.C.
National Museum of History of
Sofia, inv. no. 22467.
Open ring, two extremities covered
by a plaque which, as it widens,
forms a summarily executed human
face in relief.
Undocumented.

THE DECLINE OF THRACIAN CIVILIZATION (END OF THE THIRD TO FIRST CENTURIES B.C.)

The decline of Thracian civilization began in the year 280 B.C., the date of the death of Lysimakos, the last great king of the country. Conflicts between that ambitious strategist Alexander the Great and the Thracian kings, as well as the wars against the Diadochi, had exhausted Thrace's economic and military resources. This situation facilitated the incursion of a new group of invaders, the Celts of central Europe, who laid waste the regions of Thrace and the Greek coastal cities in 280 B.C. Their dominion was broken in 216 B.C., when the Romans gained the Adriatic coast of the Balkan peninsula. After fighting the Macedonians in three successive long wars, they occupied Macedonia in 164 B.C. and invaded Thrace, allying themselves either with the Odrysians or with other Thracian tribes. Thus in the first century B.C., when other Thracian tribes of the northwest had already been subjugated, the Odrysian kingdom became a Roman protectorate, which kept its independence until 49 B.C. This period may be called the epoch of the great invasions from the west. Little evidence of it is left. The campaigns of the Macedonians, the Celts and the Romans laid waste the region, and the burial mounds dating from between the third and the first centuries B.C. contain only common objects. The fibulae, swords and buckler appliques are identical to those found in central Europe and Italy. As in the Black Sea steppes, we find to the north of the Balkans only Sarmatian goods, such as the finds at Galiče and Jakimovo. The coins struck were imitations of Macedonian coinage and of that of Thasos.

Phalerae from Galiče, near Orjahovo. Second to first centuries B.C. Archaeological Museum, Sofia.

472

PHALERA

Silver gilt; diam. 18.3 cm. Archaeological Museum, Sofia, inv. no. 5876.
Bust of woman in relief, long hair surrounding the face; richly ornamented low-cut garment; on neck, eight folds resemble torques placed one above the other. There is a bird on each side of the bust at shoulder level. On the egg and dart border, four attachment holes.
Bibl.: B. Filov and I. Velkov, "Novoot-kriti starini," in *BIAB*, 7, 1919-1920, pp. 146-148; cf. also, in Rumania, the phalera from the Herastraü treasure, *Dacia*, 11-12, p. 35.

473

PHALERA

Silver gilt, diam. 15.8 cm. Archaeological Museum, Sofia, inv. no. 5877.
The bottom is covered with dots against which stands out the figure, in relief, of a horseman wearing several torques placed one above the other. The horse, with short hind legs, is summarily executed. On the egg and dart border, four attachment holes.

474

PHALERA

Silver gilt; diam. 12 cm.
Archaeological Museum, Sofia, inv.
no. 5878.
Small central rosette surrounded by
eight leaves with conspicuous veins.
On the egg and dart border, four
attachment holes.

475

PHALERA

Silver gilt; diam. 4.8 cm.
Archaeological Museum, Sofia, inv.
no. 5879, 1.
Four-petalled rosette with
conspicuous veins; on the border
decorated with engraved spirals,
four attachment holes.

476

PHALERA

Silver gilt; diam. 14.9 cm.
Archaeological Museum, Sofia, inv.
no. 5879, 2.
Similar to preceding.

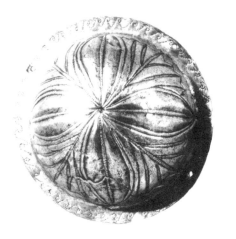

477

PHALERA

Silver gilt; diam. 15 cm.
Archaeological Museum, Sofia, inv.
no. 5879, 3.
Similar to preceding; part missing.

478

PHALERA

Silver gilt; diam. 14.8 cm.
Archaeological Museum, Sofia, inv.
no. 5879, 4.
Similar to preceding; cracked.

479

PHALERA

Silver gilt; diam. 15.1 cm.
Archaeological Museum, Sofia, inv.
no. 5879, 5.

480

PHALERA

Silver gilt; diam. 9.2 cm.
Archaeological Museum, Sofia, inv.
no. 5880, 1.
Similar to preceding, but smaller
and less curved.

481

PHALERA

Silver gilt; diam. 9.7 cm.
Archaeological Museum, Sofia, inv.
no. 5880, 2.
Similar to no. 475.

482

PHALERA

Silver gilt; diam. 9.5 cm.
Archaeological Museum, Sofia, inv.
no. 5880, 3.
Similar to no. 480.

483

Treasure from

Bohot, near Pleven.

First century B.C.

District Museum of

History, Pleven.

Bibl.: I. Venedikov, "Dve sakrovišta ot elinističnata epoha v Trakija," in Izsledvanija v pamet na K. Škorpil, *Sofia, 1961, pp. 355-358, fig. 3.*

THREE PHALERAE

Silver gilt; diam. 8.9 cm. Archaeological Museum, Sofia, inv. no. 5880, 4-6.

Similar to no. 475.

484

HEMISPHERICAL CUP

Silver; diam. 14.5 cm; wt. 236 g.
District Museum of History, Pleven,
inv. no. 57, 1.
Without decoration.

485

HEMISPHERICAL CUP

Silver; diam. 14.3 cm; wt. 124 g.
District Museum of History, Pleven,
inv. no. 57, 2.
Similar to preceding; part of mouth
missing.

486

HEMISPHERICAL CUP

Silver; diam. 13.4 cm; wt. 232 g.
District Museum of History, Pleven,
inv. no. 57, 3.
Similar to preceding.

487

HEMISPHERICAL CUP

Silver; diam. 12.3 cm; wt. 188 g.
District Museum of History, Pleven,
inv. no. 57, 4.
Similar to preceding.

488

HEMISPHERICAL CUP

Silver; diam. 14 cm; wt. 196.5 g.
District Museum of History, Pleven,
inv. no. 57, 5.
Similar to preceding; engraved line
around mouth.

489

HEMISPHERICAL CUP

Silver; diam. 13.8 cm; wt. 218 g.
District Museum of History, Pleven,
inv. no. 57, 6.
Similar to preceding.

490

HEMISPHERICAL CUP

Silver; diam. 15 cm; wt. 230 g.
District Museum of History, Pleven,
inv. no. 57, 7.
Similar to preceding.

491

HEMISPHERICAL CUP

Silver; diam. 13.6 cm; wt. 235 g.
District Museum of History, Pleven,
inv. no. 57, 8.
Similar to preceding.

492

HEMISPHERICAL CUP

Silver; diam. 13.8 cm; wt. 220 g.
District Museum of History, Pleven,
inv. no. 57, 9.
Similar to preceding.

493

PAIL

Bronze; ht. 23 cm; diam. 22 cm.
District Museum of History, Pleven,
inv. no. 58.
Lower part is missing.

Treasure of Jakimovo, Mihajlovgrad district. First century B.C. Mihajlovgrad Museum.

Bibl.: A. Milčev, "Novootkrito srebarno trakijsko sakrovište ot s. Jakimovo, Mihajlovgradsko," in Arheologija, *15, 1973, 1, pp. 1-14, fig. 1-11; V. Vasilev, "Tehnologija na sakrovišteto ot Jakimovo," dans I. Marazov,* Sakrovišteto ot Jakimovo, *Sofia, 1979.*

494

CUP

Silver; ht. 7.5 cm; diam. 14.7 cm.
Mihajlovgrad Museum, inv.
no. 38-40.
On exterior, near mouth, incised egg and dart decoration.

495

CUP

*Silver; ht. 6.8 cm; diam. 12 cm.
Mihajlovgrad Museum, inv.
no. 39-45.
Near mouth, gilded band.*

496

CUP

*Silver; ht. 102 cm; diam. 16.5 cm.
Mihajlovgrad Museum, inv. no. 37.
Similar to preceding.*

497

CUP

*Silver; ht. 10.3 cm; diam. 16 cm.
Mihajlovgrad Museum, inv. no. 46.
Inside, around mouth, engraved
decoration; outside, gilded figure in
relief: a horseman, garbed and
shod; part of horse and horseman
missing.*

498

KANTHAROS

Silver; ht. 8.6 cm; diam. 11 cm.
Mihajlovgrad Museum, inv. no. 41.
Hemispherical on a high foot;
outside, around the body, engraved
decoration; handles have horizontal
protuberances (one is missing).

499

DRINKING VESSEL

Copper; ht. 7.8 cm; diam. 11.3 cm.
Mihajlovgrad Museum, inv. no. 47.
Cylindrical; thin band of silver
surrounds opening.

500

PHALERA

Silver, traces of gilding; diam. 8 cm.
Mihajlovgrad Museum, inv.
no. 40-38.
On the border, stippled decoration;
bust of bearded man in high relief;
on the neck, three folds suggest
torques placed one on top of the
other; clasp on shoulder.

501

PHALERA

*Silver, exterior gilded; diam. 8 cm.
Mihajlovgrad Museum, inv.
no. 45-39.
Bust of winged woman in bas relief;
hair, parted in middle, falls to
shoulders on both sides; arms are
not in right place.*

502

TWO BRACELETS

*Silver; diam. 8 cm.
Mihajlovgrad Museum, inv.
no. 43-44.
Formed of narrow bands in triple
spirals; snakes' heads at ends.*

THRACE IN THE ROMAN PERIOD

After the conquest, Rome divided Thrace into three provinces, Macedonia, Mesia and Thrace. Town planning developed, and Thracian cities adopted almost all the characteristics of Roman cities—the stately architecture, the sculpture, the painting and all the minor arts, the latter still being influenced to some extent by Hellenistic art. The religion of the conquerors was also established in the urban centres: forced to retire to backwaters, the Thracian gods were no longer worshipped except in remote mountain regions. Around the cities there grew up rich necropolises with funerary steles, marble statues and painted tombs. But the Thracians mostly remained faithful to the old burial rites, and kept their burial mounds until the Christian era.

In the burial mounds of the Roman period have been found mask-helmets and appliques of the Stara Zagora type (second half of the first century B.C.), which are always of oriental style. But the most characteristic remains of this period, also discovered in the burial mounds, are the Thracian chariots, with their horses harnessed with rich trappings. The items from Šiškovci (nos. 561 to 569) give an idea of the ornamentation of these chariots, of which there are more than fifty.

Most of the relics of Roman Thrace are very like those found in all the Roman provinces of Europe: funerary vessels, weapons, gold and silver jewellery. There is, nevertheless, a group of objects which are only found in Thrace: these are the votive reliefs depicting Zeus (Jupiter) and Hera (Juno), Asklepios (Aesculapius, god of medicine) and Hygeia (Hygia, goddess of health), Silvanus (god of the woods), Dionysos (Bacchus), Pan, the Satyrs and Maenads, Herakles (Hercules), and other Greek and Roman divinities. The most interesting of these reliefs are those which show the Thracian Horseman or Hero, a strange local god who took on the characteristics of many divinities: Asklepios, Zeus, Dionysos, Silvanus, Apollo, Pluto or Mithras. The Hero is also represented in bronze: there is no doubt that these figurines, which exist only in Thrace, were made locally. Another theme frequently depicted was that of three Nymphs shown in the form of goddesses of water and fertility: the iconography is comparable to that of the three Graces.

The Roman period is represented here by typically Thracian objects. Although there was a great deal of gold and silver jewellery in Thrace, gildsmiths' work is illustrated only by the Nikolaevo treasure (nos. 527 to 549).

503

HELMET

Bronze; ht. 19.7 cm.
Brjastovec (Kara Agač), near Burgas.
1ˢᵗ-2ⁿᵈ cent. A.D.
Archaeological Museum, Sofia, inv.
no. 6176.
Conical; on skull-piece, Hermes,
Apollo, Athena, Nike and Ares, each
divinity shown under an arch; on the
cheek-guard, Poseidon.
Bibl.: I. Velkov, "Novi mogilni
nahodki," in *BIAB*, 5, 1928-1929,
p. 15 and 20, fig. 7-9, pl. III-V.

504

HELMET MASK

Bronze; ht. 21 cm.
Silistra.
1ˢᵗ cent. A.D.
District Museum of History, Silistra,
inv. nos. 509 and 607.
On the skull-piece, decoration
representing sphinxes, garlands and
eagle with outspread wings. Hair is
highly stylized. The mask represents
a young man.

505

HELMET MASK

Bronze, iron; ht. 23 cm.
Stara Zagora.
Second half of 1ˢᵗ cent. A.D.
District Museum of History, Stara
Zagora, inv. no. II C3 1116.
Back part of skull-piece is iron and
represents the hair. The mask is
bronze and beardless.
Bibl.: D. Nikolov and H. Bujukliev,
"Trakijski mogilni grobove ot
Čatalka, Starozagorsko," in
Arheologija, 9, 1967, 1, p. 21, fig. 8.

506

507

508

APPLIQUE

Silver; diam. 17.8 cm.
Stara Zagora.
1ˢᵗ cent. A.D.
District Museum of History, Stara Zagora, inv. no. II-132-7.
Hercules fighting the Nemean lion; six animals surround him: two lions, two lion-griffins and two winged lions.
Bibl.: H. Bujukliev, M. Dimitrov and D. Nikolov, District Museum of History, Stara Zagora, Sofia, 1965, p. 134, nos. 28-29.

APPLIQUE

Silver; diam. 17.5 cm.
Stara Zagora.
1ˢᵗ cent. A.D.
District Museum of History, Stara Zagora, inv. no. II-132-9.
Similar to the previous one, but with different animals depicted; in poor condition.
Bibl.: see no. 506.

CUP

Silver; ht. 9 cm; diam. 15 cm.
Collective find, Stara Zagora.
1ˢᵗ cent. B.C.
District Museum of History, Stara Zagora, inv. no. 2 C3132-2.
Badly damaged, only fragments of decorations are visible: part of a lion skin, a Satyr's head, fragment of a lion's body with tail.
Bibl.: H. Bujukliev, M. Dimitrov and D. Nikolov, op. cit., Sofia, 1975, p. 135, no. 34.

509

DRINKING VESSEL

Silver; ht. 9.6 cm; diam. 11.9 cm; wt. 209 g.
Collective find, Stara Zagora.
1st cent. B.C.
District Museum of History, Stara Zagora, inv. no. 2 C3132-3.
Comprises two parts, one introduced into the other; on the outside, relief ornaments cast in a mold.
Bibl.: see no. 508, p. 135, no. 35.

510

ASKOS

Bronze; ht. 13.5 cm.
Smočan, near Loveč.
1st cent. A.D.
District Museum of History, Loveč, inv. no. 1140.
Receptacle, the richly ornamented handle of which finishes in the head of a bearded Silenus; the eyes are inlaid with silver. A heraldic plaque below the handle bears the figure of a lioness in relief.
Bibl.: G. Kitov et al., *Trakite v Loveški okrag*, Sofia, 1980, pp. 19-21, fig. 13.

511

JUG

Bronze; ht. 19.5 cm.
Smočan, near Loveč.
1st cent. A.D.
District Museum of History, Loveč, inv. no. 1211.
Wide pot-bellied lower part, small cylindrical base, long neck. The handle is held in place by hoops, with a small iron lid attached to the top end.
Bibl.: G. Kitov et al., *op. cit.*, p. 20, fig. 21.

512

JUG

Bronze; ht. 21 cm.
1st cent. A.D.
District Museum of History, Loveč,
inv. no. 1213.
Spherical lower part tapering
towards the bottom. Short neck
ending in an elongated spout. The
handle is bent back and projects far
beyond the opening. At the bottom
end a Silenus in relief.
Bibl.: G. Kitov et al., op. cit., p. 20,
fig. 18.

513

MIRROR

Bronze; diam. 7 cm.
Stara Zagora.
1st cent. A.D.
District Museum of History, Stara
Zagora, inv. no. 2 C3542.
Round container. Small mirror
mounted on the inside of one of the
lids. In the centre of the lids, the two
sides of a medallion bearing an
effigy of the Emperor Nero.
Bibl.: H. Bujukliev, op. cit., p. 136,
no. 37.

514

EMBALMING VESSEL

Bronze; ht. 31 cm.
Varna.
Second half of 2nd cent. A.D.
Museum of Art and History, Varna,
inv. no. 11 4250.
Bust of Antinous, hole for lid at the
top of the head. The bust has a
pedestal attached.
Bibl.: M. Mirčev, "Tri grobni nahodki
kraj Varna," in IVAD, 20, 1969, p. 227,
no. 7.

515

APPLIQUE

Bronze; length 9.7 cm; width 6.7 cm.
Saraj, Pazardžik district.
2nd-3rd cent. A.D.
Archaeological Museum,
Sofia, inv. no. 6372 b.
Mask of a young woman with mouth
open, curly hair falling down either
side of her face. The mask leaves the
eyes exposed.
Bibl.: L. Manzova, "Poignées et
appliques de cassettes de l'époque
romaine conservées au musée
archéologique de Sofia," in
Arheologija, 1965, 1, p. 41, no. 6b.

516

APPLIQUE

Silver; ht. 7.5 cm.
Karnobat.
2nd-3rd cent. A.D.
Archaeological Museum, Sofia, inv.
no. 5874.
Mask of a bearded Silenus.
Undocumented.

Krumovgrad

appliques.

Bibl.: B. Filov, Drevnoto izkustvo v
Balgarija, *Sofia, 1925, p. 33, fig. 24.*

517

APPLIQUE

Silver; diam. 7 cm.
Near Krumovgrad.
2nd cent. A.D.
Archaeological Museum, Sofia, inv.
no. 3747.
Circular; bust of a bearded giant,
engraved inside a circle, the head
turned slightly to the left.

518

APPLIQUE

Silver; diam. 7 cm.
Near Krumovgrad.
2nd cent. A.D.
Archaeological Museum, Sofia, inv.
no. 3741, 1.

519

APPLIQUE

Silver; diam. 7.3 cm.
Near Krumovgrad.
2nd cent. A.D.
Archaeological Museum, Sofia, inv.
no. 3748.
The decoration around the edge is
similar, but the bust is full-face and
represents Herakles.

Treasure of Goljama
Brestnica, near
Pleven.
Second century A.D.
District Museum of
History, Pleven.

Bibl.: H. Petkov, "Novootkristoto
srebarno sakrovište ot s. Goljama
Brestnica," in Arheologija, 2, 1960, 1,
pp. 26-28, nos. 1-4, fig. 22, 24-26.

520

APPLIQUE

Silver; diam. 7.5 cm.
Near Krumovgrad.
2ⁿᵈ cent. A.D.
Archaeological Museum, Sofia, inv.
no. 3749.
Similar to preceding, with a bust of
Athena.

521

RECEPTACLE

Silver; ht. 9 cm; diam. 22 cm.
District Museum of History, Pleven,
inv. no. 113.
Cylindrical in shape; the lip curls in;
below the rim, a Greek inscription
saying that Flavius Mestrianos
makes a gift of this treasure to the
hero Pyrmerulas.

522

SMALL BOWL

Silver; ht. 6 cm; diam. of mouth 7.4 cm.
District Museum of History, Pleven, inv. no. 113, 1.
Slightly rounded; enlarged handles at either end.

523

SMALL BOWL

Silver; ht. 6 cm; diam. of mouth 7.6 cm.
District Museum of History, Pleven, inv. no. 113, 2.
Similar to previous number, but damaged.

524

SMALL BOWL

Silver; ht. 6 cm; diam. of mouth 7.6 cm.
District Museum of History, Pleven, inv. no. 113, 3.
Similar to previous number, but repaired in antiquity.

525

526

**Treasure from
Nikolaevo, near
Pleven.
249 A.D.
Archaeological
Museum, Sofia.**

Bibl.: B. Filov, "Rimskoto sakrovište ot Nikolaevo," in BIAD, 1914, pp. 1-48, pl. I-IV.

SMALL BOWL

*Silver; ht. 4 cm; diam. 9 cm.
District Museum of History, Pleven,
inv. no. 113, 5.
Concentric circles engraved on the
bottom; handle slightly enlarged at
either end, decorated with plant
motifs in relief.*

SMALL BOWL

*Silver; ht. 4 cm; diam. 9.5 cm.
District Museum of History, Pleven,
inv. no. 113, 4.
Greek inscription saying that a
Romanized Thracian makes a gift of
this treasure to the Thracian
horseman (cf. no. 521).*

527

RING

Gold; wt. 15 g.
National Archaeological Museum,
Sofia, inv. no. 4795.
Ring with a milky-blue coloured
stone.

528

RING

Gold; diam. 2.7 cm; wt. 22.1 g.
Archaeological Museum, Sofia, inv.
no. 4796.
Smooth ring, setting decorated with
plant motifs; the bezel is a small blue
stone.

529

RING

Gold; diam. 2.8 cm; weight 20.57 g.
Archaeological Museum, Sofia, inv.
no. 4793.
Resembling the preceding one, but
the ring is grooved; engraved spirals
on the setting.

530

RING

*Gold; diam. 2.7 cm; wt. 26.3 g.
Archaeological Museum, Sofia, inv.
no. 4794.
Similar to previous number.*

531

RING

*Gold; diam. 2.9 cm; wt. 23.96 g.
Archaeological Museum, Sofia, inv.
no. 4792.
Similar to previous number, but
double ring with two pale blue
stones.*

532

RING

*Gold; diam. 2 cm; wt. 11.23 g.
Archaeological Museum, Sofia, inv.
no. 4791.
Openwork with Latin inscription:
"AVRELIVS BITVS BOTV HERCVLI"
(Aurelius Bitus to Herakles).*

533

BRACELET

Gold; diam. 7.5 cm; wt. 85.29 g.
Archaeological Museum, Sofia, inv.
no. 4783.
Twisted; clasp at end.

534

BRACELET

Gold; diam. 7.5 cm; wt. 33.8 g.
249 A.D.
Archaeological Museum, Sofia, inv.
no. 4782.
Spiral of gold wire, clasp damaged.

535

BRACELET

Gold; 5 cm; wt. 33.7 g.
Archaeological Museum, Sofia, inv.
no. 4786.
Open; ends ornamented with a
spiral-form motif culminating in a
ring.

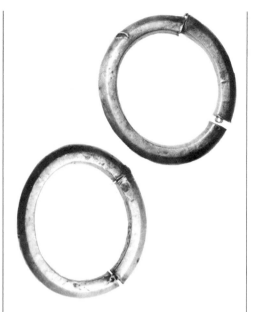

536

TWO BRACELETS

Gold; diam. 10 cm; wt. 113 g.
Archaeological Museum, Sofia, inv.
nos. 4784-4785.
Hollow (filled with resin), cross-
section a polygon. The bracelets are
in two parts joined by hinges.

537

TORQUE

Gold; diam. 12.5 cm; wt. 42.9 g.
Archaeological Museum, Sofia, inv.
no. 4781.
Twisted; ring at each end.

538

LUNULA

Gold; wt. 2.58 g.
Archaeological Museum, Sofia, inv.
no. 4804.
Crescent-shaped, with a shackle;
granular decoration.

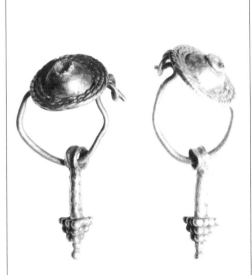

539

PAIR OF EARRINGS

Gold; length 3.5 cm; wt. 3.65 and 3.9 g.
Archaeological Museum, Sofia, inv. no. 4798 a-b.
Ring-shaped with discs attached, encrusted with blue enamel; culminate in a pendant with granular decoration.

540

EARRING

Gold; wt. 3.9 g.
249 A.D.
Archaeological Museum, Sofia, inv. no. 4799.
Small loop of spiraled wire and a drop culminating in a ball.

541

EARRING

Gold; wt. 3.85 g.
249 A.D.
Archaeological Museum, Sofia, inv. no. 4800.
Similar to no. 540, but incomplete.

542

FRAGMENT OF NECKLACE

Gold; length 17 cm; wt. 7.2 g.
Archaeological Museum, Sofia, inv.
no. 4779.
In the shape of Gordian knots
connected by rings and emeralds;
hook at either end.

543

NECKLACE

Gold; length 41 cm; wt. 20.15 g.
Archaeological Museum, Sofia, inv.
no. 4777.
Small chain ornamented with a
green stone and crescent-shaped
pendant.

544

NECKLACE

Gold; length 43 cm; wt. 40.4 g.
Archaeological Museum, Sofia, inv.
no. 4778.
Components are dodecagons
connected by links; tube-shaped
cylindrical clasp.

545

NECKLACE

*Gold; length 37.5 cm; wt. 30.83 g.
Archaeological Museum, Sofia, inv.
no. 4775.
Grooved, semi-cylindrical
components; at either end, a
triangular piece, culminating in a
hook at one end, and a ring at the
other.*

546

NECKLACE

*Gold; length 46.6 cm; wt. 91.99 g.
Archaeological Museum, Sofia, inv.
no. 4774.
Small triple chain in twisted gold
wire; ends in the shape of birds'
heads, attached to chains by studs;
central medallion; gold coin from
the time of Caracalla (211-217 A.D.)
bordered by eight precious stones.*

547

NECKLACE

*Gold; length 41 cm; wt. 29.15 g.
Archaeological Museum, Sofia, inv.
no. 4776.
Small chain with fifty-eight links;
central medallion of rock crystal;
ends leaf-shaped, culminating in a
hook at one end, and a ring at the
other.*

548

SALTCELLAR

Silver; ht. 10.4 cm; wt. 106.44 g.
Archaeological Museum, Sofia, inv.
no. 4766.
In the form of a statuette
representing a child sitting with a
dog in its arms.
Bibl.: D. E. Strong, *Greek and Roman*
Gold and Silver Plate, London, 1966,
p. 178.

549

PHIALE

Silver; ht. 29 cm; diam. 9 cm.
Archaeological Museum, Sofia, inv.
no. 4767.
With an annular base; no
decoration.

550

TELESPHORUS

Terracotta; ht. 17 cm.
Stara Zagora.
2ⁿᵈ cent. A.D.
District Museum of History, Stara
Zagora, inv. no. C3-612.
Telesphorus, Thracian god of good
health, wearing a typical hooded
Thracian garment. The face is
summarily executed. The statuette is
hollow; circular base; on the back,
an inscription in Greek.
Bibl.: H. Bujukliev, M. Dimitrov and
D. Nikilov, *Musée archéologique de
Stara Zagora*, Sofia, 1965, p. 146,
no. 6.

551

TERRACOTTA

Clay; length 15 cm; width 7.5 cm; ht.
14 cm.
Sandanski.
2ⁿᵈ-3ʳᵈ cent. A.D.
Historical Museum of Sandanski,
inv. no. 46.
Satyr playing a panpipe.
Undocumented.

552

LAMP

Terracotta; length 11 cm; width
6 cm.
Stara Zagora.
2ⁿᵈ-3ʳᵈ cent. A.D.
District Museum of History, Stara
Zagora, inv. no. 2 C3859.
Round, ring-shaped handle, the front
part forming a medallion that frames
a bust of Artemis. At the bottom, an
inscription: APTEMIC.
Bibl.: H. Bujukliev, *op. cit.*, p. 147,
no. 67.

553

APOLLO ON A HORSE

Bronze; ht. 7 cm.
Origin unknown.
2nd-3rd cent. A.D.
Archaeological Museum, Sofia, inv.
no. 412.
Head turned slightly to the left; the
left hand once held something which
has now disappeared.
Bibl.: S. Reinach, "Statuettes de
bronze du musée de Sofia," in *RA*,
21, 1897, p. 228, no. 11, fig. 11.

554

GALLOPING HORSE

Bronze; ht. 5 cm.
Dueltum, near Burgas.
2nd-3rd cent. A.D.
Archaeological Museum, Sofia, inv.
no. 2294.
Legs and tail broken; on the neck,
engraved decorations comprising
circles and lines.

555

APOLLO ON A HORSE

Bronze; dark green patina; ht. 10 cm.
Zlatovrah, near Plovdiv.
2nd-3rd cent. A.D.
Archaeological Museum, Sofia, inv.
no. 1227.
Wearing a chlamys; carrying a
quiver on his back.
Bibl.: S. Reinach, *op. cit.*, 34, 1889,
p. 121, no. 7, fig. 7.

556

THRACIAN HORSEMAN

Bronze; ht. 7.5 cm.
Drumohor, near Kjustendil.
2ⁿᵈ-3ʳᵈ cent. A.D.
Archaeological Museum, Sofia, inv.
no. 7046.
Beardless; hair in a chignon; one
hand raised, the other holding the
bridle.
Bibl.: T. Gerasimov, "Tri bronzovi
statuetki na Trakijskia konnik," in
BIAB, 13, 1939, p. 327, no. 1, fig. 369.

557

GALLOPING HORSE

Bronze; greenish patina, ht. 7.8 cm.
Čavka, near Kardžali.
2ⁿᵈ-3ʳᵈ cent. A.D.
Archaeological Museum, Sofia, inv.
no. 6231.
Tail in the air; head turned to the
left; lines and three rows of dots
around the neck; on the flanks, leaf
decorations; saddle decorated with
fringes.

558

THRACIAN HORSEMAN

Silver; ht. 6.7 cm.
Lozen, near Svilengrad.
2ⁿᵈ-3ʳᵈ cent. A.D.
Archaeological Museum, Sofia, inv.
nos. 4103-4104.
Wearing a chlamys that streams
behind his back; is making the
benedictio latina sign with his right
hand. The horseman's head is round
and flat; the eyes and mouth have
been summarily executed.

Chariot decoration from Šiškovci, near Kjustendil. Second to third centuries A.D. Archaeological Museum, Sofia.

Bibl.: I. Venedikov, Trakijskata kolesnica, Sofia, 1959, p. 27, nos. 66-75, pl. 16-19 a-g; nos. 76-81, pl. 19-20 h-n.

559

THRACIAN HORSEMAN

Bronze; greenish patina; ht. 5.5 cm.
Lozen, near Haskovo.
2nd-3rd cent. A.D.
Archaeological Museum, Sofia, inv.
nos. 4102 and 3696.
The horse is resting on its hind legs
and the front left leg. The head is
turned to the right, the upper part of
the mane is plaited. The bridle is
indicated by dots around the neck.

560

SMALL HORSE

Bronze; ht. 6 cm.
Lozen, near Haskovo.
2nd-3rd cent. A.D.
Archaeological Museum, Sofia, inv.
no. 4101.
Stallion, right leg raised, head turned
to the right, the mane gathered into
a tuft; the tail is long and bushy.

561

562

563

PIECE FROM A CHARIOT

Bronze and silver; ht. 21 cm; diam. 15 cm.
Archaeological Museum, Sofia, inv. no. 7992, 1.
Cone-shaped. At the top, a circle inscribed inside a hexagon decorated with the head of a Maenad in silver; crown, eyes and lips gilt. The lower part is also ornamented with two appliques in the form of smaller Maenad heads.

TWO CHARIOT ORNAMENTS

Bronze; ht. 14.5 and 8.3 cm; diam. 10 cm.
Archaeological Museum, Sofia, inv. no. 7992, 2.
Hexagonal shape. They originally had an applique in the form of a Maenad's head, which has disappeared (cf. previous number).

THREE CHARIOT ORNAMENTS

Bronze; ht. 11.4, 12, 11.4 cm; diam. 10.5, 10.1, 9.8 cm.
Archaeological Museum, Sofia, inv. no. 7992, 3.
Ornamented with a silver Maenad's head; the crown, eyes and lips gilt.

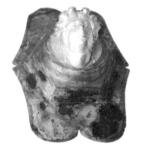

564

TWO CHARIOT ORNAMENTS

*Bronze; ht. 13 and 12 cm; diam.
10.2 cm.
Archaeological Museum, Sofia, inv.
no. 7992, 4.
Similar to no. 563.*

565

CHARIOT ORNAMENT

*Bronze; ht. 22 cm; diam. 14.5 cm.
Archaeological Museum, Sofia, inv.
no. 7992, 5.
Decorated with a bust of Hercules,
covered with a lion's skin and
carrying a baldric. The skin, baldric,
mouth, eyes and crown of vine-
leaves are gilt.*

566

TWO CHARIOT LOOPS

*Bronze; ht. with ring 8.7 and 7.2 cm;
width 13 and 13.2 cm.
Archaeological Museum, Sofia, inv.
no. 7992, 6.
Oblong in shape; decorated with
appliques in the form of Maenad
heads, two apiece, but only one
remains. On the back, a metal bar
culminating in a circular plaque is
riveted to the object; it has a ring on
top.*

567

TWO BREAST ORNAMENTS FROM HORSE TRAPPINGS

Bronze; ht. 19 cm.
Archaeological Museum, Sofia, inv.
no. 7992, 7
Ornamented with an applique in gilt
silver, in the shape of a Maenad's

head. The upper and lower parts
have openwork decorations. On top
and on either side, rings with small
chains attached.

568

TWO CHARIOT ORNAMENTS

Bronze; ht. 21 cm.
Archaeological Museum, Sofia, inv.
no. 7992, 8.
Hexagonal in shape, two sides with
semicircular hollows. In the centre,
a circle inscribed inside a hexagon
ornamented with an applique in the
form of a Maenad's head. (cf.
no. 561).

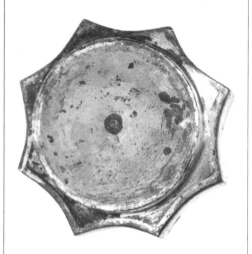

569

CHARIOT ORNAMENT

Bronze; ht. 9.5 cm; diam. 11.1 cm.
Archaeological Museum, Sofia, inv.
no. 7992, 9.
Similar to no. 562.

Matrices from the

Roman period.

570

MATRIX

Bronze; ht. 18 cm; width. 22.7 cm.
Place called Malak juk, north of
Razgrad.
2nd-3rd cent. A.D.
District Museum of History, Razgrad,
inv. no. 153.
Rectangular plaque. In the centre, a
horseman travelling to the right,
wearing a short chlamys and
holding a rhyton in his raised right
hand. In the top right corner, Luna, in
the right corner, Sol. In front of the
horse, a rooster. In the left
foreground, an altar with fire rising
round a bull. In front of the bull, a
man in a tunic holds an axe. A ram
appears between the lion's legs.
Bibl.: G. Kazarov, "Neue Denkmäler
zur Religionsgeschichte Thrakiens,"
in AA, Berlin, 1922, p. 183.

571

MATRIX

Bronze; ht. 14 cm; width 15.2 cm.
Place called Malak juk, north of
Razgrad.
2nd-3rd cent. A.D.
District Museum of History, Razgrad,
inv. no. 154.
Quadrangular plaque in the shape of
a small box. Oblique grooves at the
bottom of columns and vertical
grooves at the top. Capitals with
palmettes. Pediment arched in the
middle, with acroteria. In the centre,
a horseman wearing a phrygian hat,
tunic and chlamys. Behind the
horseman's back, a woman with a
lyre. In front of the horse, a veiled
woman holds a rhyton. An animal
appears under the horse's raised
forequarters. In front of the animal
stands a bearded man, naked, with a
double-headed axe in his hand.
Bibl.: G. Kazarov, op. cit., p. 185.

572

MATRIX

*Bronze; ht. 19 cm; width 16.9 cm.
Place called Malak juk, north of
Razgrad
2ⁿᵈ-3ʳᵈ cent. A.D.
District Museum of History, Razgrad,
inv. no. 159.
Quadrangular frame. Bust of a
goddess (Sibyl?) with folded arms
and palms turned forward. Kalathos
on her head, opening upward. The
hair rims the forehead and falls over
the shoulders and chest. Three
necklaces, bracelets on her arms.
Bibl.: G. Kazarov, op. cit., p. 191,
no. 8, fig. 8.*

573

MATRIX

*Bronze; ht. 8.6 cm; width 8 cm.
Place called Malak juk, north of
Razgrad.
2ⁿᵈ-3ʳᵈ cent. A.D.
District Museum of History, Razgrad,
inv. no. 162.
Quadrangular frame. Bust of a
goddess (Sibyl?) with three bracelets
on her arms. On the neck, a torque
with three pendants. Oblong
earrings. Long, straight hair, covered
with a veil. Wearing a grooved
crown on her head. To the right, a
three-leaf rosetta, to the left, a
broken flute.
Bibl.: G. Kazarov, op. cit., p. 193,
no. 11, fig. 11.*

574

MATRIX

*Bronze; diam. 8.4 cm; ht. 0.6 cm.
Place called Malak juk, north of
Razgrad.
2ⁿᵈ-3ʳᵈ cent. A.D.
District Museum of History, Razgrad,
inv. no. 767.
Round plaque. Herakles, naked, full
face, his right hand leaning on a
club. A lion skin is hanging on the
left arm. To the right of the hero,
an altar with a fire burning, to the
left, a palm leaf.
Bibl.: G. Kazarov, op. cit., p. 193.*

Ceramics from the Roman period.

575

THREE RECEPTACLES STUCK INSIDE ONE ANOTHER

Terracotta; ht. 20 cm; diam. 10 cm.
Pavlikeni, near Tarnovo.
2nd-3rd cent. A.D.
District Museum of History, Tarnovo,
temp. inv. no. 534.
The receptacles are deformed,
entangled in one another. A handle,
barbotine decoration: leaves. The
vessels were discovered in this
position in an oven at a large Roman
ceramics centre in lower Mesia,
abandoned in haste.
Undocumented.

576

SMALL VESSEL

Terracotta; ht. 10.5 cm; diam. of
bulge 12 cm.
Butovo, near Veliko Tarnovo.
3rd cent. A.D.
District Museum of History, Veliko
Tarnovo, inv. no. 1026/TOM/A.
Biconic in shape; enlarged mouth;
two handles, pine-cone decoration in
relief; red glaze. Part of the mouth
has been restored.
Undocumented.

577

578

579

RECEPTACLE

Terracotta; ht. 8 cm; diam. 9 cm.
Butovo, Veliko Tarnovo district.
3rd cent. A.D.
District Museum of History, Veliko
Tarnovo, inv. no. 706.
Biconic, flared mouth, two handles.
Relief decorations depicting
pine-cones. Red glaze.
Bibl.: B. Sultov, "Ceramic production
on the Territory of Nicopolis ad
Istrum, 2nd-4th century A.D.," in *Terra*
Antiqua Balcanica, 1, 1986.

RECEPTACLE

Terracotta.
Butovo, Veliko Tarnovo district.
2nd-3rd cent. A.D.
District Museum of History, Veliko
Tarnovo, inv. no. 703.
Conic lower part and cylindrical
upper part. Flat, profiled handle.
Decoration in relief comprising
ornaments in plant and geometric
motifs.
Bibl.: B. Sultov, *op. cit.*

CUP

Terracotta; diam. 12.5 cm.
Butovo, near Veliko Tarnovo.
2nd-3rd cent. A.D.
District Museum of History, Veliko
Tarnovo, inv. no. 972.
Biconic in shape, the upper part
decorated with plant motifs.
Part of the mouth has been restored.
Bibl.: B. Sultov, *op. cit.*

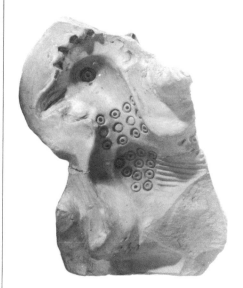

580

MOULD

Terracotta; ht. 10 cm; width 1 cm.
Butovo, Veliko Tarnovo district.
District Museum of History, Veliko
Tarnovo, inv. no. 653.
For casting an applique in the shape
of a goat.
Bibl.: B. Sultov, op. cit.

581

MOULD

Terracotta; length 16.5 cm.
Butovo, Veliko Tarnovo district.
2nd-3rd cent. A.D.
District Museum of History, Veliko
Tarnovo, inv. no. 1389.
For casting a toy in the shape of a
rooster. Restored.

582

TOY

Terracotta; ht. 15 cm.
Butovo, Veliko Tarnovo district.
2nd-3rd cent. A.D.
District Museum of History, Veliko
Tarnovo, inv. no. 724.
Wheeled horse.
Bibl.: B. Sultov, op. cit.

Thracian votive reliefs.

583

584

VOTIVE RELIEF

Marble; ht. 38.3 cm; width 31 cm. Plovdiv.
Archaeological Museum, Plovdiv, inv. no. 2103.
Rectangular arched frame. A bearded, three-headed horseman wearing a chlamys streaming out behind him, holding a double-headed axe in his right hand. The horse is moving to the right, and has placed its hoof on an altar. Under it, a dog and a wild boar; in front, two women; behind, a servant holding the horse's tail. To the right and left of the horseman, under the arch, busts of Sol and Luna (sun and moon). At the bottom, a Greek inscription: "The family has donated this relief for its health and safety."
Bibl.: G. Kazarov, "Prinos kam religijata na mnogoglavite božestva," in BIAB, 27, 1950, p. 4, no. 6, fig. 3; Z. Gočeva, "Les traits caractéristiques de l'iconographie du cavalier thrace," in BCH, 1986, 14, pp. 237-243.

VOTIVE RELIEF

Marble; ht. 30 cm; width 25 cm. Kaspičan.
Archaeological Museum, Sofia, inv. no. 1322.
Rectangular frame, a bearded horseman, holding a cornucopia, riding to the right. The horse with forelegs raised, one hoof placed on an altar. Under the horse, a dog and a wild boar.
Bibl.: G. Kazarov, *Die Denkmäler des thrakischen Reitergottes in Bulgarien*, Budapest, 1938, p. 101, no. 518, fig. 265.

585

VOTIVE RELIEF

*Marble; ht. 29 cm; width 24 cm.
Asenovgrad.
Archaeological Museum, Sofia, inv.
no. 1643.
Arched rectangular frame. Thracian
horseman riding to the right. In his
right hand, a short lance, in the left, a
crown. Under the horse, a lion
attacking a wild boar. Behind the
horseman's back, the figure of
another, smaller, horseman,
galloping to the left.*
Bibl.: G. Kazarov, *op. cit.*, p. 156,
no. 904, fig. 444.

586

VOTIVE RELIEF

*Marble; ht. 41 cm; width 24 cm.
Harlec, Vraca district.
Archaeological Museum, Sofia, inv.
no. 7518.
Rectangular frame, triangular field
divided into two parts. In the top
part, a horseman rides to the right,
chlamys streaming behind and right
arm raised. Under the horse's legs,
an altar; in front of it, a tree with a
serpent coiled round it. Below is a
veiled female figure, her long gown
pleated, holding two symmetrical
horses in front of her.*
Bibl.: G. Kazarov, *op. cit.*, p. 84,
no. 399, fig. 224.

587

VOTIVE RELIEF

*Marble; ht. 41 cm; width 26.5 cm.
Kirilmetodievo, Stara Zagora district.
2nd-3rd cent. A.D.
District Museum of History, Stara
Zagora, inv. no. 2C3 927.
Arched rectangular frame. Dionysian
scene in raised relief. On the frame a
Greek inscription: "Dedicated to
Dionysios by Flavios Perilaos."*
Bibl.: H. Bujukliev, *op. cit.*, p. 141,
no. 52.

COINS

588

589

VOTIVE HAND

Ivory; length 11 cm; width 1.5 cm.
Krasen, Tolbuhin district.
4ᵗʰ cent. A.D.
Departmental Museum of Tolbuhin,
inv. no. 204.
Hand holding a nutshell in which
there is a miniature drawing of a
horseman. The horse is in motion,
its forelegs raised. The horseman is
wearing a chlamys and is holding a
lance in his right hand. Culminates in
a handle with a small hole where it
was attached.
Bibl.: L. Bobčeva, "Nouveau
monument au cavalier thrace,"
Arheologija, 1965, 4, p. 35, fig. 1,2.

ARROWHEAD COINS

Bronze; length 3 to 4 cm.
Atija, Burgas district.
6ᵗʰ cent. B.C.
District Museum of History, Burgas,
inv. no. KVP 2055.
In the form of a point and, on the
back, a massive part instead of a
hollow socket. Fishbone the entire
length. More than 1000 were found
in a bronze receptacle, together with
a terracotta mould, which has not
been preserved.
Bibl.: T. Gerasimov, "Sakrovište ot
bronzovi streli-moneti," in BIAB, 12,
1938, pp. 424-427, fig. 211; P.
Balabanov, "Nouvelle étude des
monnaies-pointes de flèche de la
péninsule d'Atija," Th. P., 1, 1982,
pp. 40-56.

590

591

592

DERRONIAN DECADRACHMA

Silver; diam. 35 mm.
6th or 5th cent. B.C.
Archaeological Museum, Sofia, inv. no. 8739.
Obverse: man with pointed beard wearing a Macedonian wide-brimmed hat, in a two-wheeled chariot drawn by a cow; holding a whip in his left hand; above the animal, a sun symbol.
Reverse: triskele.
Bibl.: T. Gerasimov, "Nahodka ot dekadrahmi no trakomakedonskoto pleme Deroni," in *BIAB*, 11, 1937, p. 249.

ORRESCIAN STATER

Silver; diam. 20 mm.
5th cent. B.C.
Archaeological Museum, Sofia, inv. no. 6962.
Obverse: Centaur and Nymph.
Reverse: swastika in bas relief.

STATER OF AN ANONYMOUS THRACIAN TRIBE

Silver; diam. 1.9 cm; wt. 5 g.
5th cent. B.C.
Archaeological Museum, Sofia, inv. no. 10473-54.
Obverse: Silenus, one knee on the ground, holding a Maenad in his arms.
Reverse: swastika in bas relief.

593

DRACHMA OF AN ANONYMOUS THRACIAN TRIBE

Silver; diam. 16 mm.
5th cent. B.C.
Archaeological Museum, Sofia, inv. no. 2799.
Similar to the previous number.

594

SPARADOKOS (CIRCA 424 B.C.)

Silver; diam. 10 mm; wt. 1.35 g.
Archaeological Museum, Sofia, inv. no. 4545.
Obverse: protoma of a horse on the left.
Reverse: eagle with wings outstretched.

595

SPARADOKOS
(CIRCA 424 B.C.)

Silver; diam. 15 mm.
Archaeological Museum, Sofia, inv.
no. 9565-50.
Obverse: horse moving to the left.
Reverse: eagle flying to the left,
holding in its beak a serpent
inscribed in a circle.

596

SPARADOKOS
(CIRCA 424 B.C.)

Silver; diam. 15 mm.
Archaeological Museum, Sofia, inv.
no. 7219.
Obverse: horse walking to the right.
Reverse: eagle, wings outstretched.

597

KOTYS I (383-359 B.C.)

Silver; diam. 12 mm.
Archaeological Museum, Sofia, inv.
no. 121.
Obverse: head of a bearded man
turned to the left.
Reverse: vase with two handles.

598

AMATOKOS (359-351 B.C.)

Bronze; diam. 21 mm.
Archaeological Museum, Sofia, inv.
no. 8761.
Obverse: double-headed axe.
Reverse: bunch of grapes.

599

TERES II (348 B.C.)

Bronze; diam. 21 mm.
Archaeological Museum, Sofia, inv.
no. 10940-64.
Obverse: double-headed axe.
Reverse: vine bearing bunches of
grapes, inside a square in bas relief.

600

CHERSOBLEPTES
(359-348 B.C.)

Bronze; diam. 12 mm.
Archaeological Museum, Sofia, inv.
no. 10724.
Obverse: head of a woman turned to
the right.
Reverse: vessel with two handles
and wheat kernel.

601

602

603

CETRIPORIS (356 B.C.)

Bronze; diam. 17 mm.
Archaeological Museum, Sofia, inv.
no. 7220.
Obverse: head of Dionysos,
bearded, crowned, turned to the
right.
Reverse: cantharus and thyrsus.

HEBRYZELMIS (389-384 B.C.)

Bronze; diam. 18 mm.
Archaeological Museum, Sofia, inv.
no. 10430-54.
Obverse: head of a man turned to
the left.
Reverse: protoma of a lion, on the
right.

LYSIMACHOS (306-280 B.C.)

Gold; diam. 20 mm.
Archaeological Museum, Sofia, inv.
no. 6810.
Obverse: head of Alexander, at right.
Reverse: Athena sitting on a throne,
armed with a lance and holding a
Nike in her left hand; behind her, a
shield.

604

LYSIMACHOS (306-280 B.C.)

Silver; diam. 17 mm; wt. 15.72 g.
Archaeological Museum, Sofia, inv.
no. 8063.
Obverse: head of a king wearing
ram's horns and turned to the right.
Reverse: Athena carrying a Nike in
her left hand, leaning on a shield.

605

LYSIMACHOS (306-280 B.C.)

Silver; diam. 18 mm.
Archaeological Museum, Sofia, inv.
no. 8096.
Similar to previous number.

606

LYSIMACHOS (306-280 B.C.)

Bronze; diam. 20 mm.
Archaeological Museum, Sofia, inv.
no. 6238.
Obverse: Athena turned to the right.
Reverse: a doe.

607

SEUTHES III (330-300 B.C.)

Bronze; diam. 22 mm.
Archaeological Museum, Plovdiv,
inv. no. 6435.
Obverse: head of the king inscribed
in a circle and turned to the right.
Reverse: the king on a horse
galloping to the right; under the
horse, a laurel crown.

608

SEUTHES III (330-300 B.C.)

Bronze; diam. 17 mm.
Archaeological Museum, Plovdiv,
inv. no. 1370.
Similar to previous number.

609

ADAIOS (CIRCA 255-235 B.C.)

Bronze; diam. 20 mm.
Archaeological Museum, Sofia, inv.
no. 8365.
Obverse: head of Apollo, turned to
the right.
Reverse: tripod.

610

MOSTIS (LATE SECOND AND EARLY FIRST CENTURIES B.C.)

Bronze; diam. 20 mm.
Archaeological Museum, Sofia, inv. no. 6919.
Obverse: head of Apollo turned to the right.
Reverse: horse moving to the left.

611

MOSTIS (LATE SECOND AND EARLY FIRST CENTURIES B.C.)

Silver; diam. 17 mm; wt. 16.04 g.
Archaeological Museum, Sofia, inv. no. 6471.
Obverse: bust of a king, with diadem, turned to the right.
Reverse: Athena sitting to the left on a throne, holding a Nike and leaning on a shield.

612

SADALES II (FIRST CENTURY B.C.)

Bronze; diam. 15 mm.
Archaeological Museum, Sofia, inv. no. 6559.
Obverse: head of a woman with a diadem, turned to the right.
Reverse: eagle standing, turned to the left.

613

614

615

RHOEMETALCES I
(11 B.C.-12 A.D.)

Bronze; diam. 28 mm.
Archaeological Museum, Sofia, inv.
no. 4546.
Obverse: heads of the king and his
wife, turned to the right.
Reverse: heads of Augustus and
Livia turned to the right.

RHOEMETALCES I
(11 B.C.-12 A.D.)

Bronze; diam. 27 mm.
Archaeological Museum, Sofia, inv.
no. 3539.
Obverse: heads of the king and his
wife.
Reverse: head of Augustus.

KOTYS AND RESKUPORIS
(FIRST CENTURY B.C.)

Bronze; diam. 20 mm.
Archaeological Museum, Sofia, inv.
no. 47.
Obverse: head of the king with a
diadem, turned to the right.
Reverse: Nike, turned to the left.

Thracian imitations of antique coins. Third to first centuries B.C.

616

PHILIPPE II

*Silver; diam. 23 mm; wt. 13.67 g.
Archaeological Museum, Sofia, inv.
no. 2730.
Obverse: head of Zeus, turned to the
right.
Reverse: horseman riding to the
right.*

617

ALEXANDER III THE GREAT

*Silver; diam. 20 mm; wt. 2.92 g.
Archaeological Museum, Sofia, inv.
no. 5164.
Obverse: head of a young Herakles,
turned to the right.
Reverse: Zeus sitting on a throne,
holding the sceptre and the eagle.*

618

619

620

PHILIPPE III

*Silver; diam. 16 mm; wt. 2.92 g.
Archaeological Museum, Sofia, inv.
no. 1437.
Obverse: head of Herakles, turned to
the right.
Reverse: similar to previous
number.*

TETRADRACHMA FROM THASOS

*Silver; diam. 30 mm.
Archaeological Museum, Sofia, inv.
no. 8233.
Obverse: head of Dionysos,
crowned.
Reverse: Herakles naked, standing.*

TETRADRACHMA FROM THASOS

*Silver; diam. 33 mm; wt. 17.4 g.
Archaeological Museum, Sofia, inv.
no. 11157.
Similar to previous number.*

621

TETRADRACHMA FROM THASOS

Silver; diam. 33 mm; wt. 17.4 g.
Archaeological Museum, Sofia, inv.
no. 9990.
Similar to previous number.

622

TETRADRACHMA FROM THASOS

Silver; diam. 35 mm; wt. 16.2 g.
Archaeological Museum, Sofia, inv.
no. 10838-59.
Similar to previous number.

623

TETRADRACHMA FROM THASOS

Silver; diam. 33 mm; wt. 16.2 g.
Archaeological Museum, Sofia, inv.
no. 10875-60.
Similar to previous number.

THE ROGOZEN TREASURE

In the fall of 1985 Ivan Dimitrov, a tractor operator living in the village of Rogozen in northwest Bulgaria, was digging a trench in his garden when he discovered, by pure chance, a collection of sixty-five silver receptacles. A team from the departmental museum of Vraca hurried over and began methodical excavations. On January 6, 1986, in a second trench near the first one, a hundred more receptacles were found. The treasure consists of a hundred and eight phialae, fifty-four jugs and three cups. All the objects are of silver, and their total weight is twenty kilograms. The find was made on land inhabited in antiquity by the Thracian tribe of the Triballoi. The pieces were probably collected together between the fifth and fourth centuries B.C. Several of them seem to have been imported, but most were made in Thracian workshops. In their shape and decoration they resemble objects found in regions bordering the Black Sea and the Balkan peninsula, and in Asia Minor. They display scenes of figures and a whole group of images illustrating Thracian mythology, many of which are unlike anything known until now. Some of the images are emphasized by gilding. The vessels bear inscriptions and signs, sometimes engraved by stippling. The name that most often appears is that of the Thracian king Kotys I (383-359 B.C.).

The name of his son Chersobleptes (359-341 B.C.) is here mentioned for the first time, as is that of Satokos (end of the fifth century B.C.). The inscriptions also give us the names of Thracian cities: Apros, Argiskè, Beos, Geistoi, Sauthaba. And for the first time, there appears the name of a craftsman: Disloias.

Bibl.: A. Fol, P. Ivanov, B. Nikolov and S. Mašov, in Izkustvo, 6, 1986; Frakijskij klad iz Rogozena, Moskva, 1986; The New Thracian Treasure from Rogozen, Bulgaria, London, 1986; B. Nikolov, "Le trésor d'orfèvrerie thrace de Rogozen," in Archéologia, 222, Paris, March 1987.

624

PHIALE

Silver; diam. 14.8 cm; ht. 4.6 cm; weight 170.6 g.
National Museum of History, Sofia, inv. no. 22342.
To the inside, on the omphalos, is soldered a plaque with a human head in relief. Eight hollow extended gadroons (in relief) radiate outward from the omphalos. The neck has, on the outside, an engraved inscription in Greek: "ΚΟΤΥΟΣ ΕΓ ΑΡΓΙΣΚΗΣ."
Bibl.: B. Nikolov, "Fialite ot Rogozenskoto sakrovište," in Izkustvo 6, 1986, p. 48, fig. 42; The New Thracian Treasure from Rogozen, London, 1986, p. 39, no. 42.

625

PHIALE

*Silver; diam. 17.5 cm; ht. 3.8 cm; wt.
177.8 g.
National Museum of History, Sofia,
inv. no. 22394.
Around the omphalos six bulls'
heads in relief separated by almond-
shaped ornaments that incised lines
transform into acorns. The animals
are represented in realistic style,
with protruding eyes and engraved
spiraling locks on the forehead.
Bibl.: B. Nikolov, op. cit., p. 15,
fig. 94, p. 52, no. 94; The New
Thracian Treasure from Rogozen,
London, 1986, p. 47, no. 94.*

626

JUG

*Silver; ht. 13 cm; wt. 158 g.
National Museum of History, Sofia,
inv. no. 22456.
At the bottom of the neck a ring in
relief with egg and dart decoration.
The handle is split at the top and
culminates in two serpents' heads.
The base of the handle is in the
shape of a palmette. The body is
decorated with two identical scenes
in relief: a lion attacking a doe.
Gilding on the figures and
ornaments.
Bibl.: B. Nikolov, "Kanite ot
Rogozenskoto sakrovište," Izkustvo,
6, 1986, p. 58, no. 156; The New
Thracian Treasure from Rogozen,
London, 1986, p. 59, no. 156.*

ABBREVIATIONS

AA:	*Archäologischer Anzeiger* (supplement to *JdI*).
Actes du II CITh:	*Actes du IIe Congrès International de Thracologie,* Bucarest, 1980.
AJA:	*American Journal of Archaeology.*
AK:	*Antike Kunst.*
Amandry, Stathatos:	P. Amandry, *Collection Hélène Stathatos,* I, Les Bijoux antiques, Strasbourg, 1953.
Ancient Bulgaria:	*Papers presented to the International Symposium of the Ancient History and Archaeology of Bulgaria,* A. G. Poulter, Nottingham, 1981.
Aurifex:	*Études d'orfèvrerie antique,* T. Hackens, Louvain-la-Neuve, 1980.
BABesch:	*Bulletin van de Verseniging tot Bevordering der Kennis van de antiske Beschaving.*
BAR:	*British Archaeological Reports.*
BCH:	*Bulletin de Correspondance Hellénique.*
BIAB:	*Bulletin de l'Institut bulgare d'archéologie.*
BIAD:	*Bulletin de la Société bulgare d'archéologie.*
B. Deppert-Lippitz:	B. Deppert-Lippitz, *Griechischer Goldschmuck,* Mainz, 1985.
DITK:	*Dritter Internationaler Thrakologischen Kongress,* Sofia, 1984.
Duvanli:	B. Filov, *Nadgrobnite mogili pri Duvanli,* Sofia, 1934.
GNAM:	*Godišnik na Narodnija Arheologiceski Muzej, Sofia* (Annual Report of the Sophia Archaeological Museum).
GNPB:	*Godišnik na Narodnata biblioteka v Plovdiv* (Annual Report of the Plovdiv Library).
GPM:	*Godišnik na Narodnija Muzej, Plovdiv* (Annual Report of the Plovdiv Museum).
IMJuB:	*Izvestija na muzeite ot Južna Balgarija* (News of Southern Bulgarian Museums).
IVAD:	*Izvestija na Arheologičeskoto družestvo vav Varna* (Bulletin of Varna Archaeological Society).
JdI:	*Jahrbuch des deutschen archäologischen Instituts.*
JHS:	*Journal of Hellenic Studies.*
H. Luschey, Metallkunst:	H. Luschey, "Thrakien als ein Ort der Begegnung der Kelten mit iranischen Metallkunst", in *Beiträge zur Altertumskunde Kleinasiens, Festschrift für Kurt Bittel,* Mainz, 1983.
MMJ:	*Metropolitan Museum Journal.*
MPK:	*Muzei i pametnici na kulturata.*
MSB:	*Sbornik za narodni umotvorenija, nauka i knižnica na Ministerstvo na narodnoto prosveščenie, Sofia* (Collection of the Minister of Bulgarian Culture).
RA:	*Revue archéologique.*
RM:	*Mitteilungen des Deutschen Archäologischen Instituts, Römische Abteilung.*
RP:	*Razkopki i proučvanija na Arheologičeskija muzej v Sofia* (Excavations and Research of the Sophia Archaeological Museum).
D. E. Strong:	D. E. Strong, *Greek and Roman Gold and Silver Plate,* London, 1966.
Th.P.:	*Thracia Pontica.*
Tr. Izk.:	I. Venedikov, T. Gerasimov, *Trakijskoto izkustvo,* Sofia, 1973.